CHURCH HISTORY

CHURCH HISTORY

An Introduction to
Research, Reference Works, and Methods

James E. Bradley *and* Richard A. Muller

WILLIAM B. EERDMANS PUBLISHING COMPANY
GRAND RAPIDS, MICHIGAN

© 1995 Wm. B. Eerdmans Publishing Co.
255 Jefferson Ave. S.E., Grand Rapids, Michigan 49503

Printed in the United States of America

06 05 04 03 02 01   7 6 5 4 3

Library of Congress Cataloging-in-Publication Data
Bradley, James E., 1944-
Church History: an introduction to research, reference works, and methods /
James E. Bradley and Richard A. Muller.
p.   cm.
Includes bibliographical references.
ISBN 0-8028-0826-3 (paper)
1. Church history — Study and teaching. 2. Church history — Historiography.
3. Church history — Bibliography. 4. Reference books — Church history.
I. Muller, Richard A. (Richard Alfred), 1948-   . II. Title.
BR138.B69   1995
270'.072 — dc20   94-40617
                                     CIP

Contents

Preface

This book arose out of a methods seminar given in the Graduate (Ph.D./Th.M.) program at Fuller Seminary. The seminar provides an introduction to methods for research and writing, both for history and for the more systematic and philosophical disciplines in the theology division, on the assumption that historical method is common to all of these fields and that the basic tools of research used in historical study are necessary for the study of the other disciplines as well. The course was developed primarily to introduce new Ph.D. students to historical method at the very beginning of their doctoral work. It is our hope, in moving from a course outline to a book, that this study will serve as a practical resource for students beginning graduate programs primarily in the fields of church history and history of doctrine, but also for students in the areas of systematic and philosophical theology. We also trust that the bibliographical aspect of the book will be of use to established scholars, whether for the identification of traditional research tools with which they may not previously have been acquainted, or for the identification of newer tools and approaches to the many film and electronic databases now available.

Underlying many of the discussions and much of the bibliographical interest evidenced by the book is the distinction that one of our colleagues pressed on us between professional and amateur historians and the intention to further the case for professionalism in church historical studies. While granting that there is a fine line between the best of amateur historiography and the nominally "professional" essay, in this study we assume a commitment to regularity and precision in method, particularly in the identification and use of resources and tools, the critical use of theory, the placement of a particular research project into the contemporary scholarly dialogue through attention to the history of scholarship, and the careful construction of conclusions based on, and limited by, the evidence investigated — a commitment that must be an aspect of the work of the professional historian but which may often be excluded on grounds of genre and even literary style from the works of amateur or popular historians, no matter how well executed. This point is perhaps best illustrated by our emphasis on an analytical survey of previous scholarship — which we believe is a necessary element of a professional historical essay, but which may not be suitable to the more popular literature. The purpose of the original seminar and, now, of the book, is to offer guidelines to the graduate student who plans to become a professional historian.

It may also be worthwhile at this point to take note of an issue confronting the world of scholarship that has direct implications for the work of the church historian. Current debate over the character of scholarship, particularly the scholarship produced by teachers and researchers based in seminaries and graduate schools of religion, has fastened on the issue of commitment to a particular religion and the relationship of that commitment to scholarship. In short, can a Christian produce reasonably objective studies of the history of the church and its teachings? As we will argue further in our discussion of objectivity, we assume not only the possibility but also the duty of the Christian historian to develop a stance of methodologically controlled objectivity. The key issue here is method. Given the high probability that a scholar's personal religious interests will provide at least the existential reason for selecting a given topic for study, it will be the case that a sound method in the shaping of the research, in gathering resources and identifying issues, and in assessing previous scholarly opinion will be the primary basis for reaching an objective, although obviously not detached, result. We remain committed to the belief that the results of an investigation reached by a Christian historian ought not to differ appreciably from the results of a similar investigation reached by a purely secular historian — at least not because of the fundamental religious or spiritual commitment of the investigator.

Some comments about the use of this volume in the context of a graduate methods seminar are in order. The course itself is intended to introduce Ph.D. and Th.M. students to graduate level work and to give them some sense of the methodological rigor required of scholars who operate beyond the level of the M.A. or M.Div. degrees. The book, therefore, assumes a basic acquaintance with church history and history of Christian doctrine and certain basic skills in research and writing. The Fuller Ph.D. was originally conceived on the pattern of the European tutorial approach that presupposes a close working relationship between research supervisor and student, and though recently modified, the program still retains a larger component of independent research than most American degrees.[1] But whether the student is engaged in research for one year or three, we have found that the same sequence of stages in research must be observed if a satisfactory result is expected. We believe, therefore, that the following study contains sufficient matter of common interest to guide advanced students in all theological disciplines that utilize historical sources, and it should also serve in a wide variety of situations and programs.

Accordingly, the book is organized with the needs of the research student primarily in mind; it follows a logical searching sequence that will enable the student to define and narrow a topic, locate secondary literature in the chosen field, move into the relevant source materials, and turn finally to the dissertation. Following the lead of G. R. Elton,[2] we also include short sections on lecturing and the preparation of scholarly articles. We begin, however, with basic definitions of the disciplines and a rudimentary review of the nature and problems of studying the past.

The Bibliography and the Appendix that conclude this volume should be considered an integral part of the book. (Cross references to the Bibliography and the Appendix in the text of the book will appear in parentheses.) The principles for including items in the Bibliography are directly related to our purposes in writing. In the first section of the Bibliography, reference tools that must be examined by every student, irrespective of their specialization or interest, are included, as are major, well-known bibliographies and guides that may or may not be needed in some areas. When we turn in the second section of the Bibliography to specific areas that are chronologically, geographically, and topically defined, the authors' own research specializations come into play, and

---

1. One of the best short guides for students of history is G. Kitson Clark's *Guide for Research Students Working on Historical Subjects* (2nd ed., 1968; Cambridge University Press).

2. G. R. Elton, *The Practice of History* (New York: Crowell, 1967).

we apply an alternative principle of listing items that are representative of an area, or illustrative of the types of reference works that are available. Since our own work has concentrated on the Reformation, early modern Europe, and modern Britain, these fields will undoubtedly be overrepresented by illustrative material, and other areas, for example, modern French history, neglected. We believe, however, that sufficient guidance is given in most fields to enable the enterprising student to find a way into the most obscure topic.

Beyond the needs of the beginning student, the book also seeks to address the concerns of the established scholar by drawing attention to new sources and techniques in historical studies. We address the topic of computer applications in research and the new sources in microform, both in the text of the book and in the Appendix. It is noteworthy in this regard that the last comprehensive guide in Church History was published in 1931 by Shirley Jackson Case; more recent surveys of secondary literature have appeared, and many specialist bibliographies exist, but recent developments in the storage, retrieval, and manipulation of historical data require a new approach to the discipline and its methods of research and writing.[3] Established scholars will probably find the sections on microform collections and major collaborative projects like the Thesaurus Linguae Graecae most useful. Modern techniques of micro-reproduction are revolutionizing historical studies, and the computer has greatly enhanced both the ease and the speed with which students may search primary and secondary literature. Beginning students and mature scholars alike must come to terms with these new methods because in virtually every field of inquiry, advances in the past decade have transformed the traditional approach to research. This is more than a matter of convenience; in the last analysis, thoroughness of research can no longer be defended on the grounds of having visited a reasonable number of archives. Whereas in the past, an examiner during an oral defense of a dissertation might have asked whether a student had looked at a certain collection, it is now far more likely that the discerning examiner will wish to know if all relevant materials found, for example, in the *Eighteenth-Century Short Title Catalog,* have been studied.

3. *A Bibliographical Guide to the History of Christianity* (Chicago: The University of Chicago Press, 1931). G. E. Gorman and Lyn Gorman, *Theological and Religious Reference Materials: Systematic Theology and Church History* (Bibliographies and Indexes in Religious Studies, 2: Westport, CT: Greenwood Press, 1985).

Of course, convenience and time are important, and the new sources and techniques clearly enhance one's powers of research. One scholar compared the basic search for materials for an extended project by traditional methods to the searching power of a well-known data base; formerly the project would have demanded eight months compared in the new circumstance to a matter of hours.[4] We have found that in practice, an approach that utilizes both traditional and computer searches is best, and we encourage this balance throughout the book. For example, students need to be able to use the data base of the Eighteenth Century Short Title Catalog as well as *The National Union Catalog of Pre-1956 Imprints* in order not only to identify but also to locate holdings.[5] In the midst of exciting new possibilities for research, the beginner in particular must never lose sight of the fact that the latest technique will not take the place of sound deductive reasoning and good historical judgment.

The authors of this book have had the advantage of teaching the subject of church history together, but from two very different standpoints: the history of doctrine and the history of the institution of the church. Conversations over the years have illumined each other's point of departure, and in addition, our various research projects have each been typified by an emphasis on integrating the ideas of the church within their respective social and cultural contexts. We believe that in the study of church history, the time has arrived for a more systematic and self-conscious attempt to unite institutional and social history with the history of doctrine and ideas. The immediate social context for this argument is the new sensitivity to religious differences and the new emphasis on ethnic studies and women's history that have given rise to entire new fields of historical enquiry. The following chapters therefore attempt to counteract the traditional orientation of church historians toward the exclusive concentration on either the dominant ideas, or the leading institutions, that have shaped the entire tradition of the church, or specific confessional branches of the church. The convergence of the present intellectual and social climate with the development of recent

---

4. Peter Hogg, "The Abolition of the Slave Trade: A Bibliographer Looks at the ESTC," p. 96 in M. Crump and M. Harris, eds., *Searching the Eighteenth Century* (London: The British Library, 1983).

5. Scholars with the greatest experience recommend that keyword searches on machine readable files be combined with traditional bibliographical work.

technologies appears to offer us an unusual opportunity for integrating the several disciplines of church history that have heretofore been unduly isolated.

Acknowledgments

We wish to acknowledge the debt we owe to our graduate students, especially those who have served as partners in dialogue and criticism over the years. We are particularly appreciative for the energetic editorial assistance provided by Rory Randall, Richard Heyduck, and Phil Corr. We have also received a great deal of help from the Librarian of McAlister Library, John Dickason, and two of his staff, Olive Brown and Shieu-yu Hwang. A number of people read the typescript at various stages in its preparation, and we would like to thank them for their suggestions, many of which we have incorporated into the book: David Bebbington, Henry Bowden, Robert Handy, D. Bruce Hindmarsh, Julie Ingersoll, Mark Noll, Susan E. Schreiner, Susie Stanley, David C. Steinmetz, Harry Stout, and John L. Thompson.

1. Introduction to Church History and Related Disciplines

In recent years, historians have observed a growing rapprochement between institutional or social church history and the history of doctrine, and this development has occurred at a time when the disciplines of church history are increasingly influenced by new methods of research, particularly those of the social sciences.[1] This rapprochement is arguably the wave of the future. The point can be illustrated in a variety of ways: for example, one finds an increasing tendency in modern church historiography to place ideas in a wider intellectual context, sometimes broadening the latter even further, with attention to cultural symbol or "mentality." Similarly, the new areas of research opened up for us by the study of women and ethnic and religious minorities in church history have oriented us to a wider social context. Both developments are linked to new methods of investigation, and both have contributed directly to the need for re-conceptualizing the traditional taxonomy of church history and its sub-disciplines.[2] Ecumenical issues and the opportunities offered by religious

1. At the 1991 annual meeting of the American Society of Church History in Chicago, Robert Kingdon outlined recent historiographical developments in similar terms to those described here. For a good survey of the literature of the social sciences and the opportunities it presents for the church historian, see Mark A. Noll, " 'And the Lion Shall Lie Down with the Lamb': The Social Sciences and Religious History," *Fides et Historia* 20 (1988): 5-30.

2. For illustrations from the Reformation, early modern, and modern periods, see A. G. Dickens and John M. Tonkin, *The Reformation in Historical Thought* (Cambridge: Harvard University Press, 1985); Frederick Krantz, ed., *History from Below* (Ox-

pluralism and concerns for justice and equality have led us to become more sensitive to differences of opinion and approach, even as we discuss the progress of nominally orthodox dogma.

Despite these developments, the historian of ideas, and this includes many church historians, have tended to side, methodologically, with traditional techniques, while the social scientists have adopted a variety of new analytical tools to advance research and analysis. Increasingly, the more innovative techniques have revealed the inadequacies and imprecision of the traditional approaches, whether institutional or intellectual, when considered alone. We will argue that the traditional bifurcation of the field into institutional church history and history of theology or history of dogma is no longer adequate because this division itself establishes a topical grid into which the materials of history are pressed. The methods as well as the subject matters of church history will, of course, continue to be contested, because conceptualizations of the past bear so directly upon matters of our self-understanding, including our individual, social, and ecclesiastical identity. But the older arguments concerning the proper subjects and methods of the church historian, and the relationship of the social sciences to the study of history, seem increasingly irrelevant; the important question for the church historian today is the suitability of the technique to the specific task of research, which in turn is determined by the overall goal of the project and the nature of the evidence at hand. In this new context, the student should be prepared to adopt any method that appears likely to elicit the desired result, and such an eclectic approach will often require an appeal to more than one technique of analysis. This present atmosphere of diversity and freedom of investigation presents us with the need to reevaluate the traditional divisions and methods in the general field of church history and to test their compatibility with contemporary needs and outlook.

In spite of the promise we find in the contemporary academic and social settings, recent trends are also laden with no little difficulty; the broad field of church history is increasingly complex and highly fragmented. While the scholarly competence and reputation of church historians generally has never been greater, the dangers of overspecialization, as in all related disciplines in the humanities, remain very real. Competing

---

ford: Basil Blackwell, 1988); and Sherna Gluck and Daphne Patai, *Women's Words: The Feminist Practice of Oral History* (New York: Routledge, 1991).

claims with respect to methods of investigation have also resulted in a widespread malaise concerning the possibility of generally agreed upon standards in scholarship. Evidently, the increasing number and complexity of research methods are partially a product of recent innovations in technology and partially a result of the need for delicate and unconventional instruments to discern the voices of those who have left no traditional records behind them. But unless the connections between these developments are brought to conscious awareness and addressed, this complexity, and the growing suspicion of any form of objective understanding, have the potential of fragmenting historical studies even further. It is with these considerations in mind that we encourage students to consider imaginatively those research topics that have the greatest potential for drawing intellectual and social history together. We have observed that the new information sources and techniques of analysis have already proven to be a strong solvent in breaking down the older distinctions between the study of "sacred" and "secular" history.

Definitions of the several church historical disciplines are also related to the question of the objectivity of knowledge, and given the new methodological climate, this is an unavoidable question to which we will often return. The history of doctrine, for example, when construed as an independent discipline, was sustainable only on the grounds of objectivistic presuppositions. Institutional church history and the history of doctrine now demand a more holistic approach that takes full cognizance of the subtle social, political, and philosophical influences on theology. But recognizing the social location of ideas does not, in our view, necessitate the social determination of knowledge, nor does it lead inevitably to epistemological or methodological relativism. Church historians should aim at objectivity even as they acknowledge that it demands as broad and comprehensive a perspective in the analysis of ideas as it does in the depiction of complex events in the institutional or political life of the church.

The theoretical grounding for our emphases arises from reflection on the historical nature of Christianity and from considerations that are parallel to those of Wolfhart Pannenberg, who rightly observed that "no branch of history is under such pressure from its particular subject-matter to consider the whole of history as church history."[3] We have

3. Wolfhart Pannenberg, *Theology and the Philosophy of Science* (Philadelphia: The Westminster Press, 1976), p. 395. See also Pannenberg, et al., *Revelation as History* (New York: Macmillan, 1968), especially chapter 5, pp. 161-81.

also derived some insight from the modern *Annales* school, and, in particular, the influential work of Mark Bloch, who, in his unrelenting quest for a more complete reconstruction of the past, proved the truth of the maxim that "the deeper the research, the more the light of the evidence must converge from sources of many different kinds." Christianity, Bloch observed, is a religion of historians, and the concerns of the historian must be as comprehensive as the history of the human race, because Christianity places the great drama of Fall, Redemption, and Judgment on the wide canvass of world history.[4] But if the universal implications of Christianity are important for the church historian, methodological considerations necessarily follow. In a distinguished series of writings, historians of the *Annales* school have convincingly shown that the wide scope of the historian's subject matter is inevitably connected with an eclecticism in method.[5] The new environment we have briefly surveyed will not yield up its full potential apart from a close analysis of the traditional definitions of the discipline of church history and its related fields; to the extent that past definitions of the discipline have unduly contributed to the separation of contiguous and closely related fields, these definitions must be carefully scrutinized and recast. The following survey of the conventional boundaries of the field of church history will reveal that the researcher's initial orientation determines a great deal about the methods of investigation that he or she eventually adopts. We will also need to give serious attention to the history of church historical studies in order to estimate the considerable limitations of past conceptualizations. At the very outset of research, students of church history in particular need to recognize how confessional differences, when uncritically imported into the study of history, have invariably narrowed our field of vision and distorted the past.

Preliminary Definition of Terms

If the traditionally strict separation of disciplines and subdisciplines can be questioned on the grounds just noted, there remain nonetheless good

---

4. Mark Bloch, *The Historian's Craft* (New York: Vintage Books, 1953), pp. 67, 4-5.

5. For example, see Emmanuel Leroy Ladurie, *The Mind and Method of the Historian* (Chicago: University of Chicago Press, 1981), pp. 1-9.

reasons to identify the traditional disciplines and their interrelationships. In the first place, researchers and students, particularly in historical studies, cannot ignore the past, including the past of their own disciplines. As we will insist below, the analysis and presentation of the history of scholarship is an integral part of the process of research and writing. The scholarship of the past clearly did oblige traditional distinctions between institutional history and the history of ideas, church history and the history of doctrines. These distinctions remain in the present as a part of the history of scholarship and, therefore, as distinctions to be observed, and oftentimes transcended, in the process of research. It will often be the case that a contemporary historian can find grounds on which to reappraise a particular line of scholarship by looking to work done in a related but distinct area of older research not examined in previous studies of an issue because of an overemphasis on the distinction of the disciplines.

In the second place, although the boundaries between institutional, social, and intellectual history have become blurred, they have not been obliterated and, in fact, continue to exist as emphases rather than as compartments in the larger body of scholarship. Such emphases can be fruitfully employed as aids in narrowing and controlling a topic: a doctrinal or intellectual emphasis can be established and the institutional or social pole of the topic can be noted and controlled through judicious citation of recent scholarship. Third, granting that emphases or polarities continue to exist even when strict disciplinary distinctions have been obscured, it is important for researchers to recognize the gradually shifting character of these emphases or poles. Whereas the nineteenth and early twentieth centuries saw a distinct dominance of the history of institutions and the history of dogmas, the increasing importance and precision of sociology and the increasing interest in the broader history of religions have pressed social and phenomenological concerns to the fore in more recent historical study. Researchers need to be aware that such shifting interests and emphases neither negate entirely the value of older research nor absolutely define the boundaries of future research. In other words, once intellectual or doctrinal history has been modified to account for the insights of the social historians, it surely remains a viable and edifying field of research. And by the same token, social history can become a rather arid field when it ignores the life of the mind.

"Church history" is the broadest of all the traditional disciplines dealing with the church's past.[6] The discipline of church history encompasses the practice of the church as well as the thought of the church; it studies both dogma and the intersection of the church with society and the larger world. In this broader discipline we examine such matters as the liturgy of the church, its sacraments and polity; one might even include such things as preaching style or homiletics and church architecture and music. Church and state is also a topic of interest to the church historian, ranging from matters of persecution in the early church to toleration and secularization in the modern period. Anything that the church does in the world is arguably a part of church history. But we also look at what the church teaches, and thus historical theology is a subset of the broader discipline; as a church historian one is bound to study some historical theology. Most narrowly conceived, the church historian might study the teaching of individuals, but inevitably one will also examine the teaching of the church universal, or its creeds and councils. Finally, the discipline of church history embraces such matters as the mission and expansion of the church.

Like church history, "historical theology" is a general term indicating a rather broad area of study. The term itself is somewhat misleading. To some, it indicates the study of the history of Christian doctrine primarily for the sake of theological formulation in the present. To others, it has meant the analysis of the great dogmas of the church in relative isolation from the events of church history. Some definition and qualification of the term is therefore in order.

In the first place, the documents of historical theology are, with few exceptions, the same as those of church history, particularly in the patristic period. The difference between the disciplines lies in the approach the historian takes to the documents and the kinds of information that are elicited from them. For example, the works of the second-century Apologists Athenagoras and Justin Martyr can be used to understand the way in which the church conducted its mission to the pagan world. In fact, recent scholarship has tended to view these works as missionary tracts rather than as pleas for tolerance addressed to the emperor. There is no evidence that the emperor ever received these apologies and a good deal of evidence that they had considerable impact on the thought of the early church itself. In addition, they can be used

---

6. Cf. Jaroslav Pelikan, *Historical Theology: Continuity and Change in Christian Doctrine* (London and New York: Hutchinson/Corpus, 1971), pp. xiii-xviii.

as documentation of the role, the place, and the perceptions of Christians in Roman society, that is, as evidence for the construction of Christian social history. All of these areas are the proper subject matter of church history.

By the same token, these treatises can be used to elicit sacramental and liturgical practice, at least to a certain degree. The best documentation that we have of sacramental practice in the second century is Justin Martyr's *First Apology*. Finally, the works of the Apologists, in particular the *Plea for Christians* by Athenagoras, offer some of the earliest speculations leading toward the doctrine of the Trinity. Similarly, Justin provides one of the earliest examples of a technical use of the concept of *logos*. His use of *logos* language, drawn both from the Gospel of John and from Stoic philosophy, points toward the trinitarian and christological discussions of the third and fourth centuries. "History of doctrine" focuses, in other words, on very narrow, albeit significant, slices of these documents. In fact, the great burden of writing historical theology is to do justice to the sources — to the intention of their authors — while eliciting from them the materials that belong to one, somewhat artificially defined, part of this history. Historical theology or history of doctrine must be done in such a way as not to lose sight of the original location of the ideas and the original purpose behind the documents in which the ideas are found.

The "history of dogma" is the history of those particular doctrinal themes that have received normative definition from the church. There are barely three theological topics that have received this kind of definition. The Councils of Nicea and Constantinople moved toward a full dogmatic definition of the Trinity, while the Council of Chalcedon offered the church its orthodox definition of Christology. Formulated in a basic form in the patristic period, these dogmas were further elaborated in the subsequent history of Christian doctrine without any intentional alteration of the basic conciliar decisions. The other topic is the doctrine of grace. On this subject, the patristic era failed to offer a final formulation, but it did determine that salvation cannot occur apart from grace. It is orthodox to define salvation in terms of the mutual interrelationships of grace and will. But it is also within the bounds of ecumenical orthodoxy to define salvation as occurring by grace alone prior to any acts of the will. What falls outside of these bounds is the "Pelagian" assumption that salvation can arise by acts of human will apart from grace. There is, to this day, no final definition of the doctrine of grace except in the broad sense of a legitimate spectrum for the language of theological formulation. With these limitations in mind, the classic historians of dogma Adolf von Harnack and Reinhold Seeberg[7] were able to construct tightly argued histories of the fundamental dogmatic tenets of Christianity, focused on the Trinity, Christology, and grace that presented the development of Christian doctrine from earliest times to the Reformation. The Reformation, understood both as the end of a united Christendom and as a return to Scripture as a norm prior to tradition, concludes the history of dogma, except for the dogmas later enacted by the Roman Catholic church and discussed by Harnack and Seeberg as limited after-growths.

While the history of dogma does not look beyond these basic issues, the history of doctrine discusses the entirety of the body of doctrine as it moves through the life of the church in any given period. In a sense, the elements of a larger body of doctrine are capable of being identified in any period in the history of the church. It would be impossible, of course, to build a whole system of theology out of the writings of the Apostolic Fathers (A.D. 95-155). Their writings do, however, provide a body of teaching that is larger than the trinitarian, christological, and soteriological issues that typically occupy the mind of the historian of dogma: These broader elements are the proper subject matter of the history of doctrine.

The "history of Christian thought" identifies a still broader field of inquiry, inasmuch as it claims as its field of investigation the entire range of Christian thought, including those topics nominally beyond the bounds of theology. What is sometimes called history of spirituality would fit into this category, including discussion of the character of Christian life and piety, though arguably this is the subject of the church historian. Similarly, philosophical topics and the relation of Christian thought to the rise of modern science belong to this larger discussion.

Although it is the broadest field of the three, the history of Christian thought functions as the basic discipline of historical theology, without which neither the history of doctrine nor the history of dogma can really function, because the doctrines themselves (and dogmas as a special case of doctrine) can only be understood in their fundamental religious context and in relation to the way Christians were living, thinking, and acting

---

7. N.B. despite Seeberg's somewhat broader scope and title *(History of Doctrines)* his outline and closure parallel Harnack.

in society, that is, in relation to a broad Christian history of ideas. It is, for example, impossible to discuss Trinity and Christology coherently without some sense of the religious life or of the philosophical inclinations of the age. The doctrinal issues become clear only in the light of the interaction of the church with the surrounding culture and in view of the interrelationship between the doctrinal formulations and the life of the church in its historical and cultural context. The history of Christian thought is the preferred term for the larger context of intellectual history in which the history of dogma and the history of doctrine must be understood, and, in view of the methodological assumptions present throughout this introductory discussion, it must also be the basic or preferred discipline for the presentation of the teachings of the church.[8] As the broadest category, the history of Christian thought presses on the limits of what is "Christian" or "orthodox": the history of Christian thought would also include thinkers who were only marginally related to the church, and subsequently may have actually been disenfranchised by the church, such as Faustus Socinus.

When historical theology is thus defined in terms of the history of Christian thought, it is sometimes nearly identical with, and always has strong points of contact with, the discipline known as "intellectual history." Western intellectual history, by way of example, is the discussion of the life of the mind in the development of Western civilization. Learning the history of thought is essential to doing theology and church history, inasmuch as theological literature has occupied a large segment of the great literature of the West. Learning the history of Christian thought, and even the history of dogma, cannot occur apart from this larger sense of the movement of Western intellectual history, not only because of the specific documentary overlap but also because of the interpenetration of ideas and issues. For example, the impact of Aristotle

---

8. There exists no careful methodology of church history, such as is available for the history of doctrine and the history of dogma, where there is a prologue to the larger essay that describes the method. General discussions of the proper subject matter of church history are found in the classic "encyclopedias" of theology like Philip Schaff, *Theological Propaedeutic: A General Introduction to the Study of Theology, Exegetical, Historical, Systematic, and Practical* (New York: Scribner, 1894) and George R. Crooks and John F. Hurst, *Theological Encyclopaedia and Methodology, on the basis of Hagenbach* (new ed., rev.; New York: Hunt and Eaton, 1894). In terms of the history of dogma and its limits and the history of doctrine and its limits, see the first chapters on the subject in Adolph von Harnack's *History of Dogma*, Reinhold Seeberg's *History of Doctrine*, and Jaroslav Pelikan's *Historical Theology*.

on the West, beginning in the late twelfth and on into the thirteenth
century, is a crucial issue in the history of doctrine, but it is also crucial
for Western intellectual history in general, as is the loss of Aristotle (not,
of course, to everyone) in the seventeenth century. The failure of Aris-
totelianism as a world system and cosmology in the seventeenth century
has theological repercussions, but it also affects the beginnings of modern science, the changes in political philosophy, and the changes in
ethical thinking that have occurred. There is little possibility of separat-
ing the two, just as one is unable to engage in the history of doctrine
or the history of Christian thought without a grip on general intellectual
history. Western intellectual history provides a foundation for studying
the history of the church, the history of Christian thought, and systematic theology as well. Even when one moves beyond the Enlightenment
into the modern world, where there is a separation of the two major
traditions (the theological tradition and the Western intellectual tradition), the earlier history shapes the nature of the discussion, if only by
raising the issue of the authority of theology in its relation to the other
aspects of post-Enlightenment Western thought.

For somewhat different reasons, the field of study known as the
"history of religion" also impinges on and contributes to the study of
church history and its related disciplines. As developed in the late
nineteenth and early twentieth centuries, history of religions emphasized the common elements found in different religions and insisted on
the comparative study of religious movements. It is to the so-called
"History of Religions School" that included such scholars as Wilhelm
Bousset and Richard Reitzenstein that church historians owe much of
their knowledge of the ancient mystery religions and their relation to
early Christianity. More recently, Hans Jonas, Kurt Rudolf, and Simone
Pétrement have offered different and highly significant discussions of
the phenomenon of Gnosticism and its impact on Christian thought.
Such studies must be considered by historians of Christian doctrine and
institutions inasmuch as they demand the substantive modification of
earlier perceptions of the nature of the early church. In addition, as the
eminent early nineteenth-century church historian Johann August
Neander well recognized, the religious element of Christian life cannot
be excluded from the examination of the history of ideas, institutions,
or society without considerable violence being done to the historical
traces themselves: the broad religious motivation, with its social, cultural, and phenomenological ramifications, impinges constantly on the

study of Christianity and its internal life as well as its relationship to other religious movements in history.

THE EMERGENCE OF CRITICAL CHURCH HISTORIOGRAPHY

Before the mid-eighteenth century, the study of church history was uncritical; it was almost invariably written from a confessional viewpoint and it was anything but detached.[9] In the Catholic Church the tradition of the church played a far more prominent role as a norm for doctrine and theology than in Protestantism. In the study of church history, this had the effect of pressing historians toward an emphasis on continuity; there was a distinct and pervasive tendency to interpret later developments as occurring earlier than they in fact occurred. The theological assumption that links authority with antiquity has thus had a longstanding, deleterious effect on scientific investigation. The Catholic understanding of the church meant that, for many older Catholic historians (including writers as recent as Schwane and Tixeront,[10] the authors of two of the more important early twentieth-century histories of dogma), the matter of finding meaning in the past was not even posed as a question. The entire viewpoint was dominated by the concepts of a controlling providence and the unanimity of the tradition, granting the normative character of tradition for the contemporary expression of the church.

When we turn to the Protestant Reformation and its seventeenth-century aftermath, we find a more critical approach to the past, but this reorientation was laden with its own problems. The principle of *sola Scriptura* profoundly influenced the Reformers' understanding of church history as well as theology.[11] For Protestants of the sixteenth and seventeenth centuries, the Middle Ages were a particularly troublesome

9. Philip Schaff helpfully outlined the modern emergence of church historiography in the terms presented here of Catholics, radical Reformers, magisterial Reformers, and Pietism, but in much fuller detail. Philip Schaff, *History of the Apostolic Church with a General Introduction to Church History* (New York, 1854), pp. 55, 63, 69-72.

10. Joseph Schwane, *Histoire des Dogmas*, trans. (from the German) by A. Degert (6 vols., Paris: Beauchesne, 1903-4); and J. Tixeront, *History of Dogmas*, trans. H. L. B. (3 vols., St. Louis: Herder & Herder, 1910-).

11. Cf. John M. Headley, *Luther's View of Church History* (New Haven: Yale University Press, 1963).

era, and the temptation, frequently indulged, was to view the period of church history from St. Augustine, or at least from the thirteenth-century dawn of scholasticism, to the sixteenth century, in terms of apostasy. Luther's *Babylonian Captivity of the Church* critiqued far more than the Avignon papacy; indeed, he polemicized against the abuses in "this Thomistic . . . Aristotelian church," pointing directly to the captivity of the church to scholasticism.[12] Protestant dogmaticians, beginning with Andreas Hyperius (d. 1564), consistently argued a decline of thought in the era of scholasticism, a view repeated by Protestant writers throughout the late sixteenth and seventeenth century, who distinguished their "scholasticism" from that of the Middle Ages.[13] The great Protestant chronicle, the *Magdeburg Centuries*, scanned the Middle Ages for a few faithful forerunners of reform. The radical Reformers embraced this approach as well, but pressed it to its extreme conclusion: the *Chronicle* of Caspar Braitmichel (1542) placed the fall of the church at A.D. 150. In this view, the entire church, including the first three centuries after the apostles, fared very ill, and the promise of Christ that the gates of hell would not prevail against the church was conveniently ignored.

Church historians throughout the sixteenth and most of the seventeenth century, then, viewed the church's past in terms either of orthodoxy or heresy. In Catholic thought, the crucial idea of development was present; but in the polemical atmosphere of the sixteenth and seventeenth centuries, it was vitiated by a providential view of superintendence that allowed for little or no error in the past. (The great exception to this generalization is the historian of doctrine, Dionysius Petavius, who recognized, for example, that the trinitarianism of the first three centuries was quite different from that of Nicea.) The Anabaptist view denied the possibility of development and had little patience with the study of the past at all, while various antitrinitarian heretics of the day looked at the pre-Nicene era as a source for their views, leaving the orthodox of the day, Protestant and Catholic alike, with little sympathy for careful, historical examination of the earliest church such as had been done by Petavius. The major Lutheran and Reformed churches also tended to view developments that were not in

---

12. Martin Luther, *The Babylonian Captivity of the Church*, LW 36, p. 29.
13. Richard A. Muller, *Post-Reformation Reformed Dogmatics,* vol. 1: *Prolegomena* (Grand Rapids: Baker Book House, 1987).

some way related positively to Protestantism in an excessively negative light. These three approaches to historical understanding, represented by Catholic theologians, the radical Reformers, and the magisterial Reformers, are of more than merely passing interest; even today it is not uncommon for students of church history to be controlled by viewpoints such as these.

Two basic alterations of perspective were necessary to produce the modern, critical church historiography of the mid-eighteenth century: first, a greater scientific concern for the analysis of original documents, and second, the freedom to interpret these sources in a way that did not lead to a predetermined, or at least predictable, goal. The latter of the two developments emerged in part from the Pietist distinction between piety and doctrine which, despite its inherent difficulties, did allow for a positive evaluation of a group or movement with which the historian did not agree theologically. Thus, the Pietist historian Gottfried Arnold's *Impartial History of the Church and of Heretics* (1699-1700) defended a number of medieval sects on the strength of their religious experience. Since the heart of religion for Arnold was subjective, experimental piety rather than strict orthodoxy, he strove for a fair presentation of the religious motives of various heretics and schismatics. The corollary of this generosity, however, was that Arnold frequently treated the orthodox with undue severity.[14] A similar emphasis is found in the works of Joseph Milner, an Anglican historian of the eighteenth century. For him as for Arnold, sects frequently provided significant examples of Christian piety. Milner, however, was not nearly as polemical as Arnold. His object was even more popular and practical than Arnold's, and he omitted everything from his history that failed to edify. Said Milner, "Nothing but what appears to me to belong to Christ's Kingdom shall be admitted; *genuine piety is the only thing which I intend to celebrate.*"[15] This was selectivity with a vengeance, and neither Arnold nor Milner

---

14. Schaff, *History of the Apostolic Church*, pp. 69-70.

15. Schaff, *History of the Apostolic Church*, p. 71. Milner's approach resulted in a great many errors. S. R. Maitland wrote an entire book entitled *Strictures on Milner's Church History* (1834). Maitland admits that Milner's work is typified by piety (pp. 8, 79). Milner claimed, in his own words, to consult the "original record," and to eschew the statements of "modern historians." Maitland (pp. 15, 51) shows just how partial and slipshod a job he did. The value of Maitland's critique of Milner is that it shows us just how far competent criticism of sources and modern assessments of the relative weight of ancient authorities had come by 1834.

really grasped the need for an objective handling of original sources. But in both, a new approach to the past freed them from arriving at a predetermined, predictable conclusion.

The beginning of the Enlightenment, concurrent with the development of Pietism, had a profound impact on historical studies. The Enlightenment brought both a more tolerant atmosphere and a more empirical approach to the source materials. The genuine objectivity that was lacking in Arnold and Milner was fully developed in the work of Johann Lorenz von Mosheim (1694-1755), for much of his career chancellor of the University of Göttingen. On the grounds of his exceptionally erudite, detailed, and balanced four-volume *Institutes of Ecclesiastical History*, Mosheim is often called "the Father of church history."[16] Mosheim's work was the preeminent text for more than a century and, in its English translation, was used in most American seminaries throughout much of the nineteenth century.

Although the critical, objective use of documents was not new in Mosheim's work, his *Institutes* made this critical objectivity a central methodological concern. "My principal care," he wrote, "has been to relate events with fidelity and authority. For this purpose I have gone to the very sources of information, the best writers, that is, of all ages, and such as lived in, or near, the times which they treat of." Mosheim looked critically at the approach of many of his predecessors who had simply rested their work on the chronicles of earlier writers. Such a practice, he continued, "is attended with this evil, that it perpetuates the mistakes, which are apt to abound in very large and voluminous works, by causing them to pass from a single book into numerous others."[17] Mosheim not only went to the original documents for information, he was also very careful to cite his sources in order to aid his readers in evaluating his work. Mosheim's attempt to attain methodological objectivity, in contrast to that of virtually all of his predecessors, including Arnold and Milner, is most evident in his comments on the treatment of heresies:

> The history of these commotions or heresies, should be full and precise. This labour, if wisely expended, and with impartiality, will

16. Johann Lorenz von Mosheim, *Institutes of Ecclesiastical History, Ancient and Modern*, trans. J. Murdock, ed. H. Soames, 4 vols. (London: Longman & Co., 1841). The first edition, in Latin, appeared in 1726-55.

17. Mosheim, *Institutes*, vol. 1, p. 10.

well repay the toil: but it is arduous and difficult. For the leaders of these parties have been treated with much injustice; and their doctrines are misrepresented: nor is it easy to come at the truth, in the midst of so much darkness; since most of the writings of those called *heretics* are now lost. Those, therefore, who approach this part of church history, should exclude every thing invidious from the name, *heretic:* and consider it as used only in a more general sense for a man, who, by his own, or by another's fault, has given occasion for wars and disagreements among Christians.[18]

Mosheim's approach to the materials of history also went considerably beyond the mere narrative or chronicle to attempt historical explanation. The historian, he argues, "must not only tell *what was done,* but also *why this or that thing happened,* that is, *events* are to be joined with their *causes.*" As far as Mosheim was concerned, "naked facts" only served to amuse readers, while the explanation of the "reasons" behind the facts, with due care not to "fabricate causes," serves the reader by "sharpening discriminating powers, and rendering [him or her] wise."[19] Even so, Mosheim was acutely aware of characteristic dangers that face the historian, such as anachronism, undue reverence for authority, and bias:

> The *times* in which we live often have such ascendancy over us, that we measure past ages by them, thinking that formerly either to have been done, or to be impossible, which now is either done, or is impossible. Then *persons,* whose testimony one must use, especially those of them who have long been famed for holiness and virtue, often lead us into error by their authority. Lastly, the love of *opinions* and doctrines, which have our own affections, often so constrains our minds, that even unconsciously we may give erroneous views of facts. This triple servitude must, therefore, to our utmost power, be driven from the mind.[20]

The Enlightenment thus contributed a critical, analytical approach to historical study. In their enthusiasm for their own enlightenment, however, many of Mosheim's contemporaries and successors evince a certain

---

18. Mosheim, *Institutes,* vol. 1, p. 18.
19. Mosheim, *Institutes,* vol. 1, p. 18.
20. Mosheim, *Institutes,* vol. 1, pp. 20-21.

contempt for the past; or, alternatively, were tempted to view all history progressing toward the goal of enlightenment.

In very short order, the eighteenth century saw the development of historical-critical method in the works of Baumgarten and Semler[21] and the beginnings of the historical approach to biblical theology and to Christian doctrine in the writings of Gabler and Münscher respectively.[22] Gabler and Münscher were able to perceive that the materials of the past, whether biblical or churchly, could only be brought into the service of contemporary formulation if they were first understood in their own right and independently, without the interference of modern theological categories and opinions. This perception, refined considerably beyond the views of Gabler and Münscher by biblical and historical scholars of the nineteenth and early twentieth centuries, is fundamental to modern theological scholarship and provides the primary rationale for the study of history in seminaries and in graduate programs in religion.

The Romantic movement took a different avenue to the study of the past. Generally speaking, it was typified by a deeper appreciation for the past understood on its own terms and by a greater recognition of the way that the historical environment shapes individuals. Johann Gottfried Herder's *Ideas Toward A Philosophy of the History of Mankind* (1784-91) was especially influential in this respect.[23] Whereas the Enlightenment preferred mechanical analogies, Herder stressed the analogy between history and living things. By viewing history organically, he engendered a love for the past in its entirety, since presumably one cannot destroy part of a living organism without destroying the whole. The impact of Herder's ideas on the study of church history can be seen in August Neander (1789-1850). Neander was a student at the University of Halle in 1806, and there he fell under the influence of Schleiermacher; later, at Göttingen, he studied under Gesenius, the Hebrew scholar. In 1813, having published a monograph on Julian the Apostate, he was called to the University of Berlin as professor of church

21. See the discussion in Hans W. Frei, *The Eclipse of Biblical Narrative: A Study in Eighteenth and Nineteenth Century Hermeneutics* (New Haven: Yale University Press, 1974), pp. 88-91, 111-12, 157-61, etc.

22. On Gabler see Frei, *Eclipse*, pp. 159, 163, 165-67, 248-51; for a discussion of Münscher, see Adolph von Harnack, *History of Dogma*, 7 vols., trans. Neil Buchanan (New York: Dover, 1961), vol. 1, pp. 13, 31-32.

23. According to Schaff, *History of the Apostolic Church*, pp. 90-91.

history, where he worked until his death in 1850.[24] Neander is most well known for his multivolume *General History of the Christian Religion and Church* (1826-52).

Neander's indebtedness to the Romantic movement is seen explicitly in the dedication of the first volume of his *General History of the Christian Religion and Church* to Schelling. Says Neander: "In striving to apprehend the history of the church, not as a mere juxtaposition of outward facts, but as a development proceeding from within, and presenting an image and reflex of internal history, I trust that I am serving a spirit which may claim some relationship to your philosophy. . . ." Neander's indebtedness to Schleiermacher is made explicit when he discusses the purpose or the end of church history. "To exhibit the history of the church of Christ, as a living witness of the divine power of Christianity; as a school of Christian experience; a voice, sounding through the ages, of instruction, of doctrine, and of reproof, for all who are disposed to listen: this from the earliest period, has been the leading aim of my life and studies."[25] Moreover, organic metaphors and the theme of development are found throughout his work. "It shall be our purpose to trace, from the small mustard-grain, through the course of the past centuries, lying open for our inspection, the growth of that mighty tree, which is destined to overshadow the earth, and under the branches of which all its peoples are to find a safe habitation."[26]

Neander's hermeneutical sophistication and his relation to Schleiermacher is noteworthy. He works as a historian out of a conviction concerning the inner connection between spiritual life in Christ and scientific inquiry. "Our knowledge here falls into a necessary circle. To understand history, it is supposed that we have some understanding of that which constitutes its working principle; but it is also history which furnishes us [with] the proper test, by which to ascertain whether its principle has been rightly apprehended."[27] Neander's organization of

24. Leopold von Ranke (1795-1886) was also at the University of Berlin at this time. His work as a modern historian is noteworthy primarily for his emphasis upon the original sources. Von Ranke brought a strong objective attitude to the study of history. It was said of his famous *History of the Popes* that though written by a German Lutheran, it pleased many Catholics.

25. August Neander, *General History of the Christian Religion and Church,* 5 vols. (Boston, 1872), vol. 1, dedicatory page.

26. Neander, *General History,* vol. 1, p. 1.

27. Neander, *General History,* vol. 1, p. 1.

the material is also far superior to that of Mosheim. He casts all of his data on a single topic, for example, persecution, together in one place, and then covers an extended time frame, within reasonable bounds. Then he treats different topics in their relation one to the other; for example, the structure of the ministry or the clerical hierarchy is followed by a discussion of the doctrine of penance in relation to the hierarchy and the institution. One finds in Neander the adoption of vitalistic, organic categories as a way of construing historical development; there is, in addition, a strong stress upon the importance of primary sources and accurate documentation; and as with those who preceded him, he adopts a separation between piety and doctrine that enables him to judge a movement favorably without agreeing with it theologically. All these features combine to bring the study of church history into the modern world. The enormous influence of Neander is documented in the work of Friedrich A. G. Tholuck (1799-1877), friend of Neander and professor of theology at the University of Halle. Tholuck delivered a series of lectures at the University of Halle in 1842-43 that were translated and published in *Bibliotheca Sacra* as "Theological Encyclopedia and Methodology." Edwards A. Park, the translator, noted that the system adopted here "was in some respects, far more scientific and extensive than that adopted in other lands."[28] In this lecture Tholuck lays out the major tasks for one who wishes to be "a worthy historian" of the church. First, "one must consult the original authorities." The second prerequisite for a historian who "would be master of his art" is that he or she exhibit individual facts "with individuality of style; he describes times and persons in detail rather than in general."[29] This requirement amounts to an early plea for historical analysis. Tholuck was surprisingly bold to criticize the great Neander himself on this account; Neander, said Tholuck, exhibits "only a small degree of such vivid individual portraiture."[30] To defend his point, Tholuck quoted Herder, who said: "As the most beautiful acts of the individual Christian will be those of which the world ha[s] no knowledge, so the most interesting operations of Christianity will be those which are unnoticed

28. Introductory comments by Edwards A. Park on Friedrich A. G. Tholuck, "Theological Encyclopedia and Methodology: From the Unpublished Lecture of Prof. Tholuck," *Bibliotheca Sacra* 1 (1844): 178.
    29. Tholuck, "Theological Encyclopedia," p. 570.
    30. Tholuck, "Theological Encyclopedia," p. 571.

in general history, those which are performed in the quiet circle of family friends."[31]

A third prerequisite is that the historian have no "party prejudices," though "party preferences" are important, since without a point of view, history will be colorless and lifeless. A primary example is found in Neander, who "manifests a noble and true freedom from blind partisanship. It must be confessed, however, that Neander is sometimes too desirous of exhibiting impartiality, and is therefore more favorable to the heretics whose character he describes, than the truth will warrant."[32] Finally, Tholuck ventures into the difficult realm of causation and advances a position not unlike that of Wolfhart Pannenberg.

> A fourth requisite for an ecclesiastical historian is, that he accompany his narration of events with a reference to their causes and consequences, and that he make this reference on psychological and religious grounds; in other words, that he display a psychological and religious *pragmatism*. He is said to give a psychological explanation of the causes of events, when he describes the mode in which these events result from the character, and the individual peculiarities of the persons to whose agency they are ascribed. He is said to make a religious reference of events to their causes, when he refers the events to the directing providence of God, and to some definite moral and religious final cause.[33]

Philip Schaff (1819-93) is sometimes considered the father of American church history, not because he wrote much on the American church, but because he brought together the best advances in the study of church history and set new standards for the discipline in the United States. In 1846 he published an essay entitled *What Is Church History?*, subtitled "A Vindication of the Idea of Historical Development."[34] Here he chronicled his dependence on Herder, Neander, and Tholuck (in

---

31. Tholuck, "Theological Encyclopedia," p. 571.
32. Tholuck, "Theological Encyclopedia," p. 572.
33. Tholuck, "Theological Encyclopedia," p. 572.
34. Philip Schaff, *What Is Church History?* pp. 17-144 in *Reformed and Catholic: Selected Historical and Theological Writings of Philip Schaff*, ed. Charles Yrigoyen, Jr., and George M. Bricker (Pittsburgh: The Pickwick Press, 1979). For the influence of Philip Schaff and a series of excellent historiographical surveys, see Henry W. Bowden, ed., *A Century of Church History: The Legacy of Philip Schaff* (Carbondale: Southern Illinois University Press, 1988).

addition, the views of Hegel are everywhere evident) and set forth his own understanding of church history, called "The Reformed-Catholic Perspective." Schaff's essay is still valuable today, and it will probably never be superseded as a stimulus to the sympathetic reading of church history. Yet while Schaff represented the best in post-Enlightenment historiography, the influence of Hegel was so pervasive that the work suffers from at least three characteristic weaknesses, all related to Hegel's schema and the optimism typical of the nineteenth century. Schaff understands history in terms of steady improvement, but he is, in the first place, naively optimistic. While on the one hand he clearly sees how differently the idea of organic development can be used (compare, he suggests, Neander to F. C. Baur), on the other hand he believes that Christianity never loses, nor can lose, anything of real value. Second, the historian is able to comprehend past events truly, and to unfold them, just as they originally stood, before the eyes of the readers. Finally, Schaff is overly optimistic about the historian's ability to discern the hand of providence and the guiding spirit of Christianity in history. Since the mid-nineteenth century, historians have generally become a good deal more sober about the likelihood of discerning the final outcome, the factual accuracy, and the inner causes of historical events. Nevertheless, historical scholarship reached a level of maturity by the mid-nineteenth century that in many respects has not been surpassed to this day. In terms of the utilization of primary sources, energy in accumulating these sources, critical power in comparing them, and detachment in their interpretation, the accomplishments of a hundred years ago, particularly in Germany, are seldom surpassed today. Indeed, much that is written today falls far below those standards.

In the discipline of church history in the nineteenth century these emphases on the possibility of detachment and the discovery of the actual truth about the past became increasingly central. One finds a growing optimism about what the historian could actually hope to accomplish. In 1851, Henry Boynton Smith could write an article entitled "The Nature and Worth of the Science of Church History."[35] Smith demonstrated a tremendous confidence in the possibility of historical objectivity: the first duty of the historian "is to present the facts them-

35. Henry B. Smith, "The Nature and Worth of the Science of Church History," *Bibliotheca Sacra* 8 (1851): 429. Here he acknowledges his indebtedness to his "venerable and beloved teacher," Neander.

selves in the order of their occurrence."[36] The next duty of the historian is to verify the past; the past is to "live again upon the historic page." The historian, in fact, can so present the past that we may read of the events "better than did the very actors in them."[37] Besides facts, the historian must discover and set forth the events "in the light of their principles and laws. These he is to seek out with a patient, a sympathizing, a reverential, and a truly inductive spirit." Finally, the historian is to discern the ends that the general laws or principles produce.[38] Thus the general laws of history are to be deduced from the facts, and from these one may infer the ends that are to be accomplished by them. Such are the major ingredients of "scientific history." This was a confident, not to say audacious, outlook that characterized many of Smith's colleagues. Scientific church history seems here to be excessively confident about both the nature of research, that is, getting the "facts" straight, and the outcome of the results, which meant establishing general laws of development. E. H. Carr's comment about nineteenth-century historians in general applies equally to church historians: "Historians walked in the Garden of Eden, without a scrap of philosophy to cover them, naked and unashamed before the God of history. Since then we have known Sin and experienced a Fall."[39]

The scientific preoccupation with objectivity was characteristic of much of the late nineteenth century as well.[40] For example, in 1884 another article entitled "Church History as a Science," John De Witt, professor of church history at Lane Theological Seminary, called for movement beyond a series of historical laws and principles to the identification of "the single law which binds together this uncounted multitude of cause and condition."[41] By the turn of the century the emphasis on objectivity and ascertaining the facts had led many church historians toward an explicitly secular understanding of church history. Here, all theological presuppositions were to be eliminated from the study of

---

36. Smith, "Nature and Worth," p. 415.
37. Smith, "Nature and Worth," p. 417.
38. Smith, "Nature and Worth," pp. 417, 421.
39. Edward H. Carr, *What Is History?* (New York: Vintage Books, 1961), p. 21.
40. For the late nineteenth century, see Henry W. Bowden, *Church History in the Age of Science: Historiographical Patterns in the United States, 1876-1918* (Chapel Hill: The University of North Carolina Press, 1971).
41. John De Witt, "Church History as a Science, as a Theological Discipline, and as a Mode of the Gospel," *Bibliotheca Sacra* 41 (1884): 105.

church history, and though this was a large step away from what Neander, Tholuck, and Schaff had envisioned, it can be construed as the logical extension of the emphasis upon objectivity and detachment.

There were a handful of church historians who continued to accept the reality of spiritual causes and would talk about God's activity in history. But those who did so from the 1880s forward spoke with less confidence than their mid-nineteenth century forebears. In Williston Walker's *History of the Christian Church,* first published in 1918, one detects "the absence of any sense of his writing from the interior of the Church."[42] From roughly 1900 through the 1930s American church historians ceased to talk about providence or general laws that could be deduced from factual data. There was still, however, great confidence in history as a science and the ability of the historian to get the facts straight. One finds a few exceptions to this generalization, as with the historical writings of Walter Rauschenbusch. But even in the case of Rauschenbusch, the exception was not so much in the area of how he interpreted church history, as in how he applied it. Rauschenbusch wanted to apply the lessons of history, especially the social lessons, to the present. Scholars at the University of Chicago, in particular, emphasized the social aspects of Christianity in the early decades of the twentieth century, and they were especially interested in discovering the natural, environmental causes for developments in the church. Through 1930, even in the books of such an obviously devoted churchman as William Warren Sweet (University of Chicago Divinity School) there was very little theological and interpretive content.[43]

In surveys of recent trends, scholars have observed a change in this approach beginning about 1930, and it is clearly related to the impact of neoorthodoxy in this country. Henry Bowden, for example, found that following 1930 the new emphases in church history were parallel to similar developments in the study of secular history, and they may be conveniently summarized under four general categories: a new emphasis on cultural influence; a greater stress on the theological significance of the church in history; an appreciation of the church's role in preserving cultural values; and a fresh emphasis on the importance

42. George H. Williams, "Church History: From Historical Theology to the Theology of History," p. 154 in Arnold S. Nash, *Protestant Thought in the Twentieth Century: Whence and Whither?* (New York, 1951).
43. Williams, "Church History," pp. 159-60, 162.

of ideas in explaining the church's past.[44] Thus as we move into the period from 1933 to 1950, historians like John T. McNeill (Union), Sidney E. Mead (Chicago), James Hastings Nichols (Chicago, then Princeton), and Cyril Richardson (Union) all defended the importance of addressing meaning in church history.[45] Cyril Richardson, for example, wrote that the church historian "cannot, if he tries to write sacred history in its fullest sense, be content to confine himself to that bare record of events which we know as *scientific* history [italics mine, says Williams]. . . . he has to tell the story against the background of ultimate meanings." In other words, "the events with which he deals are transfigured by the holy."[46] But at about the same time that we find a new interest expressed in the meaning of history, and specifically, church history, fresh reservations arose in some quarters about the possibility of an objective view of the past. In 1933 Charles Beard's presidential address before the American Historical Association was entitled "Written History as an Act of Faith." He and Carl Lotus Becker provocatively challenged the idea that there were such things as "facts" at all.

In the period since 1950, there is some evidence to suggest that there was yet another reaction to this emphasis on meaning among church historians, and it is entirely likely that the reaction was a result of the growing impact of the social sciences on history.[47] But the historiography of the church from the 1950s to the 1990s is yet to be written in detail. Provisionally, we can say that this forty-year period is typified by several important developments. First, the emergence of the study

---

44. Henry Warner Bowden, *Church History in an Age of Uncertainty: Historiographical Patterns in the United States, 1906-1990* (Carbondale: Southern Illinois University Press, 1991), pp. 222-26. See also Williams, "Church History," pp. 162-63, for a similar evaluation.

45. Williams, "Church History," pp. 170-73.

46. Williams, "Church History," p. 173.

47. Evidence from conferences and articles in the 1970s and 1980s suggests a reaction to a perceived objectivism; these include Clyde Manschreck's presidential address before the American Society of Church History, "Nihilism in the Twentieth Century: A View from Here" (*Church History* 45 [1976]: 85-96); Gordon Wright's presidential address before the American Historical Association in December 1975, entitled "History as a Moral Science" (*American Historical Review* 81 [1976]: 1-11); and Lee Benson, a leading proponent of cliometric history, in the spring of 1981, before the annual meeting of the Organization of American Historians, who urged historians to act as moral philosophers. Benson went so far as to say that scholars should organize themselves into "communities of historians" that would "work with nonscholarly activist groups to solve social problems" (*The Chronicle of Higher Education*, April 6, 1981).

of women in history, though traceable in its origins to earlier in the present century, was undoubtedly the most important feature of the historiography of these years. The related fields of the study of African Americans and ethnic minorities and their institutions took major steps forward during the same period. In secular history, the years 1950 to the present were dominated by the "new" history, that is, by the introduction of quantitative techniques, heretofore applied only in the social sciences; we also find in this period the beginnings of such new approaches as psycho-history. This rich multiplicity of approaches and techniques not only allows the scholar to choose an appropriate technique for a given topic, whether psychology, sociology, or statistical analysis, but also allows some of the best works to combine a number of them in a single project. Because of this attention to detail, and because of the introduction of empirical tests of statistical significance, some scholars have expressed a renewed optimism about obtaining a true, objective understanding of the past. Critics, however, have charged that these approaches tend to minimize the influence of ideas in history and drain the past of meaning. In the discipline of church history, the use of the new techniques has been introduced reluctantly, in part, we must suppose, because of the reigning paradigm of church history as preeminently the history of Christian thought.[48] Given the tremendous variety of methods and new topics, the historian is now challenged with the perplexing question of whether there remain any viable norms in scholarship. Or, in Henry Bowden's words, "The troubling element is that historians of all kinds now tacitly accept the fate of being dismissed by those who do not share their perceptions and priorities."[49]

Because of the exacting demands of these new techniques and the isolationist tendencies of the new fields, the historical monograph that dissects a very small period or topic of history continues to dominate the field. Very few scholars belonging to the present generation of church historians have worked at general history because of the dominance of the historical monograph, and, as a result, we have tended to become isolated in our specialties. If the church historian's slowness to embrace the social sciences is related to a reluctance to subject the church to the

48. A rigorous defense of this observation would prove difficult: it is based on the relative lack of quantitative research in the leading journals of church history. See the further discussion in chapter 3 below.

49. Bowden, *Church History in an Age of Uncertainty*, p. 228.

profane techniques of science, our inability to write general histories is probably related simply to the enormity of the task, given the present conditions of the discipline.

The ecumenical environment in which we presently work is a very favorable one, and it represents a final characteristic of the historiography of the period. The interest in the history of minorities and women's history is highly complementary to this intraconfessional context, since both favor freedom of investigation. The diversity of method noted above is related in part to this welcome diversification in topic, with an ever expanding interest in the "underside" of history. The present atmosphere is clearly conducive to a more thorough, less biased, approach to investigation in a wide range of fields. A Protestant author cannot write today about the history of the doctrine of justification without consulting what is being said by Catholic and Orthodox scholars both in relation to history and among themselves. The ecclesiastical and social contexts in which we work demand an empathetic, sensitive study of other traditions, and presumably, this may be accomplished without compromising one's own confessional distinctives.

Finally, the ecumenical context, combined with the interdisciplinary, technical, and highly specialized nature of research in church history, may offer a partial solution to the problem of overspecialization. It seems clear that in the future, church historians will be able to address the need for general studies only through collaborative efforts. The understanding of fragments of the human past is necessary, but it "will never produce the knowledge of the whole; it will not even produce that of the fragments themselves."[50] The goal of the historian will remain the same: the reintegration of the parts that must be disentangled for the sake of analysis. Moreover, historians have always collaborated in an informal sense, since no one historian is able to "seize the whole." But given present trends, the need for formal collaboration will make itself increasingly felt. Large-scale cooperative scholarly projects now appear to be the only satisfactory way of producing general church histories.

50. Bloch, *The Historian's Craft*, p. 155.

Methods and Models in the History of Doctrine

If the church historian's point of view with respect to providence, meaning in history, and confessional loyalty has often significantly shaped the outcome of research, so, too, specific methods of construing the materials of history, as distinct from the specialized techniques of analysis, have had a profound influence on the general contours of the disciplines we are studying. Students who hope to make a genuine contribution to historical understanding must consider the various ways in which historical materials have been used, and, in the process, sometimes removed from their essential context and thereby distorted. It is surely the case that the history of doctrine lends itself to a more systematic development and builds more upon previous methodological analysis than the history of the church broadly construed. Church history typically takes a more topical, episodic approach than the history of doctrine. Topics need to be developed at length, sometimes parallel to other topics, without a perfectly clear or consistent relationship between them.[51] As is sometimes said, the history of doctrine lends itself more to a synchronic and developmental approach, while church history is necessarily diachronic.

Even so, the discipline of church history has never produced lengthy methodological prolegomena like those found in the classic histories of doctrine. In fact, there remains a significant methodological relationship between the history of doctrine and the disciplines of biblical theology and the history of the religion of Israel over such issues as the propriety of a diachronic doctrinal method, and the preferability of a synchronic and developmental study of the complex of religious beliefs belonging to a particular community in and through various historical contexts — a relationship that has little parallel in the more general presentations of church history.

There are, accordingly, several approaches to the method and organization of the history of Christian doctrine. (As will also become more evident below, the various methods noted here in detail for the

---

51. It is worth noting, however, that the dominance of the monograph identified in the preceding discussion of church history is also characteristic of contemporary historical theology — and that some recent projects in the field have moved toward the multi-author model: for example, Hubert Cunliffe-Jones et al., *A History of Christian Doctrine* (Edinburgh: T. & T. Clark, 1978).

history of doctrine are of fundamental importance for an understanding of systematic theology as well.) At least four basic patterns have been used for the presentation of the history of doctrine: (1) the general/special, (2) the special, diachronic, or systematic, (3) the great thinker, (4) and the integral, synchronic, or organic model.

a. The General/Special Pattern

There is a historical trajectory of meditation on the history of doctrine that began in the late eighteenth century and extended into the nineteenth. The first historian to worry profoundly about the method of historical theology was Wilhelm Münscher. His basic approach was followed by most of the historians of doctrine in the nineteenth century. Two major examples of the method are the histories by Neander and Karl Hagenbach, both of which were translated into English in the nineteenth century and exerted a major influence on British and American studies of the history of doctrine.[52] All three followed a method which has come to be known as the general/special method because it divides into two distinct discussions, one offering a general outline of thought, the other a discussion of particular issues. The first step that these writers took was to break the history of doctrine down into periods for the sake of identifying historical types of theology. Then, within each period, they provide a general survey of authors, their ideas, and the forces that impinged on the history of doctrine. As the second part of their exposition, remaining within the same period, they present the "special history of doctrine." This "special history" typically took the form of a system of theology, beginning with preliminary thoughts on the nature of the theological task in a particular period, moving on to the doctrine of Scripture and the sources of theology, and then to the doctrines of God, creation, providence, and so forth, as far as the last things. Neander and Hagenbach offer this outline for the period of the Apostolic Fathers, the era of the pre-Nicene theologians, of the post-Nicene theologians, and then of various periods, down to the present.

The model has the advantage of very neatly lining out the ideas

---

52. Johann August Wilhelm Neander, *Lectures on the History of Christian Dogmas*, trans. J. Ryland, 2 vols. (London: Bohn, 1858); Karl R. Hagenbach, *A History of Christian Doctrines*, trans. Plumptre, 3 vols. (Edinburgh: T. & T. Clark, 1880-81).

from an individual period and showing in considerable depth the various theological and systematic ramifications of the thought of the church at different times in its history. This model also provides very useful preparation for doing systematic theology. If a theologian needs to understand the patristic reflection on a particular issue, he or she can look to Hagenbach or Neander for a clear presentation.

The problem with the method concerns its location of meaning. The location of meaning is, moreover, a basic issue to be addressed in all historical endeavor. Where does the historian's method locate the meaning of what has happened, of what has been stated and intended in a particular time and place? The general/special method quite pointedly locates meaning in a view of theological system virtually contemporary with the historian. Hagenbach and Neander knew and debated the theological systems of eighteenth- and nineteenth-century Protestantism, most of which began with prolegomena and moved on to the doctrine of Scripture and the doctrine of God and concluded with the doctrine of the last things. The problem with the method, bluntly stated, is that Ignatius of Antioch, who lived in the early second century, never imagined such a thing as a theological system. The general/special method operates under the profound disadvantage of wedging the thought of particular periods of the history of the church into a model that was unknown in the period and is not reflected in the writings of the time. Neither Ignatius of Antioch nor Clement of Rome, nor even the second-century Apologists, ever considered such a thing as theological prolegomena. They did not ask rudimentary questions such as, "How do I go about doing theology?" and "What are my presuppositions?" It is not historically accurate to consider the documents of the second century in a way that is unrelated both to the structure and the intention of the documents and to the intellectual and spiritual milieu of their authors. This does not mean that the method completely lacks usefulness, but it does embody a major methodological problem.

The problem is, moreover, inherent to the method. It is entirely legitimate to take a thinker or a group of thinkers who belong to the same era and culture and to ask what body of doctrine is taught by them. Once this is done, however, the topics must be elicited from the documents and the thinkers, and never imposed on them from without. Such an approach is particularly useful in the discussion even of the ages of the church before the beginnings of systematic theology when, for example, an author like Cyril of Jerusalem can provide an entire body of doctrine in the form of catechesis. Cyril of Jerusalem's catechetical outline, or Gregory of Nyssa's, can be used as the basis of an examination of a particular period in theology. In following a model such as this, thinkers would not impose on the materials issues and topics that were not discussed or understood as distinct issues and topics in the fourth century. At the same time, central doctrinal issues such as the Trinity and Christology would not be discussed in isolation from the rest of Christian thought.

b. The Special or Diachronic Model

An outgrowth of the "general/special" model is the "special," diachronic, or systematic model for examining the history of doctrines. Examples of this model are the histories by W. G. T. Shedd, Louis Berkhof, and Bernhard Lohse. Each of these treatises, particularly Shedd's, discusses individual doctrines in detail. Indeed, Shedd's history could almost be composed out of Hagenbach's by drawing together each of the sections of the special history that deal with one doctrine into a continuous history of the doctrine. The result would be a history of apologetics and prolegomena, followed by a history of the doctrine of God, a history of Christology, and so forth. The histories appear in a topical order and in the shape of a theological system. Louis Berkhof's follows the same pattern, and ought, in fact, to be understood more as a prolegomenon to his *Systematic Theology* than as an independent historical exercise. Both Shedd and Berkhof were, after all, primarily systematic theologians searching out the historical roots of their theologies.

This model has the same failing as the general/special history: it imposes a modern, systematic grid on the subject matter. This failing or problem belongs to all histories of individual doctrines, like R. S. Franks's *History of the Doctrine of the Work of Christ* or Sydney Cave's *The Doctrine of the Person of Christ*. All such books abstract a doctrine from its context and then cease to examine the larger context as a basis for understanding the doctrine. They can address the person of Christ quite independently of the work of Christ, and vice versa, which is something really quite impossible given the character of the historical materials. Or, similarly, they can discuss the doctrine of the person of Christ apart from a sacramental context, an illegitimate endeavor whether one is working in the period of the early church or in the sixteenth century. Nonetheless, if this method is utilized with a candid recognition of its limitations, it does serve as a useful approach to particular doctrines and a good prologue to the study of systematic theology.

c. The Great Thinker Model

The third, and by far the most problematic, of the methods can be identified as the "great thinker" method. An example of this model is A. C. McGiffert's often brilliant *History of Christian Thought*. McGiffert was a fine historian, and it needs to be stated that the problematic character of his method does not give contemporary students of history permission to ignore his work. Justo Gonzalez's three-volume history of doctrine also tends toward the examination of individual thinkers. The problem with this method is that it locates meaning in individual persons; but meaning, arguably, does not reside in individuals. Meaning resides in the materials and ideas used by individuals and mediated by them to others after further meaning and significance have been added by their own efforts. Thus, a chapter on the teaching of Bonaventure as representative of thirteenth-century theology, followed by another chapter on the doctrine of Aquinas as also representative of the thirteenth century, followed by other almost identical chapters on other thinkers, loses sight of the fact that these writers are living out the results of a long tradition, interacting with one another and with any number of other writers, and using the same ideas but in somewhat different ways. It is far more useful (and methodologically justifiable) to follow the history of ideas and the way those ideas develop and change in a particular time, noting the contributions of the various writers who contributed to the development, than it is to discuss a host of similar thinkers individually or to claim that one writer can represent an entire age.

Besides locating meaning in the wrong place, this method adopts a culturally and chronologically imperialistic view of the past. Historians of philosophy are far more guilty of this than historians of doctrine. They tend to move through the materials of history by thinker as if, for example, the thirteenth century can be reduced to Bonaventure, Albert the Great, Thomas Aquinas, Henry of Ghent, and Duns Scotus. The approach is inappropriate because the thinkers themselves did not share such an assumption. A still more extreme example (in a generally superb survey) is Frederick Copleston's treatment of seventeenth-century continental philosophy as moving from Descartes through Geulincx and Malebranche, to Spinoza, and then to Leibniz. Copleston asked the question, "What was really important to the seventeenth century?" This question leads to the investigation of such writers as Francis Suárez and Clemens Timpler, and to the recognition that Descartes was virtually without influence until the second half of the century. Timpler is unknown only because of the intellectual imperialism of modernity. The great thinker model loses track of the interrelationships of ideas and, indeed, of the host of "lesser" minds whose work may have been far more important to their contemporaries than the "great thinkers" identified by later generations. On the other hand, the great thinker method remains extremely useful because it is a way of understanding how ideas cohere in one person's thought. A history of doctrine or a history of philosophy must offer such cohesion, although, surely, not at the expense of the interrelationships of thinkers and ideas in the context of a larger intellectual development.

It is worth noting that a well-trained historian of doctrine or of philosophy ought to be able to follow an idea through its development throughout history (the "special" model) and to focus on an individual thinker in an almost systematic way (the "great thinker" model). At the same time, the well-trained historian will also be able to look for the optimum pattern for the organization of materials and to search out the best location of meaning for the sake of understanding the larger body of materials or sources.

d. The Integral, Synchronic, or Organic Model

The best model for the history of doctrine is certainly the integral or organic model that attempts a synchronous understanding of the development of the central ideas of Christianity. While it was developed primarily by historians of doctrine, this model holds the most promise for reconceptualizing the task of the church historian on a broader scale. The foremost practitioners of this model were Adolf von Harnack and Reinhold Seeberg, although their histories do evidence occasional acknowledgment of the great thinker or the special model. But by and large, however, it is the matrix of ideas in a particular period that controls the exposition of the history of doctrine in Harnack's and

Seeberg's works. Both writers were concerned primarily with the development of the doctrine of God as Trinity and of Jesus Christ as one person in two natures in the early church, granting that these doctrines were the major foci of debate. Other doctrines (which Seeberg in particular examines) are laid out in subsidiary relation with some discussion of individual thinkers. The major methodological issue for both was to trace out the large issues addressed by groups of thinkers and to indicate how those issues were brought to a conclusion.

In many cases the guiding force in the development of a doctrine is not the inner logic of the doctrine itself, as might be gathered from the special history model, or the force of personality of one individual thinker. A broader dialogue took place with other theological topics and other issues, such as social concerns, politics, and the interaction of parties in the church in confrontation with one another. This approach provides a more complex view of history, but the complexity belongs to the materials themselves and ultimately yields a clearer sense of why ideas developed as they did. In the final analysis, the integral method provides a firmer basis for answering even the more systematic questions at the root of the other methods, granting that attention to context and development accounts for the forms of theological statement and, indeed, for the maintenance of certain forms and the rejection of others.

Students can usefully think in terms of employing several different grids or what might be called mental retrieval systems. A periodizing grid, for example, will recall Christian thought in the thirteenth century as distinct from Christian thought in the sixteenth or eighteenth centuries. A topical grid might retrieve information about the doctrine of God in its historical development. Yet another grid might recall the thought of Thomas Aquinas on a variety of different topics. In addition to that, some sense is needed concerning the intersection of different grids: Thomas Aquinas stands as a thirteenth-century thinker who examined the doctrine of God together with a series of other theological and philosophical problems in a particular context. Each of the methods noted contributes something to our larger understanding, but the synchronic method offers the greatest potential for bridging the subdisciplines of church history and embracing the actual complexity of the past. The location of meaning lies in the interaction of ideas, in a particular period as understood by particular individuals, but always as contributory to the larger development.

2. Perspective and Meaning in History

THE PROBLEM OF THE PAST

The relationship of present-day account to past event raises the question of the meaning of "history." Just as with the case of the basic definitions of the historical disciplines, the answer is more complex than one might imagine. The term "history" itself is ambiguous. Initially, there are at least two histories that we must consider: past event and written contemporary account. But it requires little reflection to realize that even this is an oversimplification, because the past is never simply the past. When we talk about the past, for example, we inevitably project our present perspectives into the past; we encounter the problem of what Carl Becker called the "specious present." Historians cannot simply block off the past and study it objectively as if it were an object under the microscope, because we ourselves are a product of that past. There is thus a complex, ambiguous boundary between past event, our present circumstance resulting in part as a product of the past, and our interpretation of the event.

Students of history sometimes assume that the recent past is more accessible than the distant past, and this viewpoint is grounded in the common belief that the passage of time makes understanding more difficult. But a case can be made for the opposite viewpoint as well. The ancient or early modern world may be studied more objectively because we have a greater distance from those periods of time. On the other hand, the study of past cultures raises the question of the unfamiliarity of the habits and customs of those cultures, and hence a heightened inability to understand them because of a greater distance between the observer and the thing observed.

The tension we find between our too facile understanding of the familiar, on the one hand, and the objectivity associated with our attempts to understand the unfamiliar, on the other, probably means that it is easier to study reasonably distant history than very distant history or very recent history. If the events are too recent, although the documentation may be easy to come by because either written evidence or the oral reports are still accessible, nonetheless the level of personal involvement in the events may be so great that it is difficult to step back toward objective interpretation. In fact, the level of one's own involvement may be so great that stepping back is impossible. If the event is too far distant, not only have we lost an enormous amount of material about the event, but the social, political, intellectual, and spiritual context may be so far from our own approach that we have difficulty understanding and reconstructing what happened. In the middle it becomes much easier, granting that patterns of thought and patterns of society are not altogether different. Biases, particularly our own involvement in the issues, are reduced. In addition, there is a reasonably large amount of material still surviving. Nevertheless, biases can never be completely suspended, and modern historiography has properly concluded that the issue of interpretation begins the moment we think about the past.

The problem of the past is not only related to the subjective question of the present interpretation; it is also related to the nature of historical evidence. The minute we say that history is "what happened" it begins to dissolve between our fingers, because we no longer have "what happened." All we have are scattered traces left by "what happened" or people who were involved in "what happened." In the history of Christian thought there are many ways in which the student must reckon with an idea as an event. In one sense we can say that the idea happened. It was generated in a person's head. At least in terms of that person's life or the lives that the person touched, it is the generation of that idea and the liveliness of that idea that had a particular effect. Nonetheless, all that we have is the written record that resulted at some distance from that idea being generated. It is very much the same with other events belonging to "what happened." All that we have are results and traces. From those results and traces we then construct something that we call history, which is no longer so much "what happened" as the way we construct connections between the surviving traces. The work of the historian is enormously difficult given that the connections between the traces are the points at which meaning is inferred — whether it is meaning for us or meaning for whatever happened in the past. And yet, those are precisely the points that do not appear in the documentation.

Historians deal without exception (if we are dealing with human history) with human remnants and human artifacts, much of which falls into the category frequently identified as "brute fact" or simple data. Nonetheless, virtually all such forms of evidence are products of the mind. Perry Miller, the noted American intellectual historian, has said that history is the history of the human mind and no more. Even the study of political behavior that is based on an examination of how people voted at the polls can be construed as a study of the mind, since the seemingly hard quality of quantifiable data like poll books still reflects an element of interpretation. The past does not exist, and all we have is a set of surviving traces of the past. All traces of evidence already reflect some level of interpretation — perhaps in the character of the documentation, the style, or the design. If you use a coin from the Roman Empire and you view that coin as a hard datum, you must recognize that the design of that coin says something. What is on the coin says something about the mind of the designer. Far from being a "brute fact," it is already filled with interpretations of the meaning of the empire. The mind of the emperor, or the public image desired by the emperor, or even a particular artist's conception of the image of imperial Rome, is seen in the way the face on the coin is portrayed. Similarly, the words on the coin are intended to convey a meaning. A recent, analogous case for American history is the design of the abortive Susan B. Anthony dollar. The honored subject of this monetary portrait would hardly be able to recognize herself if she were able to return to this world and look at the coin. The artist's original, lifelike portrait was altered and a large protruding jaw given to Ms. Anthony in order to make the coin a suitable symbol of the liberation of women. The coin is hardly a "brute fact."

Another example of physical evidence that is not quite "brute fact" is the grave marker. On the one hand, a grave marker may offer information about the birth and death of an individual that is just as accurate as the state bureau of vital statistics. And in the case of very old cemeteries, grave markers may well offer information not found in the state offices. The grouping of graves may offer information about families, not merely the size of family, but also evidence of problems of infant mortality and disease. The high infant mortality rate in nineteenth-century rural America is often graphically evidenced by numerous small graves — many of which bear sorrowful carvings of little animals, sometimes even of dead birds. Beyond this kind of information, there is also the highly subjective aspect of grave monuments: an inscription on the grave of a dishonest shopkeeper might read "Dear Husband and Beloved Father." Or, also on the subjective side, information may be given about likes and dislikes of the deceased — or perhaps of relatives, granting that the deceased have no control over mottoes or verses of hymns inscribed on their monuments.

On the other hand, some historians are more interested in human behavior than in the development of thought, and clearly, different forms of evidence yield different aspects of written history. A written document is, of course, from one perspective just as much a datum as a coin or a grave monument, and it is just as likely to mix more or less objective data with interpretation. The document is, at one level, an evidence of the thought of its author and of the various cultural, religious, social, and political forces that had an impact on his or her mind.

A written document will also be capable of chronological placement in the life of its author given the changing context of his or her thoughts. Thus, the writings of Tertullian that offer little direct evidence of their date can be placed in some order given his interest in and eventual espousal of Montanism, ca. A.D. 207. The treatise *On Modesty*, for example, argues that sins such as apostasy, murder, fornication, and adultery cannot be pardoned by a bishop and will not be pardoned by the Spirit. Tertullian gives as one of his grounds of authority the presence of "the Paraclete himself in the persons of the new prophets."[1] The treatise can, on the basis of these statements, be dated in Tertullian's Montanist period, granting both that the statements are typical of the prophetic perspective of Montanism and that they are not characteristic of treatises known to have been written by Tertullian before his conversion to Montanism.

Nonetheless, the critical historian must recognize that documents can and sometimes will intentionally or unintentionally stand in the way of a clear understanding of their author's mind. For example, Arminius's negative comments about scholastic theology as antithetical to true and apostolic Christianity and his statements that he never

---

1. Tertullian, *On Modesty (De Pudicitia)*, 21, in *The Ante-Nicene Fathers*, vol. 4, p. 99.

recommended works by the Jesuits but consistently encouraged students to read Calvin's *Institutes* and Scripture commentaries mask his significant appreciation and use of the writings of Thomas Aquinas, Francis Suárez, and Louis Molina — all scholastics, and the latter two, Jesuits.[2] Given his historical context, Arminius could not have openly advocated Roman Catholic authors without bringing considerable condemnation on himself, but his adamant denial of interest in such works has led generations of historians to ignore their impact on his thought.

The upshot of what we have been saying is that history is not nearly so concrete as we would like to think it is. As Carl Becker observed, the so-called "facts" of history are not objects like bricks that can be readily handled and manipulated. There are numerous problems inherent in the documents that demand critical reading and analysis and, most importantly, the document itself may point only indirectly toward the event or action that inspired it. The document, in other words, is not an event but a trace, a result from which the historian attempts to identify and describe a historical occurrence. A series of documents and other traces is, then, not like a neat row of matched bricks that fit together with precision. Each document or trace may well be unique and replete with distinctive problems.

If the traces of history are not concrete, neither are they complete. We preserve what we view as important. The history of the church is filled with the fragmentary remains of individuals and movements that have been regarded as heretical and almost the complete remains of individuals and movements that have been viewed as orthodox (minus of course the potential remains that the individuals in the movements decided to exclude).

Individuals frequently decide which of their works they want to have survive and which they do not: we have, for example, no musical compositions from the pen of the late Romantic composer Gustav Mahler from a time before 1880, although we know of an early complete opera, two other operas at least partially sketched out, and a piano

2. Cf. James Arminius, *The Works of James Arminius,* trans. James and William Nichols, intro. by Carl Bangs, 3 vols. (1825-75; repr. Grand Rapids: Baker Book House, 1986), vol. 1, pp. 295-301; cf. Geeraert Brandt, *The History of the Reformation . . . in and about the Low Countries,* 4 vols. (1720-23; repr. New York: AMS Press, 1979), vol. 2, pp. 49-50; and see the discussion in Richard A. Muller, *God, Creation and Providence in the Thought of Jacob Arminius: Sources and Directions of Scholastic Protestantism in the Era of Early Orthodoxy* (Grand Rapids: Baker Book House, 1991).

quintet for which the young Mahler had won the composition prize at the Vienna conservatory in 1878. Mahler destroyed all of these works and identified his *Das klagende Lied* of 1880 as opus 1.[3] Early influences on Mahler's style are, therefore, impossible to identify. Historians very often attempt to discover precisely what people unaccountably left behind, and distinguish these remnants from what they intentionally left. Unintentional remains of the human record are obviously considered more valuable for understanding human motivation, but such records are comparatively rare, and this fact, of course, heightens the problem of interpretation. The field of oral history provides a contrasting example. Oral history is by its very nature necessarily intentional with respect to what is recorded, and it is this characteristic that has necessitated the use of unusually rigorous safeguards in the practice of oral history.

A healthy skepticism concerning the factual quality of historical data should be balanced, however, with some confidence concerning what can be learned about the past. Although E. H. Carr surely goes too far to one extreme when he says that history is a hard core of interpretation surrounded by a pulp of disputable facts, it remains the case that the very evidences the historian examines are far from neutral. This absence of neutrality, however, can often lead to a greater clarity concerning motivation and direction in human events, and the masses of evidence that do remain can be examined and, often, clearly understood from the perspective of the present. In some areas of study it can even be shown that we now know more about the past than the contemporaries who lived in the past. For example, today we know more about how people voted in eighteenth-century England and how their religious persuasion influenced their vote than observers who lived at the time. Before the advent of the computer it was simply impossible to crunch thousands of bits of data into a synthetic picture of what was actually going on in the eighteenth-century electorate. No individual or group of individuals was capable of cross tabulating religion or occupational status with voter preference, but today this task is readily accomplished. The historian can thereby accurately corroborate or discount the vague impressions of eighteenth-century political observers.

3. Kurt Blaukopf, *Mahler* (London: Futura, 1974), pp. 20, 25, 31.

HISTORICAL SOURCES — THEIR USE AND ASSESSMENT

Historical research assumes both the value and the significance of sources. After all of the qualifications noted in the preceding paragraphs and all of the distinctions and cautions to be made in the following discussion have been taken into consideration, the basic point remains: historical study consists in the examination and evaluation of sources — and the sources themselves are interesting. They contain the traces of the human story in all of its remaining detail. The distinctions that can be drawn between primary and secondary sources and various forms of evidence serve to emphasize the significance of the best sources and the importance of cultivating a critical attitude over against source materials, particularly over against those of a secondary or tertiary nature. The primary sources, the documents and traces left by people and events, remain the focus of historical interest and the last court of appeal for historical judgments. History at its best is the careful analysis of sources that allows them to convey their message and reveal their significance to the present. The humanist motto of the Renaissance, *ad fontes*, "to the sources," is the watchword of historiography.

An initial criterion used in the assessment of evidence is the quality of the source. Distinctions must be drawn between primary, secondary, and even tertiary sources, between unwritten and written sources, between intentional and unintentional evidences and, in addition, between manuscripts, printed sources contemporary with the author, and subsequent editions, critical and uncritical.

"Primary" and "secondary sources" are sometimes distinguished from each other as the data or traces are distinguished from an account based on them — or as Barzun and Graff state, the historian uses primary sources to produce a secondary source.[4] This definition is correct as far as it goes, but it does not cover all of the cases, nor does it allow that historians do, also, use secondary sources in compiling an account. In addition, it omits reference to sources that fall so far below the level of primary reference that they can be called "tertiary." The "primary source" is a document, datum, or artifact that belongs to the era under examination and that offers the most direct access to the person or issues being studied.

This definition does not, of course, exclude modern editions of

4. Barzun and Graff, *Modern Researcher* (4), p. 124, n. 18.

older works. Thus, manuscript copy of an original transcript of one of
Calvin's sermons is surely a primary source — but so also is the sixteenth-century printed text of the sermon, the sixteenth-century English
translation, a microfilm or microfiche version of any of the sixteenth-
century forms of the text, and any modern edition or translation. Modern critical editions may often be more accurate than old uncritical
editions, or even more accurate than an old transcript of a sermon.
Translations must always be checked against the original, if possible, but
they do fall into the category of primary sources. An old translation —
such as the sixteenth-century translations of Calvin — may very well
offer fundamental documentation about the reception of Calvin's
thought in England and, indeed, about the importance of translations
in conveying or, perhaps altering slightly, a person's thoughts. The relative value of original manuscripts, printed texts, critical editions, and
translations will also figure significantly in the construction of proper
footnotes.[5]

By the same token, electronic media forms of a text, such as
Migne's *Patrologia* on CD-ROM, are also primary sources, although
here, as with printed editions, careful scholarship may often demand
recourse to early printed texts or modern critical editions. The *Patrologia*
itself is not the best critical text; much of it was taken from the better
text of the Benedictine edition of the fathers and in the transcription
process some problems crept in. Yet another transcription, even one
done as carefully as the CD-ROM version, removes the reader from
immediate contact with the original text of the author and, therefore,
despite the significant research advantages of the CD-ROM, will
frequently require examination of a critical edition or at least an earlier
printed edition. A source like *Corpus Christianorum* has the advantage
of offering a significant critical edition later entered on CD-ROM and
supplemented by a major Thesaurus.

This definition of primary sources does, moreover, allow for the
existence of "secondary" sources dating from the era under examination:
Theodore Beza's *Life of Calvin* is a secondary source for Calvin's life
even though it is a sixteenth-century document written by a close colleague of Calvin. A letter by Calvin is a primary source for examining
the life of Calvin, but it would have to be regarded as a secondary source
when it describes events in Strassburg or Zürich to which Calvin was

5. See below, chapter 4.

not an immediate party. Indeed, any description of an event, even one written later by a contemporary, has a certain secondary character when contrasted with remains or evidences of the event itself — such as a transcript or a juridical record.

Secondary sources, therefore, are sources that offer information about an event but stand removed from it either in time or by a process of transmission of information. The secondary source is not a direct result of an event but itself rests on other sources such as documents, oral reports, or historical investigation of artifacts. In other words, a secondary source is *secondary to* or in some sense removed from the event in question; it is not a direct or primary trace of the event. Thus, secondary sources include not only such older works as Beza's *Life of Calvin* or Brandt's *History of the Reformation . . . in the Low Countries,* but modern histories, scholarly monographs, articles — and, yes, dissertations.

The "secondary" character of such works gives them a substantively different place in the work of research than that occupied by the primary sources. Secondary works are, of their very nature, indirect sources of information. They must be used with care inasmuch as they embody elements of selectivity and interpretation beyond the interpretive tendencies already present in the primary documentation. Secondary works also introduce their own errors and misconceptions into narrative accounts.

In addition, some works are so indirect in their relation to materials and so reliant on secondary works themselves that they ought to be designated as tertiary sources. This category of source includes historical surveys so broad that the author cannot be well acquainted either with the documents underlying his inquiry or even with the development of scholarly literature in a field. Will Durant's *Story of Civilization* and Williston Walker's *History of the Christian Church* fall into this category. So also do standard encyclopedias with unsigned articles, like the Britannica, Americana, or Collier's. Tertiary works, while often valuable sources of information at an introductory level, cannot typically be used to good effect in scholarly research.

A very important rule, therefore, in the research and writing of dissertations, monographs, and scholarly articles is that *secondary and tertiary sources must not be used to fill gaps in one's knowledge of the primary sources.* Of course, all rules must occasionally be broken; this particular rule is consistently broken in the writing of survey texts, granting that the author of a survey or general history cannot be a specialist in all of the areas covered and must, of necessity, rely on secondary sources in the construction of his narrative, and granting that monographs will include surveys of context and background not researched in the detail of the body of the monograph. Judicious use of well-researched secondary sources must occur at the edges of one's own research, always measured against one's broader knowledge of the field. The exception, however, proves the rule. Survey texts and general histories are notoriously out of date and unreliable on particulars.

The proper use of secondary and sometimes tertiary works in scholarly research leads not to the construction of arguments based on evidences gleaned secondarily, but to the development of an educated context for argument about the meaning and implication of the primary sources. If they have any place at all in scholarly work, carefully chosen tertiary sources provide a generalized background of knowledge — but it is a background that the researcher will frequently find inadequate not only in detail but also in accuracy and will need to modify constantly under the impact of both primary documents and scholarly essays and monographs. The secondary sources, ideally, become the basis of a scholarly dialogue about the documents and ideas of history and, insofar as the history of scholarship on a point is mastered by the researcher, a beginning for further discussion. When the secondary literature is used in this way the researcher becomes part of the ongoing history of scholarship and contributes substantively to the investigation of a subject. Conversely, when the secondary literature is not analyzed or reviewed, the researcher may fail to contribute anything new either to the current scholarly dialogue about a historical topic or, indeed, to the general fund of human knowledge. When the secondary materials are not mastered, a researcher is in danger of both accidental duplication and a naive approach to conclusions.

As a corollary to this rule, it is unwise to cite texts as quoted in secondary sources (and, of course, quite improper to cite such texts as if they had been taken from the original source itself). Secondary sources frequently edit, misquote, mistranslate, and abbreviate sources without giving any indication of the liberties taken with the text.

By way of example, one recent historian of Christian thought, in attempting to prove that various post-Reformation Reformed and Puritan writers held a voluntaristic soteriology, has argued that the Puritan theologian, William Ames, placed repentance (an act of the will) definitively prior to faith (which necessarily involves the intellect). He cites Ames as follows: "While repentance is indeed an 'effect' of faith, 'Repentance in respect of that carelessness, and anxiety & terror arising from the Law which it hath joyned with it, doth goe before Faith, by order of nature, as a preparing and disposing cause.'"[6] The sentence in which the citation occurs itself raises questions. If Ames could say that repentance was an "effect" of faith, does Ames think that effects can precede causes, and how does this statement relate to the sentence apparently cited in full by Kendall? When the citation is checked out against Ames's actual text, however, all becomes clear. In the first place, what appears to be a full sentence is in reality only the first of three independent clauses in a single sentence. In the second place, the sentence, when cited in its entirety, actually proves the opposite point: the "order of nature" to which Ames refers occurs only in the unregenerate and it relates to the so-called second or pedagogical use of the law. Understood, however, as an effective and genuine turning from sin, repentance, Ames makes clear, must follow faith as an effect follows its cause. Contrary to Kendall's conclusion, this rather neatly mirrors Calvin's view. Woe to the unsuspecting writer who trusts the secondary source for citations of primary sources!

There are also, of course, numerous forgeries and impostures available to befuddle the historian. This problem is somewhat different from that of the mistaken secondary account; it is instead a problem of fabrication, either at the primary or the secondary level. The "Cardiff Giant" and the "Piltdown Man" are cases of primary fabrication. Both were produced before the modern development of the science of paleontology, but at a time when people were first entranced with pre-historic archeological discoveries. The Cardiff Giant began as a five-ton block of stone ordered by George Hull of Binghamton, New York, to be carved out of the gypsum deposits near Fort Dodge, Iowa, and sent to Chicago to be fashioned into the shape of a ten-foot-tall man. Hull then had the statue transported to Cardiff, New York, and buried in the ground for a year. In 1869, it was unearthed by well diggers and displayed by Hull as a petrified prehistoric "giant." After touring for several de-cades and amazing hosts of spectators, the Cardiff Giant was shown to be a hoax in 1900 by Othniel March of Yale University.

---

6. R. T. Kendall, *Calvin and English Calvinism to 1649* (Oxford and New York: Oxford University Press, 1979), p. 160, citing William Ames, *The Marrow of Sacred Divinity* (London, 1643), p. 128.

The "Piltdown Man" had a longer and far more successful history. In 1912, Charles Dawson reported his discovery of cranial fragments and a jawbone on Piltdown Common, near Lewes, England. Near these fragments were other humanoid bones and the remains of various animals not extant in England. In addition, the animal remains showed evidence of having been worked on with tools made of bone and flint. At the time, the Piltdown Man was hypothesized to be an ancestor of modern *Homo sapiens* dating from the Pleistocene age. Although the gravel in which the remains were found was eventually dated from a later era, the Piltdown Man entered textbooks and standard encyclopedias as a genuine human ancestor. Thus, in the 1944 edition of *Webster's Collegiate Dictionary* we read that "Piltdown" is "a prehistoric station in Sussex, England, yielding remains of an extinct species of man, Piltdown man *(Eoanthropus dawsoni)*, characterized by a retreating, apelike chin and thick cranial bones, but a humanlike cranium." It was only in 1954, as scientists found and studied genuine ancient remains and became more adept at identifying bones and at reconstructing and restoring humans and animals from partial skeletal remains, that the hoax was exposed. The cranial fragments were human, but not ancient; the jawbone was from an orangutan. Together with these and the other bones, various primitive tools had been buried in the gravel of Piltdown Common. Although the discoverer of Piltdown Man, Charles Dawson, has been suspected as the perpetrator of the fraud, no final proof has ever been offered. Such frauds lie at the edge of historiography and responsibility, for their exposure falls into the hands of paleontologists. Nonetheless, fraud belongs to the study of history on two counts and establishes the dependence of historiography on collateral fields of study. The existence of an unexposed fraud relativizes the worth of essays on the subject of prehistoric humans from the era in which the remains were accepted as genuine. Subsequent generations of researchers, including historians of the period, must be careful to take into account the state of knowledge at the time of the fraud, and, second, they must be careful to balance their accounts with a critical recognition of the findings of later scientists.

Chatterton's *Rowley Papers* and Macpherson's epic *Fingal,* attributed to the bard Ossian, are notable examples of imposture — both of which have maintained their place in English literature for their contribution, not to the eras from which they purported to come, but to the beginnings of Romanticism in the late-eighteenth century. James

Macpherson (1736-96) was a schoolmaster whose literary talents were stimulated by old Gaelic poems that he heard in the Scottish highlands. In 1760 he presented to the literary public *Fragments of Ancient Poetry Collected in the Highlands.* Not only was the work a success, but the interest in ancient lore, bards, and heroes typical of the beginnings of Romanticism was such that money was raised to send Macpherson to the highlands to find more of these wonderful fragments. In 1762 Macpherson published his *Fingal* and in 1763 *Temora,* two epic poems attributed to the bard Ossian.

When Samuel Johnson and others demanded that Macpherson produce the manuscripts, he refused and was condemned in literary circles as a forger. Despite these accusations, Macpherson gained renown as a student of ancient poetry and was given a government post with a lifetime salary for his efforts. On his death he was interred in Westminster Abbey. Then, in 1807, after Macpherson's death, the Gaelic text of the epics was published, still without any trace of manuscripts. The Gaelic text was quickly judged to be a translation of parts of Macpherson's work back into the ancient language of Scotland. From the perspective of history, we can allow that Macpherson's critics were partially correct; the epics were indeed forgeries, but, contrary to the claims of his detractors, Macpherson had considerable talent and his works had an enormous impact on the rise of Romantic poetry. William Blake, Thomas Gray, and Robert Burns were admirers of the Ossianic poems, and Goethe read the German translation with admiration. In this case, the forgery did not lose its value on discovery, but took a place in the history of literature slightly different from the one intended by its author.

Of a somewhat different order are the *Rowley Papers* by Thomas Chatterton (1752-70). The gifted young Chatterton began, at about the age of eleven, to produce medieval ballads, family histories, and other documents relating to Thomas Rowley, a priest, and to William Canynge, a merchant, both from the era of Henry VI. The explanation given for the documents was that they had been found in an old English church. As in the case of the Ossianic poems, the ancient style brought immediate interest and the papers were a considerable literary success. Here again, Thomas Gray took an interest, but this time of a more critical nature. He recognized that, despite the usually fine style of the papers, there was occasional misuse of a fifteenth-century word and an occasional anachronistic usage. Here again, however, the imposture had its effect and, like *Fingal* and *Temora,* contributed to the rise of English Romanticism. The young Chatterton was, undoubtedly, a literary genius of the first order. His early and tragic death is mourned in the forty-fifth stanza of Shelley's "Adonais."

Even more significant among the ranks of forgeries are the *Pseudo-Isidorian Decretals* and the *Donation of Constantine.* In the mid-ninth century, pope Nicholas I appealed to a collection of the letters and decrees of the church of Rome attributed to bishop Isidore of Seville (d. 636), in which the "chair of Peter" was identified as the seat of power in the church, and the bishop of Rome as the convener of councils, the final court of appeal in all controversies and the "universal bishop." The *Decretals* also contained the so-called *Donation of Constantine* in which Constantine reputedly gave all power in the West to the pope. From the time of Nicholas to the close of the Middle Ages, these documents were viewed as genuine and used as the basis of papal claims to ecclesiastical and civil supremacy. The validity of the documents was questioned in the later Middle Ages by the English scholar Reginald Pecock and finally disproved on linguistic grounds in the Renaissance by Lorenzo Valla. Here again, the identification of the forgery in no way lessens the impact of the documents on history — and the historian becomes responsible for the understanding of the documents and their impact as well as for the knowledge of their later exposure and their decreasing impact on later generations. The historian also becomes responsible, generally, for the critical examination of evidences for the sake of identifying forgery and imposture.

One less famous but quite insidious imposture is the contribution of one of the anonymous writers for *Appleton's Cyclopaedia of American Biography.* Presumably, he became aware that the editorial board of the *Cyclopaedia* was more anxious to receive short biographies of interesting individuals and to improve their style editorially than to check the veracity of the research that had produced the essays in the first place. In addition, writers were paid for each short biography. This particular writer went so far as to invent interesting lives, such as that of the French scientist Nicholas Henrion (1733-93), who studied medicinal plants in South America, served as physician during the plague in Callao, Peru, in 1783, and surveyed the silver and sulphur mines of Peru before returning to France in 1793. Henrion was rewarded by the governor of Peru for his work against the cholera with "letters of nobility," but executed on his return to France for suspected royalist sympathies. So detailed is the essay that it notes even that Henrion's *Herbier expliqué des plantes du Pérou* was published in two volumes, quarto, in 1790.

The problem here is that Henrion, like the explorer Bernhard Hühne and some forty other entries in the encyclopedia, is pure fabrication.[7] Not only might one wonder how his several books on South America were published in French before his return home — but more careful research would reveal that he battled cholera in Peru nearly a half century before its first reported occurrence there. The unwary student's life is immeasurably complicated by the presence of a genuine Nicholas Henrion in French biographical and bibliographical sources of the time; the real Henrion was a military engineer during the Revolution who published several treatises on that subject. The genuine Henrion is in danger of being reduced to yet another of the accomplishments in the already distinguished career of his nonexistent namesake. In this case, there is little useful historical impact of the imposture and much potential harm. At the very least, students must be warned of the careless use of secondary sources and reminded of the rule that secondary and tertiary sources ought not normally to be used in dissertations, monographs, and scholarly articles as sources of information not available from primary sources. When the rule is not observed, Henrion's exploits become a significant part of the history of Peru and other details from the essay embellish the works of careless scholars.

The close examination of these episodes in the history of hoax and fraud show us once again how the social and cultural assumptions of an era influence our thinking and contribute to various forms of credulity. Hoaxes, however, reveal less about credulity at the individual level than they do about what the majority of people in a given age were prepared to see and what they expected to understand. The Piltdown Man was accepted in an age that was enamored with the advances of science and the perception that evolution possessed an uncanny power to make sense of things otherwise mysterious. In this regard, it is well to remember that the specific cases of hoax and fraud we have examined in this chapter pale in significance when compared to the unveiling in the mid-twentieth century of several of the greatest hoaxes of all time. It has taken the work of women historians and African American theologians to convince us that a person's socio-political setting and per-

7. See the discussion in Allan Nevins, *The Gateway to History* (New York: Heath, 1938), pp. 131-32.

sonal history profoundly shape both the content and the methods of his or her scholarship.[8] The rapid maturing of the new fields of women's history and the history of ethnic and religious minorities has raised in an acute form the question of whether it is possible for historians to attain any reasonable degree of detachment and objectivity in reconstructing the past.

THE PROBLEM OF OBJECTIVITY IN HISTORICAL STUDY

In specific cases, historians today may attain to a more objective, accurate understanding of the past than either the individual participants in history or earlier historians, but the question naturally arises, is entire objectivity ever attainable, and, more importantly, how may we approach it methodologically? There are, in the first place, several barriers to total objectivity, or what might be called impartiality. Renier correctly notes that "absence of bias is not the same thing as secure knowledge," granting that "the historian's narrative cannot possibly be a faithful and total reproduction of a section of the past."[9] The selective nature both of the traces and of the historian's reconstruction stands in the way of total reproduction, and selectivity, whatever its source, stands in the way of totally secure findings. History is continually being rewritten through the use of newly discovered or previously neglected sources; it is of the very essence of sound historiography that it be selective. Renier observes: "no story can be told till a selection has been made among available events, and . . . the selection of facts is a judgment passed upon their importance."[10] With selection and individual judgment comes partiality.

Nonetheless, most contemporary scholars have also resisted the inclination of some early twentieth-century historians and of some modern hermeneuticians to become lost in a mire of subjectivity and relativism and to claim that the materials of the past mean whatever can be made of them. Certainly, the significance of materials changes over time and new levels of significance are added as materials are

---

8. James H. Cone, *God of the Oppressed* (San Francisco: Harper & Row, 1975), p. vi.

9. G. J. Renier, *History: Its Purpose and Method* (New York: Harper & Row, 1950), p. 249.

10. Renier, *History,* p. 250.

carried forward in a tradition of interpretation, but the meaning of the document in its original situation not only does not change but also continues to limit the significance of the document in the present. Objectivity arises out of a willingness to let the materials of history speak in their own terms while the historian, at the same time, exercises a combination of critical judgment and careful self-restraint. Her objectivity is not measured by a canon of absolute truth; it arises as a standard of the relationship between data and its interpretation.[11]

This objectivity, so important to the understanding of both past and present, results neither from an absence of presuppositions, opinions and existential involvement, nor from an ability to set aside such biases. Rather, it results from an honest and methodologically lucid recognition and use of the resident bias as a basis for approaching and analyzing the differences between one's own situation and the situation of a given document or concept. In other words, involvement in the materials of history can lead to a methodologically constructed and controlled objectivity that is quite different from, and arguably superior to, a bland, uninvolved distancing of the self from the materials that must, ultimately, remove the importance from history.

Objectivity, rightly understood as a methodological stance, does not, therefore, remove the relationship of historical study to one's own self-understanding. Instead, a methodologically cultivated objectivity, coupled with and instructed by an awareness of one's own subjectivity, can and should result in an increased sense of the ways in which events and ideas of the past have been woven into the fabric of our present. The goal of the student is to pursue balance and objectivity without abdicating one's personality or losing entirely one's sense of involvement in and with the events of history. It is, after all, involvement with past events that engenders continued historical interest. Objectivity in historical study does not, and cannot, exist if it is defined as an absence of involvement with or opinion about the materials. Instead, historical objectivity results from a methodological control of the evidence, of the various levels of interpretation both inherent in and related to the evidence, and of one's own biases and opinions concerning the evidence and the various known interpretations.

The issue of objectivity can be understood, initially, in terms of a

11. Edward H. Carr, *What Is History?* (New York: Vintage Books, 1961), pp. 158-59.

balance between what is considered to be a concrete datum with questions of interpretation — ours and someone else's — together with a personal evaluation of the question of empathy and bias. On the one hand, we move toward the creation of a methodological distance between ourselves and the sources. We encounter sources. We write about the sources and deal with them, usually because of a root issue of empathy or bias. We are attracted to writing about something either because we like it or dislike it, because it moves us positively or negatively. The issue in writing is to try to transcend that basic problem of motivation, and in many ways to *use* the motivation to understand the materials.

For example, a historian may initially study Jacob Arminius in order to understand more about his or her tradition. But the student should not ask whether or not Arminius is ultimately doctrinally right or wrong. Rather, the question is, "Why does he say what he says?" One can find out a lot about why he says what he says by comparing his thinking to the Reformed thinking of his day, and then asking the objectivizing questions, "What is the reason that he moves in one particular direction as opposed to another? What is going on in his mind that leads him in this other direction?" These questions raise the further question of what is fact and what is interpretation. Several elements of the written record are data and fact. We have (1) Arminius's own comments about his own theology, what it is and what it is not, including his comment that he did not read Roman Catholic authors and that he admired John Calvin as much as anybody else. We have (2) the printed catalogue of his library as auctioned off by his widow after his death. In his library we find a wide selection of Roman Catholic books, by the very authors that he said he did not read and did not recommend to his students: Aquinas, Bellarmine, Suárez, and Molina. Finally, we have (3) his own writings, which are virtually unfootnoted, a fact that (while typical of the time) makes it very difficult to analyze the documents. The absence of annotation means that one has to have a hands-on knowledge of a whole series of potential sources in order to check them out against what one is reading. Granting his library and his statements about his work and his theological intentions, and granting the material, so to speak, in the middle — mediating between the books of the library and Arminius's intentions and offering a basis for our interpretation — his own writings, plus (4) the comments of his adversaries, plus (5) the larger theological and philosophical context, one then attempts (very painstakingly) to match his statements with statements in the literature. The result is an Arminius who is very different from the Arminius defined by his opponents, very different from the Arminius that Arminians have wanted to find, and very different from the public Arminius created by Arminius himself during the theological debates. One finds a modified Protestant Thomist, a scholastic thinker, who did indeed read Catholic materials.

The historian, thus, always has to deal with the questions of interpretation that are lodged in the sources themselves, questions of interpretation that are present in the writings about these materials, and a hard core of data in which there is already interpretation, all of which provide the historian with clues for directions in his or her own thinking. On the one hand, we do not want ever to say that there are facts, or a past, without interpretation. On the other hand, we do want to say that there really are hard data, hard data that have some level of interpretation already in them that has to be critically examined, but data nonetheless.

The approach to objectivity can be enhanced by a candid recognition of the fact that empathy and bias belong to our work, from beginning to end. Yet the issue of objectivity, empathy, and bias does not rest with a simple discussion of our own empathies and biases, but rather on the empathies and biases that are detectable in the materials themselves, and in the way that our own feelings relate to the empathies and biases in the materials. All of these issues have to be brought to the level of critical consciousness as one is writing.

It is methodologically important that one's empathy or one's bias be registered as an initial issue in method at the very beginning of research, so that the method can begin to cancel out its effects. In research on a doctrinal issue, if one disagrees with the teaching of the writer who is the object of research, the disagreement ought to be drawn into conscious relation to the analysis of the document and methodologically controlled. In research and writing, rather than registering disagreement, what one should register is the way in which one's own understanding of the reasons for a particular intellectual construction are different from the reasons for someone else's intellectual construction. This understanding can then become a tool for asking the question, "Why does this other person formulate the way he or she does?" What one writes about is not the difference of opinion, but what has been discovered about the logic of the other person's formulation, by asking the basic question, "Why is that formulated differently from the way that I have been accustomed to seeing the issue formulated?" One's own writing should not register one's own theological opinion, pro or con. Rather, whatever that opinion was, it merely serves as part of the method in encountering what the other person is thinking or doing. As a historian, one makes no judgment about the rightness or wrongness of the person's teaching on an absolute scale — rather, all such judgments are to be made against the background of standards contemporary to the author being examined.

Finally, the success with which an historian attains objectivity is often related to the specific type of task in which he or she is engaged. When the historian works at the level of simple description, a high degree of objectivity is often possible. It is not difficult to describe certain events in history, or to establish beyond a measurable doubt that a person acted in a specific way. To return to the example of eighteenth-century England, let us say that although England had an Established Church in the eighteenth century, we know beyond a doubt that Presbyterians voted in parliamentary elections. Objectivity becomes more difficult when we move from the realm of description to that of explanation. Here we are interested in the cause or motivation of a certain behavior; we wish to know why Presbyterians voted and whether or not they were motivated primarily by religion or by economic elements or, what is more likely, by both. Thus, establishing the fact of a particular behavior is relatively easy, but determining whether or not the action was intrinsically religious is far more difficult. A third step that the historian often takes removes the goal of objectivity even further from reach; namely, when historians address the question of significance, or larger historical meaning, they almost inevitably invite debate. If the Presbyterian merchant who voted during the American Revolution was motivated primarily by his socio-economic status, can we conclude more broadly that economic elements were more significant in determining voter preference than ideological or religious elements? In this case, a conclusion one way or the other will almost certainly be contested, and the possibility of actually proving the case will remain highly unlikely. The historian's dual tasks of assigning causes and construing significance thus put the greatest strain on the goal of objectivity, and yet these tasks are by far the most interesting aspects of the discipline.

MEANING IN HISTORY

The question concerning what difference it makes for historians to write from a Christian or non-Christian perspective has been a vital issue in the history of historical writing, and it is properly construed as a particular case of the larger problem of objectivity. Wolfhart Pannenberg has rightly observed that "Church history faces in a way no other branch of history does the question of the relevance of the religious concern to the understanding of history because it deals with the history of a religion the essence of which is belief in a God who acts in history."[12] In the past, historians who wrote with Christian convictions wrote very different kinds of things from those who wrote from a non-Christian perspective. We have seen that in the sixteenth, seventeenth, and eighteenth centuries, Christians in one tradition had a difficult time understanding Christians in other traditions, to say nothing of those who stood outside these traditions. Since the Enlightenment, great advances have been made along the lines of detaching our Christian commitment from our writing of history, and yet the degree to which one can or ought to interpret texts along the lines of one's own confessional viewpoint provides grist for an ongoing debate.

In a helpful article on this topic, Harry S. Stout distinguishes between method, empathy, and point of view.[13] One could start at the most objective level and ask, "Does Christian commitment or a Christian perspective have anything to do with the methods we use?" In other words, does a Christian perspective have some intrinsic connection with methodological distinctives? Few people today would wish to argue in favor of this proposition. Then we might ask, "Does a Christian perspective have any bearing on our empathy for the subject of study or bias against it? Does a Christian historian, for example, write about the Christian church with more empathy than the non-Christian?" Some historians have argued that a Christian scholar may write with deeper empathy when treating Christian subjects than the non-Christian; a great deal of attention has been paid of late to the so-called "participant-observer" model of writing church history. Clearly, however, a

12. Wolfhart Pannenberg, *Theology and the Philosophy of Science* (Philadelphia: Westminster, 1976), p. 396.

13. Harry S. Stout, "Theological Commitment and American Religious History," *Theological Education* 25, no. 2 (1989): 44-59.

non-Christian may write with more understanding than Christians have ever previously written, depending upon how good a historian he or she is and the current state of research and level of sophistication in the secondary literature. The classic case used by Stout in this regard is Perry Miller and the writing of Puritan history in this century. Seventeenth-century Puritans had suffered a great deal of grief at the hands of nineteenth-century historians; as late as the early part of the twentieth century, Puritans were still commonly considered humorless, repressive, and tyrannical. While he could do nothing about the Puritans' characteristic lack of humor, Perry Miller, writing from an agnostic viewpoint, examined the minds of his chosen subjects with remarkable empathy, and he thereby resuscitated the entire reputation of three or four generations of Puritans in colonial America. Evidently, a person writing from a non-Christian perspective can have a powerful impact on reviving an entire segment of the Christian tradition.

We might put the matter rather differently and think of the religious perspective of the scholar as an undesirable handicap, rather than a potentially desirable asset. In this case we should ask whether it is even possible for Christians to write objectively about Christianity? Can Christians deal with their own history in such a way as to discern accurately and responsibly its meaning, even when that meaning does not oblige their preconceptions? If so, can they build on what they have found? The answer to these questions must certainly be "no," if providential or supernatural causes are assigned to events that will never, by their very nature, submit themselves to the methods of the historian. On the other hand, if the religious element is entirely excluded from church history, the historian's conclusions might become so many arguments for atheism.[14]

One could argue that Christian faith *might* lead to greater empathy for a subject and thereby greater understanding than a non-faith perspective, but this is clearly not a necessary corollary of faith. What may be claimed as a safe minimum is the ideal that the Christian scholar, assuming that he or she possesses sufficient analytical gifts and literary abilities, may bring a point of view to a topic that a non-Christian might not bring. If we return to the basic question of the way that the historian goes about selecting materials, a Christian might bring a point of view to the selection and to the organization of those materials that a non-

14. Pannenberg, *Theology and the Philosophy of Science*, p. 396.

Christian would not bring, simply because a person's own history and training ultimately do say something about how the materials are selected and ordered. But the entire question of the role of Christian faith in writing history must be examined at different levels. Methodologically, there does not appear to be much of a debate. Similarly, when we consider the question of empathy in the modern climate of rigorous analysis and detachment, few, if any, differences between a Christian and a non-Christian approach to scholarship should appear. Even when we put the question in terms of one's point of view, it is not at all obvious that a Christian historian's faith will have a positive bearing upon the work that is done.

While it is not unlikely that the point of view the Christian historian brings to the study of the past will shape what is finally produced in subtle ways, it is impossible to determine ahead of time whether the result will be salutary or not. We have seen the deleterious effect of nominally "Christian" convictions in our study of the slow emergence of critical historiography, and students who are anxious to locate providence in history should be ever mindful of, and loath to return to, that long and tortured process. The theological element that may find its way into the narrative and analysis of the church historian must be recognized as such and introduced only tentatively, and one would hope, winsomely. Adopting for our purposes the contention of Wolfhart Pannenberg concerning the theologian's religious convictions, we believe that these convictions properly belong to the heuristic, not the probative, context of historical analysis and argument. Conclusions that are sympathetic to religion, no matter how great the sincerity of the historian, can be recovered for church history only "when they are studied as a disputed theme in history itself."[15]

UNDERSTANDING THE PAST

Students who are eager to find traces of providence in history from which they may elicit personal meaning have commonly failed to give sufficient attention to the historical problem of the discipline of history in relation to theology. The scholarly or critical study of the history of the church and Christian doctrine is a relatively new phenomenon in

15. Pannenberg, *Theology and the Philosophy of Science*, pp. 321, 399.

theology. The discipline is barely two hundred and fifty years old in an intellectual community that has been studying theology for more than seventeen centuries. Before the early eighteenth century when Mosheim wrote his *Institutes of Ecclesiastical History* and Walch produced his introduction to the religious controversies both in and beyond the Lutheran Church,[16] the history of Christian teaching and religion was, typically, a function of dogmatic theology. A portion of each locus of the dogmatic system was devoted to a polemical description of the "state of the controversy" in which the views of opponents of all sorts, ranging from the perpetually refuted arch-heretics of the patristic period, through various writers of the Middle Ages, to contemporary adversaries, were ranged in chronological order as part of an etiology of error. The construction of such etiologies is, of course, a time-honored practice, dating back to the classical period and observed by the fathers of the church from the late second century onward. Hippolytus dispensed with the Gnostics by arguing the origins of Gnosticism in the errors of Greek philosophy, and Athanasius expounded the virtues of Nicea in his survey of the materials and debates of subsequent councils during the battle against Arianism.[17]

The object of all these early attempts at the history of Christian doctrine or of heretical opinion was not history as such, but rather a nonhistorical truth standing outside and above the chronology of a problem. History, in other words, has always been recognized as having some importance for the identification of truth, but only in recent times has history been recognized as having an importance in itself as the embodiment of a kind of truth. This latter recognition was, in its initial form, the contribution of Mosheim, Walch, and the historians and theologians of the eighteenth century who followed in their steps.

The importance of history and the dominance of historical method in the contemporary study of religion and theology bear witness, therefore, to the realization that a right understanding of the documents and

16. Johann Lorenz von Mosheim, *Institutes of Ecclesiastical History, Ancient and Modern,* trans. James Murdock, 4 vols. (London: Longman, 1841), originally published in 1755; Johann Georg Walch, *Historische und theologische Einleitung in die Religionsstreitigkeiten der evangelisch-lutherischen Kirche,* 5 vols. (Jena, 1730-39); and idem, *Historische und theologische Einleitung in die Religionsstreitigkeiten, welche sonderlich ausser der evangelisch-lutherischen Kircheentstanden,* 5 vols. (Jena, 1733-36).

17. See Hippolytus of Rome, *The Refutation of All Heresies,* Book I, prooemium, in *ANF,* vol. 5, p. 10; Athanasius, *De Synodis,* in *NPNF,* series 2, vol. 4, pp. 448-80.

of the concepts with which theology works is a historically defined and historically governed understanding. The fact that this is a comparatively recent realization means, however, that very few of the documents and concepts of theology will themselves contain or, in their fundamental intellectual direction, oblige a historical model for understanding their own contents or implications. At one level, then, the importance of history is that it provides a context of meaning that was not immediately or even fully available to the creators of the documents.

The people of the fourth century, for example, certainly knew collectively more about the events of their time than we today can ever reconstruct. Much of the past is lost to us forever. Nonetheless, when we pose the question of the meaning and implication of recorded events, we are today in a position, through the use of historical method, to know more about the fourth century — or about any past century — than any individual who lived at that time. It is not simply that we know the course of events beyond the life span of individual people. We also are able to understand trajectories of ideas and patterns of debate free from the blinding biases of the moment.

We can draw, by way of illustration of the point, on one of the previously mentioned examples: Athanasius's chronologically organized analysis of the fourth-century councils has little understanding of either the Arian or the Nicene or the non-Nicene, non-Arian views of the relationship of the Father and the Son as growing out of an earlier history of developing Christian God-language. It never occurred to Athanasius that the Arian and the various non-Nicene views of the Godhead had roots in the undeniably orthodox teachings of such writers as the Apologists of the second century, Hippolytus of Rome and Irenaeus. Such views even had some affinities with the pronouncements of Tertullian. Tertullian, after all, saw no difficulty for Christian theism in the statement that "there was a time when . . . the Son was not," the very sentiment for which Arius was condemned.[18] It also most probably never occurred to Athanasius that the gnostic and hermetic use of the term *homoousios*, still remembered by the church at the time of Nicea, may have exerted a positive influence on ecclesiastical usage.[19]

---

18. Tertullian, *Against Hermogenes*, 3, in *ANF*, vol. 3, p. 478; cf. Arius, *Letter to Alexander*, in Athanasius, *De Synodis*, 16. (N.B., Tertullian's language is clearer in the Latin original: "Fuit autem tempus . . . et filius non erat" in PL, 2.200.)

19. On the history of the term *homoousios*, see G. L. Prestige, *God in Patristic*

History and Self-Understanding

Historical understanding of documents and ideas will, therefore, frequently be rather different from the self-understanding of those who held the ideas and who produced the documents, although it will try to analyze and to grasp that original self-understanding as part of the task of historical interpretation. These two elements of historical understanding are crucial to the work of reconstructing the past, whether for the sake of an accurate representation of the past in and for itself, or for the sake of the present-day use of the materials of the past. On the one hand, accurate reconstruction entails the establishment of a legitimate vantage point for the analysis of an idea or document. This vantage point will allow the historian to take into consideration the cultural context, antecedent to, contemporary with, and subsequent to, the particular object of study.

In the study of the history of doctrine, the methods of intellectual history demand attention to the development and use of particular vocabularies and to the way in which those vocabularies function in a specific, historically discerned and reconstructed context of meaning. The past, in other words, cannot mean what we want it to mean — its ideas cannot be forced, certainly not as an initial stage of interpretation, into our contemporary context of meaning. The very terms of an argument, even if they continue to be used in seemingly identical arguments today, will have changed in meaning, if ever so slightly, with the result that our contemporary understanding of those terms will stand in tension with our right understanding of the way in which they functioned in a different time and place.

On the other hand, present-day use of the materials of the past also requires a clear sense of the difference and distinction between the setting of the document and the contemporary setting, as well as a knowledge of the historical path that connects the document with the present and that, in addition to enabling it to speak with a continued relevance to our situation, accounts for the differences between the perspective of the document and our present-day perspective. In those

---

Thought (London: SPCK, 1952), pp. 197-201; and for the usage in the hermetic literature see *Hermetica*, 4 vols., edited and trans. Walter Scott (repr. Boston: Shambhala, 1985), vol. 1, p. 118 (Poimandres, 10).

cases when the contents of a document are totally or nearly totally strange to us, the cultural context of the document in its social, religious, political, and linguistic particularity will most certainly provide the best, if not the only, corridor of access to the meaning and implication of the document. Without a grasp of that context, the contents of the document will either remain utterly puzzling to us or they will be assimilated to, and therefore misinterpreted by, our own cultural and intellectual milieu. The point is particularly telling when a specific document or set of ideas, despite the remoteness of its situation from ours, so belongs to the foundations of our own thinking that its right interpretation is necessary to our own self-understanding.

An example of this latter dilemma (again, remaining within the bounds of the historical problems already noted) is the attempt of a fairly well-known contemporary theologian to argue that the Nicene or Athanasian *homoousios* means "that God himself is the content of his revelation in Jesus Christ" and that the "Gift" is "identical" with the "Giver."[20] In the first place, the term *homoousios* implies no particular theory of revelation, most certainly not a theory of revelation as "personal" rather than "propositional," such as appears to underlie these statements. In the second place, although the term certainly does indicate the essential (although not the individual or personal) identity of God the Father with the divine Logos incarnate in Jesus Christ, it in no way implies either the identity of God with Jesus Christ, who was both divine and human, or the identity of Jesus Christ with the entirety of God's revelation. After all, Athanasius strongly affirmed, in agreement with virtually all of his predecessors in the patristic era, the revelatory work of the Logos *asarkos,* that is, of the Logos apart from the flesh, in and through the created order. Moreover, inasmuch as revelation is the work and not the being of the Logos, the Logos itself cannot be identical with revelation. In addition, Athanasius's clear distinction of divine persons, together with his assumption that the Logos, as second in order, serves a mediatorial function, precludes any theory of a total revelation of the transcendent Father and therefore also precludes any thought of an identity between God and his self-revelation.[21] Whatever the merit

20. Thomas F. Torrance, *The Trinitarian Faith: The Evangelical Theology of the Ancient Catholic Church* (Edinburgh: T. & T. Clark, 1988), pp. 138, 305.

21. Cf. G. L. Prestige, *God in Patristic Thought,* pp. 214-18, especially p. 218, with Jaroslav Pelikan, *The Christian Tradition: A History of the Development of Doctrine* (Chicago: University of Chicago Press, 1971-), vol. 1, pp. 202-6.

of a twentieth-century theory of the identity of God with his self-revelation, it is an example of badly done history to thrust the theory upon Athanasius. It is also exceedingly unlikely that badly done history can be the basis of well-done theology.

THE IMPORTANCE OF HISTORY

The point of this discussion is not that history "teaches lessons" about the good and the bad, the moral and the immoral. Such lessons are the province of ethics, not of history. The importance of history lies instead in the realm of the identification and definition of issues and of the cultivation of objectivity in judgment. The assignment of value — whether ethical, philosophical, or theological — to the ideas and events of the past is not, per se, a historical task. Where the ethicist, the philosopher, or the theologian judges crime or error or heresy, the historian reports analytically with a view toward meaning in the original context. When a historian does write of crime or error or heresy, those judgments arise not out of the opinion of the historian but out of the clear presentation of the views of the contemporaries of the individual, idea, or event in question. Thus, Arianism is not a heresy and the teaching of Athanasius not orthodoxy because a contemporary historian says so, but because the church of the fourth century, represented in two ecumenical councils, offered that opinion.

When, moreover, historians reappraise decisions of the past, they do so on the basis of evidence drawn from the past, not on the basis of present-day assumptions. Thus, several twentieth-century scholars have argued that Nestorius was, at least in his intentions, essentially orthodox. Their point is not that the councils of Ephesus and Chalcedon were incorrect in their assignment of boundaries to christological orthodoxy in the fifth century — and certainly not that the twentieth century can claim, on historical grounds, that what was once heterodox can now be appropriated as useful teaching. Instead, these scholars have examined a recently rediscovered treatise by Nestorius and have reexamined the evidence from Nestorius's debate with Cyril of Alexandria and have concluded that Nestorius's views may have been misconstrued for political reasons. In other words, the theological rectitude of the councils is not an issue for the historian, but rather the accurate representation of the views of the historical Nestorius and of his relationship to the views known as Nestorianism.[22]

The importance of history, therefore, in general and in its specific relationship to the graduate study of the Christian church and its tradition, can be found both in the importance of the remains of times past and in the importance of the cultivation of an objective approach to the materials of religion and theology. If Leopold von Ranke's maxim concerning the reconstruction of the past "wie es eigentlich gewesen" (as it really was) is understood not as an attainable object but as the description of the fundamental intention of historical method, it ceases to be an unattainable dream and becomes a practical guide. More than that, it becomes the first step in a process of education or, perhaps, a hermeneutical circle, that moves from the materials of history to the historian or theologian in the present-day context and then back again to the materials; that creates a perspective for understanding the materials themselves, the larger tradition to which they belong, and in addition one's own situation in the present; and that provides an attitude and a set of intellectual tools for the better evaluation of all of the ideas and materials of theology.

If the graduate study of the Christian church and its tradition is to be designed to train teachers and leaders for service in seminaries, universities, and churches, the balance and the objectivity together with the understanding of materials, past and present, and of one's self that are to be gained from historical study are indispensable. History provides, on the one hand, a source of breadth for contemporary theology inasmuch as its vast resources of ideas and perspectives manifest a variety and a range of insight quite beyond the reach of an individual mind or of a community of minds at a particular time. When approached by means of a balanced and objective historical method, these resources, simply by reason of their breadth and of their cultural and intellectual relation to our present, lend a certain balance and objectivity to our own discourse.

On the other hand, history offers a source of limitation inasmuch as its resources frequently manifest the failure of plans, projects, ideas, and systems, or demonstrate the inability of certain teachings to bear

22. Cf. J. N. D. Kelly, *Early Christian Doctrine,* rev. ed. (San Francisco: Harper & Row, 1988), pp. 310-17.

an intellectual freight for which they were not designed. It has sometimes been said that the modern church, usually because of its ignorance
of the patristic period, has tended to duplicate in its theology most of
the errors and problems of the first five centuries of Christian thought.
When approached in a balanced and objective manner, history provides
insight into the limitation of our powers, if only by preserving the
reasons for the failures of the past and, in the case of the theological
tradition, showing the boundaries within which the community has
chosen to formulate its views.

The importance of objectively recounted history lies, therefore,
both in the task itself and in the use of its result. From the task itself
not only is there gained a knowledge that has its own value as knowledge,
but also the mind of the investigator is trained in an approach to
materials that yields balance and solidity of judgment as well as clearer
self-understanding. From the result of objective historical investigation
comes an indispensable tool for the exercise of critical judgment and
for the formulation of ideas in the present. Theological and religious
understanding have profited immensely from the revolution in historical thinking that took place during the eighteenth century. Training in
theology, especially at the advanced level of a graduate program,
whatever the field or subdiscipline, gains its substance and its perspective from history.

3. The Initial Stages of Research and the Use of Bibliographic and Reference Sources

We proceed from a formal consideration of the various subject matters and their subdisciplines to the practical task of research itself. Once a student has chosen to work in the broad field of church history or theology, he or she will soon encounter the need to select and narrow a viable topic of research. In some respects, the mental processes of choosing and limiting a topic are time-honored and traditional; in other respects, the use of computer-assisted searches has influenced even our preliminary considerations. This chapter sets forth the methods by which students may delimit a topic; we then introduce a wide variety of bibliographical tools, including those that utilize the latest techniques of storage and retrieval, and we show how the judicious use of these tools and techniques should contribute to a successful outcome. We will find that traditional resources and guides, when used in conjunction with computer databases and materials in microform, offer advantages in both the method of selecting a topic and in the creation of new areas of research.

SELECTING AND NARROWING A TOPIC

When the research student first considers selecting and narrowing a field of study, personal interest in the topic is an important beginning point, because in most cases engagement with the field will extend considerably beyond the three- or four-year period of graduate studies. Students will commonly continue academic work well beyond the completion of the degree and may thus be involved in the general area of research chosen for the dissertation topic for ten or even twenty years. An individual's personal interest in the research topic raises once again the issue of bias and the theological and/or Christian commitment of the researcher. Indeed, the student's own theological or scholarly pilgrimage ought to come into play at some point, since an investment in the worth of the topic is often necessary for sustaining an interest in an area for a long period of time. This chapter will show, however, that the problem of bias and personal interest can be brought into fruitful tension with the process of narrowing and selecting a topic.[1]

Students should be able to answer with some sophistication the question of why they are engaged in advanced historical or theological studies. The specific reason that one finds a topic interesting is less important than the interest itself. Everyone should take the time to ponder the wide variety of circumstances that lead to the decision to study a particular topic, ranging from objective matters largely beyond one's control to highly personal and subjective choices. If, for example, a professor's advice about a topic is alone determinative, the student may not fully adopt the topic as his or her own possession. On the other hand, a degree of tentativity about the viability of a subject should be cultivated, especially in the early stages of research, because it is imperative that the particular shape of the project be determined primarily by the evidence, rather than by a predetermined notion about the results of research.[2] The best approach is characterized by a healthy tension between genuine commitment to the value of the subject, and the integrity that comes into play when one examines a topic with detachment. Nothing is more difficult for the researcher than maintaining a balance between interest and detachment, and yet nothing is more valuable in the quest for objectivity.[3]

It is not uncommon for a student to begin on a topic, only to find

1. The following paragraphs reflect similar concerns to those expressed in G. Kitson Clark, *Guide for Research Students Working on Historical Subjects,* 2nd ed. (Cambridge: Cambridge University Press, 1968), pp. 10-22.

2. Kitson Clark, *Guide for Research Students,* p. 12.

3. Carl Becker rightly observed that the "really detached mind is a dead mind"; see *Detachment and the Writing of History: Essays and Letters of Carl L. Becker,* ed. Phil L. Snyder (Ithaca: Cornell University Press, 1958), p. 24.

after a significant investment of time and energy that it is less compelling than originally thought. In such a case, it is essential that both mentor and student be sufficiently flexible to start afresh on a new topic. Even six months or more of time spent on a topic that ultimately proves abortive is not lost, because by this time the basic method of research is well established and the student will have acquired a good familiarity with scholarly tools. The fact that much of the energy that is devoted to an advanced degree is properly focused upon developing the skills of research is in itself a salutary motive for the endeavor. Indeed, almost any topic will serve this purpose, even those for which the student can muster little enthusiasm. But without a positive interest in the field, students are not likely to be able to maintain sufficient interest in a long-term program of research. Thus a willingness to turn to a different topic at a relatively early stage in scholarly production may actually help preserve a career of scholarship that would otherwise be jeopardized. It is also well to remember that if the general area of the dissertation does not carry a scholar for a decade or more beyond the Ph.D., the area of research can serve as the point of departure for writing articles and monographs in adjacent areas. Students should not be intimidated by the consequences of their choice, but they should think seriously about how their topic will bear upon the whole future of their academic career in one way or another.

The value of staying with the original topic for several years beyond the Ph.D. is revealed by the second book that will begin to show what a person can really do in his or her chosen field. To make a significant breakthrough in any scholarly field one has to move past the dissertation. Only *after* the dissertation does one finally learn the discipline well enough to play with the materials, and it is the long-term investment in a field of research that is really productive. Not infrequently, students will produce a good dissertation only to turn to other things, but it is the long-term investment in a specialized area that will produce lasting results.

The long-range view of scholarly activity we are advocating here is important for another reason. At the beginning of a research project, when mentors require a student to narrow the topic down, the common fear is that the subject will become so narrow as to lose all relevance. Thus existential interest in the area seems to be threatened by the need to find a heretofore unexamined field of primary research. This tension between relevance and originality is highly salutary, and if at times the first is sacrificed to the second, the student will have the assurance that at least he or she is acquiring a proper methodology. But it is at this point that a consideration of the long-term perspective can help alleviate the student's anxiety. In time, the narrow study will broaden in scope, and if at the outset of one's career the first piece of research examines only a decade, the second book may cover the period of a generation. Only mature scholars should attempt to write the history of a century or an era, or a system of theology, and thus the inculcation of a proper method at the outset will one day lead to a much broader sweep with even greater relevance.

If some students worry about the narrow focus of their dissertation topic, others may feel that their course of study is too broad and not directly germane to their primary purpose of producing a publishable piece of research. These people may need to be reminded that they are not only learning the methods of technical research, but acquiring the skills of comparison, balance, and a due sense of proportion — in a word, the characteristics of a teacher.[4] These are qualities that can only be acquired by wide reading and broad-ranging reflection. The greatest benefits in graduate work thus come to those who expend considerable effort in both detailed, close reading of texts that cover perhaps merely months of time or a single doctrinal locus, and reading that ranges at least across the decades of the century in which they work.

The second step in selecting a topic involves asking the question, "Does it exist?" and this question should be put at the same time we ask "What is it?" Is the topic the student wishes to write about a real topic, or is he or she moving into an area that by its very nature will not sustain research? For example, one might consider the topic "The View of the New World Reflected in Dante's *Inferno*." Granting that Dante died in 1321, there cannot be views of the new world reflected there. It is not uncommon for students to imagine topics that are in fact not topics, because they may believe there are sources available for a topic that in fact do not exist. When once it is clear that the topic is viable, then one has to ask, "Is what I have thought of as topic something that everybody in the field already knows about? Is my chosen topic covered exhaustively in somebody else's monograph, or in a major article in *Dictionnaire de théologie catholique?*" and if so, the topic must be abandoned. One might then ask the question, "Can I deal with a

4. Kitson Clark, *Guide for Research Students,* p. 11.

subtopic of this issue that appears to be common knowledge, the subtopic not being common knowledge? Is there a ramification of it that someone else has not seen?" From the very outset of research, students must think about the distinction between a discovery that is new to them and a discovery that makes a genuine contribution to a field. The majority of one's early insights will fall into the former rather than the latter category, and in one sense, the entire goal of the search in secondary literature is to enable the student to make this critical discrimination with certainty.

These questions raise the issue of the scope of the topic. "The History of the Necessity and Extent of the Atonement from the First Century to the Present" is not a dissertation topic, but a multivolume series, probably written by more than one established scholar. The question must be asked, "Am I choosing a topic that can be examined in some 200-350 pages?" That may be hard to do at the beginning, and one has to be aware of the need to adjust as progress is made on the project. A person might begin a doctoral dissertation on "Spiritual Gifts in the Early Church," assuming that there was just enough material in the sources to sustain the dissertation. After several months of research, it might become evident that the materials were rich to the point of embarrassment, and thus it should be admitted that the early church was far too great a period for the scope of the dissertation. The doctoral advisor should be able to help with the matter of scope and the general outside parameters of a topic. But students themselves should constantly ask, "What is the extent of this topic? How can I narrow it down?" One of the ways of doing this in dissertation research is to think about the various parts of the dissertation, and ask, "Is this piece of research a thirty-page chapter? Or is this piece a two-hundred-page topic? Do I need to readjust?" These are questions that should be asked at the outset, but they also need to be asked over and over again. Selecting a topic is not a separate matter from narrowing a topic; these tasks actually interrelate, and one should keep on asking such questions as the project develops.

We have alluded to a number of ways of narrowing a topic. The most obvious way for the historian is chronology. It is not uncommon today for dissertations in modern British political history to be confined to a single administration that may extend to only three or four years. Students may also narrow their area by means of a subtopic. This approach allows one to examine the broader field while concentrating in more detail on specific aspects that have heretofore been neglected, and for this reason, it holds great promise for maintaining a connection with the student's interests. Within the chronological period of the eighteenth century, for example, one might concentrate on a single denomination or movement. Another way of narrowing a topic is to focus on a particular method that has not been used before. Today this often involves quantification. A researcher begins with certain impressions about an area of historical study, but these impressions are based upon qualitative, impressionistic evidence. It is then useful to look at that data and say, "Is there a way of quantifying this?"

A topic may also be narrowed by the specific type of subject matter to be studied (which is closely related to method, but somewhat different). Is there a possibility of bringing a new set of documents or source materials to bear on a topic that has already been examined? One example of this is found in the distinction between printed and manuscript sermons. In colonial America, printed sermons have been quite thoroughly examined, but the study of manuscript sermons is currently an active area of research. In late eighteenth-century Britain, however, neither published nor unpublished sermons have been examined in any detail. In this case, a student would probably wish to select a representative sample of sermons of either the published or unpublished variety, though it might well make sense to draw from both types of sources. In any case, the type of source examined may serve as one method for narrowing a topic. This method is particularly useful in light of the vast new collections of source material that are available in microform and on CD-ROM.

Research topics ought also to be narrowed on the basis of a careful consideration of the level of detail necessary to the proper analysis of the topic. This level of detail must be understood, moreover, in terms both of primary and secondary sources. In the first place, the detail, technical level of argument, and scope of a topic must relate directly to the detail, technical level of argument, and scope of the primary sources being examined. By way of example, an essay on Calvin's exegesis of the Epistle to the Romans will encounter problems relating to the interpretation of the Greek text of Paul, to Calvin's own work as translator in the context of other extant translations (notably, the Vulgate, Erasmus, and Bucer), to Calvin's own understanding of the text in the light of his exegesis, his reading of the exegetical tradition, and his grasp of the larger theological context into which various passages of Romans had come to be placed over the centuries. It is clear that a study involving all of these elements of Calvin's interpretation of the entire epistle will be a rather lengthy book. Similarly, in the investigation of a theological or philosophical topic like the scholastic doctrine of the divine attributes, a researcher will observe differences in approach between theologians, a variously interpreted problem of predication, a lengthy series of attributes, and an even lengthier set of distinctions concerning the attributes. Thus, Aquinas and Duns Scotus differ over the way in which attributes are predicated of God and over the way in which attributes are said to be distinct from one another and from the divine essence. Among the attributes themselves, an attribute like the divine will can be distinguished into an absolute and relative will, a hidden and revealed will, an antecedent and a consequent will, and so forth. A discussion of the scholastic doctrine of God that does not understand these and other issues — at the level of detail and technique employed by the scholastic theologians themselves — will be unable to do justice to the topic. In addition, the level of detail just noted leads to the conclusion that "the scholastic doctrine of God" is the topic not of an essay, and not even of a monograph or dissertation, but of many volumes. The dissertation or the essay must take as its subject a part of this larger whole in order to deal adequately with the detail.

Similarly, the secondary sources dealing with a topic will also dictate the length and character of a study — again, on grounds of detail. A large body of secondary literature on a point will demand considerable analysis: the issue of Luther's *Turmerlebnis,* the "tower experience" in which he gained his understanding of the Pauline language of righteousness, for example, might not appear to be an enormous topic given the nature and extent of the primary sources that deal directly with the experience. Once, however, the scholarly examination of Luther's early theological development has been examined, the various ways of interpreting the difficulties in Luther's own account have been evaluated by examination of other writings of Luther from the period, and the number of different scholarly results noted, the task of wading through and evaluating all of the arguments of many scholars in the light of a large number of texts not originally related to Luther's account, the study takes on dimensions not of a short article but of a monograph. The issue here is that any subsequent study of the problem ought to take its place in the history of scholarship — and, in order to do that, a detailed evaluation of generations of work by scholars becomes imperative. A study that does not pay close attention to the level of detail in primary and secondary sources runs the risk of appearing naive and of failing to do justice to the materials.

Finally, one may narrow geographically. Suppose one wished to study the relationship of church and state as expressed through preaching during the period of the American Revolution. The topic could be studied in the North American colonies; or it could be confined to England. One might also choose to study church and state in Wales or Scotland and have a legitimate topic, granting that the conclusions one draws are geographically as well as chronologically specific. But by the same token, we should note that it is probably not a valid dissertation topic to examine all four of these countries. The examination of two countries, in the form of a comparative study, could work, and we thereby arrive at yet another delimiting factor. Two discrete dissertations may have already been done on two of these countries, but there is the possibility of a dissertation arising from a comparative study, a study that looks at parallels, influences, and differing outcomes. On the other hand, a dissertation that is historical in orientation and that deals with institutions or movements, as distinct from ideas, will not often be attempted on both America and Britain. Of course, there are exceptions. One might realistically address the transatlantic community, a topic of recent, high interest among scholars, but if the geographical spread is too broad, it will commonly take the beginning student too far afield. Even in the case of North America, it would be critically important to distinguish between Canada, New England, mid-Atlantic, and Southern regions; attitudinal differences will be found related to the different political contexts, to say nothing of the difficulty of handling the vast body of literature and properly nuancing it.

In philosophy, the history of ideas, or the history of doctrine, there are additional ways to limit a topic. No one will be able to write a dissertation on the entire philosophy of Thomas Aquinas or the entire thought of David Hume. When we consider the philosophy of a great thinker, then we begin to ask about the impact of other materials on that writer. Naturally, we are limited by which materials the person had access to, which may not be geographical. But then again, the question of the influences on a person's thought may have certain relationships to geography. At different periods in history the flow goes in different directions. It is obvious, for example, in late seventeenth-century British philosophy, that the impact of Cartesianism must be registered somewhere after 1660: rather than write a subsidiary essay on Descartes, the researcher should ascertain how Descartes's philosophy was transmitted across the Channel and how it was received, interpreted, and adapted. At the same time, the impact of British philosophy on the continent should be registered. For example, one can observe the impact of Hume on Voltaire. But there is far less impact of German philosophy on the French in the eighteenth century than English philosophy on the French. Christian Wolff does not significantly impact the French, but Hume definitely does. In the history of thought, it is not so much the geographical limitations as the lines of communication that are important, and these have to be clearly traced out.

It is entirely legitimate to discuss late seventeenth- or eighteenth-century British philosophy, or nineteenth-century British philosophy, on the condition that the student is careful to note continental influences. That is a proper limitation in that it permits one to restrict the main lines of analysis to British thinkers and not have entire chapters on individual continental thinkers. A student can build in geographical limitation, even in those areas, as long as the lines of influence are defined. By the same token, one might discuss late eighteenth-century German biblical criticism, as long as one carefully notes the impact of the English deists; but this does not necessitate having separate chapters on the deists. The student can refer, analytically or critically, to the large body of research that has already been done on the deists and focus instead upon their impact on the Germans. Proper footnoting handles the comprehensive survey of secondary sources, rather than exposition in the text. In this case, then, the geographical distinction does work, as long as one is careful about it.

In the process of selecting and narrowing a topic, research students may now take advantage of the powerful new tools of computer-assisted searching. The new techniques and databases are so important that they already have become, in and of themselves, one means of finding and delimiting a viable topic. On the one hand, this technology simplifies certain aspects of the initial search process, but on the other hand, because of the comprehensive and extensive bibliographic reach of these vast databases, it adds new and sometimes daunting complexity to the task. Neither the possibilities nor the pitfalls of these new sources can be adequately grasped apart from a thorough acquaintance with the traditional tools of research.

A caveat must also be made about the process of narrowing: the topic *must* be narrowed; the mind and the perspectives of the re-searcher should not be. As one of our teachers has reminded us, a researcher ought not to be in so great a hurry to narrow a topic that knowledge and appreciation of the surrounding territory is lost or, indeed, never gained. Balanced research requires a certain amount of breadth — and "circling around" a topic is often as important as narrowing it. In other words, the intellectual, social, political, or re-ligious context around a topic remains a significant source of insight into the topic itself, a significant source of collateral topics for future research, and, in addition, a reservoir of materials that enlighten and stimulate the interest of the researcher in a general way. The process of "narrowing" ought to be a process of focusing a topic without the loss of its larger context.

The crucial issue, therefore, in narrowing a topic is the estab-lishment of a well-focused perspective on the topic that considers care-fully both the topic itself and its proper context. Beyond the recognition of the larger context of any given topic, moreover, there must be an identification of the immediate context for historical analysis; thus, a discussion of a point in Calvin's theology must, of course, hold in focus the larger context of the Reformation and of the movement of thought from the later Middle Ages into the sixteenth century. But the immediate context of the point may well be an event taking place in Geneva or in France at the time that Calvin wrote, the publication of a particular book or tract with which Calvin felt the need to take issue, or the history of the exegesis of a particular text in Scripture — or, indeed, all three of these possible contexts. Events in Geneva might well have pressed Calvin to examine closely a tract written elsewhere and, in answering its teaching, he could have recourse to the interpretation of a particular text in Scripture — and find himself either in accord or out of accord with the older tradition of interpretation. In any case, the analysis of any point, whether theological, political, or philosophical, in isolation from its immediate context can lead to profound misunderstanding or, at least, to a partial and unsatisfactory analysis. It is simply not useful to write about Calvin's theology in isolation from its context, as if it were a set of archetypal ideas. Such an approach fails to indicate either the originality or sameness of Calvin's thought and fails also to present the real basis for the thought itself.

It is also at this point that the process of narrowing and estab-lishing the topic relates or connects directly with the issue of tools and methods in research. The immediate context of the topic and, therefore, the topic itself must be examined with attention to the necessary research tools and the requisite pattern or method of approach to the materials. Thus, identification of an exegetical context for the understanding of a passage in Calvin points directly toward the identification of the biblical commentaries and the lexical and textual tools used by Calvin — and, by extension, toward both the history of exegesis and the rise of Renaissance humanism. Lexical tools and a resource like Stegmüller's *Repertorium biblicum medi aevi* will play a significant role in such a study.

CURRENT RESEARCH TECHNIQUES AND NEW BIBLIOGRAPHIC DATABASES IN CHURCH HISTORY AND THEOLOGY

Major methodological advances in the humanities are usually not as frequent, nor as dramatic, as advances in the natural sciences. Two notable exceptions to this rule are found in the Enlightenment and in the current revolution in the storage and retrieval of information. For over 200 years the basic methods of historical investigation have remained essentially the same, but while the mental tools of the Enlightenment have not been superseded, they are no longer sufficient for critical historical study. Advances in technology are currently influencing the humanities on a scale comparable to the impact of the scientific method during the Enlightenment, and scholars are now talking about the influence of the computer on the study of history as a paradigm *defining* change.[5] Ten years ago it was commonly thought that the use of computers and sources in microform applied only to certain types of historical investigation, such as economic and social history, or more narrowly, to those areas that were susceptible to quantification. Research on the impact of religious belief on voting behavior is one example of the use to which quantitative data was often put. But a number of well-known scholars resisted the so-called "new history" with a passion that bordered on paranoia. They feared that the new methods would drain history of meaning; most of the critics worked in the field of intellectual history, and in their apprehensions,

5. Janice L. Reiff, *Structuring the Past: The Use of Computers in History* (Washington: American Historical Association, 1991), p. 4.

the specter of economic determinism was always standing in the wings.[6]

Church historians have been even more reluctant than historians of ideas to embrace the new technology, and apparently for the same philosophical reasons.[7] Recent innovations in storing and searching documents have simply passed these critics by and placed the debate on an entirely new footing. It is now evident that scholars in most areas of history and theology must become familiar with at least the rudiments of the new techniques. The revolution in the manipulation of information made possible by the computer is clearly transforming the nature of research, though, to be sure, the mental habits of disciplined study and critical judgment remain unchanged. The unparalleled access to sources in the mediums of microfilm, microfiche, and compact disk is a closely related phenomenon. We believe that the newer technology, understood broadly, is no longer optional. The scholar who neglects current technological advances in the manipulation and accessing of sources puts himself or herself in the position of the student who refuses to adopt the methodological advances of the Enlightenment; they become, by definition, precritical. The areas in which students can safely ignore the new methods and source mediums are becoming fewer, and even those scholars working in areas as yet untouched by this technology can still benefit from an exposure to the conceptual elegance of un-impeded research, and exhaustive, near-perfect bibliographies.

In many, if not most, fields of historical and theological inquiry, the nature of critical study today thus necessarily entails the utilization of new searching techniques based on modern technology. The new techniques and sources have considerable relevance for research students in a variety of ways. For example, given the contemporary ease with which personal computers are linked to databases, and given the growing bulk of material that is now available in microform through

---

6. Jacques Barzun, *Clio and the Doctors: Psycho-History, Quanto-History, and History* (Chicago: University of Chicago Press, 1974); G. R. Elton, "Two Kinds of History," in Robert W. Fogel and G. R. Elton, *Which Road to the Past?* (New Haven: Yale University Press, 1983); Gertrude Himmelfarb, *The New History and the Old* (Cambridge, Mass.: The Belknap Press, 1987). Recent quantitative research in popular religion and popular politics has in fact demonstrated the influence of ideas on behavior, but with far greater authority than the old analysis of literary sources.

7. The briefest survey of major periodicals like the *Journal of Ecclesiastical History* and *Church History* suggests the lack of interest in these topics.

interlibrary loan, the need for students to locate themselves near large research libraries is proportionately reduced. Above all, however, the new technology bodes well for the creation of new research projects alluded to throughout this book. Indeed, old topics can now be reexamined, but with more extensive documentation and, hence, greater precision. New areas of research are opening rapidly as the capabilities of the new techniques are recognized. It is now possible to study the number of editions of religious pamphlets and the place where they were published, and this in turn will allow us to offer new interpretations concerning the influence of religious ideas. The entire written corpus of less well-known persons can now be examined, and these works will often provide enough new material to sustain a thesis or dissertation. Clearly, the use of the new techniques for identifying people in the past has implications for the study of minorities and women's studies in church history. The power these tools offer the historian in primary research is simply unparalleled in history, and the same observations apply to searches of secondary literature, both unpublished (dissertations) and published (articles and monographs). Clearly, traditional hard-copy bibliographies will remain useful, but given the current rate of proliferation of monographic literature, it is entirely likely that computerized searching will soon be mandatory. It is currently impossible to use large research libraries without an elementary introduction to computer searching and microfiche readers.

The obvious merits and advantages of databases ought not, however, to be allowed to obscure the continuing importance of hands-on study in great libraries and archives. The contemporary excitement over the new availability of bibliographical resources and actual documents must be balanced by the realizations that the establishment of a superb bibliographical base for research through the use of various databases merely leaves the researcher without excuse and that vast stores of books and manuscripts are not and will probably never be available on film or fiche: the materials themselves still need to be procured and, not infrequently, they will have to be procured through the services of major libraries. In the case of rare books, manuscripts, and archival materials, the researcher will have to turn from the computer screen to the original hard copy in a library or archive.

Church History and Theology: Research in Secondary Sources

Dissertations and Theses

One of the first steps in doctoral research is to determine whether the proposed topic of one's dissertation has been researched by someone else at the doctoral level and whether her or his dissertation covers the topic in such a way as to make further research unnecessary. Logically, one might begin with a bibliographical search for scholarly monographs, or even with a search of the periodical literature. By far the best approach, however, is to begin with a search of the dissertation literature.

This is a simple piece of advice that offers several advantages to those who follow it. It is, in the first place, a salutary exercise because it leads the student to think about the character and scope of dissertation topics, and to begin to look at what other students have done at other seminaries and universities across the land. The dissertation search ought to lead to conclusions about what can be accomplished in a dissertation and about the length and breadth and depth of research topics at the doctoral level. In the second place, in view of the exhaustive cataloguing done by University Microfilms International for *Dissertation Abstracts International,* the current character of the listing of titles and abstracts, and the careful bibliographical work required in most doctoral research, together with the availability of all catalogued dissertations from University Microfilms, the dissertation search can offer the most convenient access to recent work, whether in the form of dissertations or in the form of references to the monographic and periodical literature. It is not a crime — in fact, it is a prerequisite to good research — for a student to pay close attention to the bibliographical work of previous scholars.

The bibliography at the end of this book lists the most important items, including *Dissertation Abstracts International,* which is the most generalized source for American dissertations: it indexes dissertations in every academic field (Bib. I.A). *Masters Abstracts,* typically, need not be consulted; there are very few cases when a master's thesis ought to give anyone pause for concern. This observation would be less true in the case of British commonwealth countries than it is in the United States; M.Litt. theses from Oxford or Cambridge, for example, are usually of high quality. Most American master's theses, however, will be fairly superficial treatments of a topic, and even if they cover precisely the topic that one is dealing with, the Ph.D. dissertation should supersede any master's work considerably.

Dissertation Abstracts International is organized around two basic subject categories, the humanities and the sciences. A third section lists European abstracts, and although *Dissertation Abstracts* is referred to as an "international" guide, the coverage for the period before 1976 is limited almost exclusively to dissertations produced in North America. Students in church history and theology will obviously be concerned primarily with the humanities. New titles and abstracts are published in hard copy every month, so that even in its traditional format, this reference is relatively up to date. For a small fee University Microfilms International also provides a computerized search service that is more current. In this form, the database is more extensive: it contains dissertations dating back to 1861 and can search by keyword both the titles of dissertations and the contents of the abstracts. Most research libraries now have *Dissertation Abstracts International* on CD-ROM for even more convenient and less expensive searching (although the CD-ROM version does not allow abstract searches before 1980), and on-line services such as DIALOG also provide access to the latest edition. Once the appropriate dissertations are chosen, they may be ordered in the form of either soft cover hard copy, or 35 mm. positive microfilm. Many dissertations in the UMI database may also be borrowed on interlibrary loan through OCLC (see below, under Computerized Databases).

Several ancillary tools are also of use in obtaining titles of dissertations in history, and specifically in church history and historical theology. For a number of years, the journal *Church History* offered a survey of recent doctoral dissertations in the history of the Christian church, though most of the dissertations found here will also be located by a thorough search in *Dissertation Abstracts International*. The standard work in historical studies for the United States and Canada is Warren F. Kuehl's *Dissertations in History,* now available in three volumes with coverage through 1980. The British counterpart to *Dissertation Abstracts International* is the *Index to Theses Accepted for Higher Degrees by the Universities of Great Britain and Ireland,* which begins in 1950 and carries through to the present. Researchers who are working on topics centered in other foreign countries will have recourse to the specialized dissertation guides for those specific countries. Similarly, limiting a topic by century will assist the beginning student in locating important guides to dissertations. For example, *Scholars of Early Modern Studies* (formerly *Historians of Early Modern Europe*) is an annual publication that includes the Newsletter of the Sixteenth Century Studies Conference and the Society for Reformation Research. *Scholars of Early Modern Studies* publishes the names of Ph.D. candidates, their advisors, and dissertation topics.

The question of the retrospective extent of these volumes raises a further issue: the dissertation search can safely be concentrated upon the last thirty years, or forty years at the most. Dissertations that were written before 1950 are usually of much less concern. Given the technological and methodological advances typical of most disciplines in the humanities in the last generation, one can be fairly certain that a dissertation written before 1950 is not going to pose a major threat to current research efforts. In addition, the best dissertations of the past have, typically, either been published in book form or consistently noted in subsequent studies of the same topic.

The main scholarly achievements of older dissertations, whether they are good dissertations or not, will thus commonly have already been brought into the history of research between the date of the writing of the dissertation and the present. The topic will have been covered in some way, and most often the dissertation will be superseded by someone else's research. But occasionally one finds older dissertations that have not been surpassed. Two that belong to the field of seventeenth-century theological studies are Charles McCoy's 1956 dissertation on Johannes Cocceius, the seventeenth-century covenant theologian, which continues to be referred to as the only English-language source on Cocceius's thought; and John W. Beardslee's two-volume 1957 dissertation on Francis and Jean-Alphonse Turretin. Neither, of course, was written before 1950 — but both are nonetheless exceptions in the field and both serve to illustrate the difficulty of identifying older dissertations that have not been superseded. The existence and quality of such works, moreover, becomes readily apparent from the rest of one's research in the other forms of secondary literature. The exceptions to the "rule of 1950" will therefore easily be dealt with in the subsequent stages of one's literature search. Almost without exception, students will find ways to cover the literature examined in dissertations produced before 1950 without difficulty, and they will readily improve upon them.

As with almost every kind of search that will be discussed in this chapter, one should start with the most recent references and work back in time. The briefest experience in theological or historical research reveals the logic of this procedure. The more recent studies will have many references to previous dissertations as well as to recent monographs and articles. Students will, therefore, save themselves a good deal of time and energy if they begin with the most recent references.

An examination of recent scholarly bibliographies will make it very clear that the relative ease of this initial search process in no way diminishes its importance for the final product of one's own research and, certainly, in no way implies that the reading of dissertations belongs exclusively to the dissertation phase of scholarship. We are in the midst of a bibliographical revolution that has as much to do with unpublished as with published materials. Those of us who went through graduate school in the early 1970s used many scholarly books that failed to refer to a single dissertation. But because of the publication program of University Microfilms International, this is becoming less and less true. Good books and good contemporary dissertations will almost always refer to at least a half dozen dissertations. Indeed, references to dissertations in a scholarly monograph are one indication of the currency of its research.

Students must not assume that dissertations that have not been revised for publication are of no value. Graduate schools make and retain their reputations on the quality of their dissertations. The vast majority of dissertations are never revised for subsequent publication as books, and this occurs for a range of reasons: sometimes scholars move on to other topics, sometimes the dissertation is too long to be turned into a book, and sometimes the extent of the changes necessary to induce a publisher to accept the dissertation as a monograph is not appropriate to the subject. (The advantages and disadvantages of turning dissertations into books will be the subject of a subsequent discussion.) When it is published, then the dissertation becomes a monograph, and then it belongs to a different literary genre that requires different searching tools.

Undoubtedly the most important reason today that dissertations are not published is that University Microfilms has rendered publication unnecessary. The assumption is commonly made that contemporary dissertations ought to be the final product of advanced research: University Microfilms provides copyright services and, in effect, an on-demand publication service. In a sense, the form of citation frequently used in references to doctoral research — "Unpublished Ph.D. Dissertation, University of X" — no longer accurately represents the case. Word processing, desktop publication, and the photolithoprinting of so-called "camera-ready copy" have resulted in dissertations that are more like books and books that look more and more like visually improved dissertations.

In addition to the main guides, we have listed a few indices in the bibliography that deal with specialized fields. These references are to be understood only as illustrative of a vast host of specialized bibliographies of dissertations.[8] For example, V. F. Gilbert and D. S. Tatla, *Women's Studies: A Bibliography of Dissertations, 1870-1982,* would be a critical source for anyone working in women's studies. Michael Montgomery's *American Puritan Studies: An Annotated Bibliography of Dissertations, 1882-1981* is also a significant bibliographical effort. Both of these works used *Dissertation Abstracts International* extensively, and most of the annotations in Montgomery's book are from *Dissertation Abstracts International.* Montgomery has added a few annotations of his own, but the main contribution of this book is its convenience; though it must be supplemented by a search for the past decade, in Puritan studies, it is the best initial point of departure.

Constant vigilance is required to insure against the chance that others are working on the same topic, and this is not a concern that can be settled definitively in the early stages of one's research. However, if a student does find that another scholar is working on the same body of literature, it may well be that the specific topic or methods of research are sufficiently different to justify several monographs. Open discussion is required, and much can be accomplished in this respect by a candid exchange through correspondence.

Once a student has determined that his or her subject has not been treated by someone else's dissertation or, if it has been the topic of someone else's dissertation, that its thesis is capable of modification or reappraisal either in whole or in part, the bibliographical search moves on to the next stage, that is, to published discussions of the particular subject and its collateral subthemes. Just as one's topic can be ruled out at the dissertation level, it can also be ruled out at the level of scholarly articles and published monographs. Commonly, we gather materials in

8. See, for example, chapter 7, "Dissertations and Theses," in Ronald H. Fritze, Brian E. Coutts, and Louis A. Vyhnanek, eds., *Reference Sources in History: An Introductory Guide* (Santa Barbara: ABC-Clio, 1991).

the two categories of articles and monographs at the same time, but we have chosen to examine articles before monographs because periodicals are themselves an excellent tool in the search for pertinent books and because recent articles often provide the most up-to-date research available on a given topic.

Periodical Directories and Abstracts

In the general field of religion, including Church History, History of Christian Doctrine, and Systematic or Philosophical Theology, probably the best single source for references to articles in the field is *Religion Index One* and *Religion Index Two* (Bib. I.B). The first of these tools deals with periodical literature in about 500 different journals. *Religion Index Two* is arguably the more valuable of the two references since it deals with articles and essays published in multiauthored books and *Festschriften,* sources that are notoriously difficult to catalog and hence to use effectively. Both sources are indexed and edited by the same consultants and both are standard references used by all scholars in a wide range of fields having to do with religion.

These indices do, however, have their limitations, both in the number of journals indexed and in the system of topics and cross-references used. It would be worthwhile for the beginning student to scan the list of indexed periodicals that is found in the front of each volume and to note omissions as well as inclusions — and to make a mental note that other indices will need to be consulted. Students who use the topical section of the index should recognize that the researcher's topics and the indexed topics will not always be identical in definition or parameters; the index will often use a different name for a topic and proceed on different assumptions than the researcher. Continental Protestant theology in the seventeenth century, for example, can be identified as "Protestant Scholasticism," alphabetized with other things Protestant, as "Scholasticism, Protestant," listed as a subcategory of "Scholasticism"; it could be listed as "Protestant Orthodoxy" or "Orthodoxy, Protestant," with the same qualifications; or alternatively, as "Lutheran" or "Reformed Theology, Seventeenth Century," or, somewhat differently again, as "Post-Reformation Protestant Theology, Reformed" or "Lutheran." In seventeenth-century England, many Puritans became "Nonconformists" following the Act of Uniformity of 1662, but Nonconformists may be properly referred to as "Dissenters" or "Protestant Dissenters." Occasionally "old Dissent" is used as a catchall phrase for the earlier denominations (Presbyterians, Congregationalists, and Baptists), and "new Dissent" is the term most commonly applied to the Quakers and Methodists. The researcher must be aware of all of these possibilities and be prepared to look for *all* of these terms, *even after* a preliminary search under one of them yields some useful references. *Religion Index One* and *Religion Index Two* are both available on-line and via CD-ROM, but the use of these media raises the specter of even greater pitfalls, and, to be sure, enormous advantages, that will be discussed below under "Computerized Databases."

A further limitation of *Religion Index One* relates to the word "religion" itself. A student can be very seriously misled if she uses *Religion Index One* and *Religion Index Two* as the only sources for articles and essays in the field of religion. There will be numerous articles with titles that conceal the fact that they contain crucial religious content that, for one reason or another, was not indexed under "religion." Virtually everything that is published in the fields of Western history and philosophy before the eighteenth century — politics, economics, recreation — has some kind of religious content or implication, and articles on these topics will also have religious implications. The compilers and abstractors may not have caught an article that deals with religious issues historically or philosophically — or the article may be listed in a historical or philosophical index simply because of the journal in which it was published — and yet it may have tremendous relevance for one's own research in "religion." No researcher can safely depend exclusively on the use of tools like *Religion Index One* and *Two*.

Among the other tools that must be consulted are the *Catholic Periodical and Literature Index, Ephemerides Theologicae Lovanienses,* and the *Philosopher's Index.* In contrast with these indices, *Religion Index One,* with a few important exceptions, is oriented more toward Protestant thought and history. There are, therefore, quite a few major periodicals dealing with religious and philosophical subjects that are indexed only in the *Catholic Periodical Index.* The *Philosopher's Index,* with coverage beginning in 1940, also deals with nominally religious topics, such as the existence and attributes of God, the problem of evil, and so forth, but it references primarily philosophical periodicals and frequently identifies important essays not listed either in *Religion Index One* and *Two* or in the *Catholic Periodical Index.* The *Philosopher's Index* is available on-line and it is also now accessible on CD-ROM, thus placing more than 150,000 articles, books, and contributions to anthologies before the bewildered student. Thankfully, tutorial guides are available for searching such databases as *The Philosopher's Index* (see App. I below, under DIALOG and the Philosophy Documentation Center). *Ephemerides Theologicae Lovanienses*, which is known to scholars as the larger publication that includes *Elenchus Bibliographicus Biblicus* (since 1985, *Elenchus of Biblica*), is a massive bibliographic tool from the University of Louvain that indexes both articles and books and offers very fine year-end cross-referencing. It contains more references to European materials than either *Religion Index One, Catholic Periodical Index,* or *The Philosopher's Index.* All of those reference tools should be consulted regularly for current bibliography in the field.

In more strictly historical studies, *Recently Published Articles* is probably one of the best, more recent research tools, which has, unfortunately, ceased publication. Published by the *American Historical Association* from 1976 through 1991, it is based upon a search of thousands of periodicals that draws together all the materials on history and organizes them by country and then by standard periodization, such as, Britain, 1714-1815. In a given year, some 200 articles would typically appear in that one section alone. *Recently Published Articles* is a very fine indexing tool that can still be used for the brief period of its tenure in research in the area of church history (as distinct from theology).

Students occasionally wonder whether all of these indices are in English: an index will characteristically cite all articles and books in their original language, unless the language is one not normally used in the scholarly community addressed by the index. For example, articles written in Eastern European languages will typically be cited with translations of their titles. A quick glance at *Ephemerides* will serve to underline the importance of the use of several modern languages in almost all areas of religious, historical, and theological study, particularly English, French, and German. Students in advanced studies need to come to grips with the fact that modern languages are not an "official" problem. They are the necessary means of obtaining essential information and there can be no excuse for not using them. However, one does not need to be an expert in several foreign languages in order to use most of the tools discussed in this book. A biographical essay in a German dictionary can, for example, be read to find out when an individual was born and died, where the person studied, and so forth, without great linguistic

skills. It is also worth noting that particular fields of study are dominated
by specific languages: the French virtually own patristic and medieval
theological and philosophical studies. Similarly, German scholarship has
tended to dominate Reformation and biblical studies, and naturally the
tools reflect these areas of emphasis and strength.

Besides general knowledge of a broad field, students need to accept
the fact that specialized knowledge, such as foreign languages, quantitative techniques, or skill in reading handwritten manuscripts, is often
required. It might be discovered, for example, that vital records, such
as birth and baptismal registers, have a great value in identifying the
social strata of individuals, a datum which in turn has relevance for
questions of religious motivation. Vital records, however, especially in
seventeenth-century handwriting, are difficult to read without training,
and a student might be tempted either to avoid the difficulty altogether,
or muddle along without acquiring a technical understanding of early-
modern handwriting. The acquisition of specialized knowledge for the
purpose of research must be taken in stride, at whatever cost, and this
rule applies to the newer techniques as well as to the old.

Computerized Databases of Secondary Literature

We have previously alluded to the computerized databases of University
Microfilms International and the American Theological Library Association.[9] Just as with dissertations, bibliographic databases comprising
periodical and monographic literature can be searched, and these services are available through most libraries or, with a modest investment
in computer modem hardware and software, through one's own personal computer (App. I.-III). For more than a decade, numerous indexing projects have been storing bibliographic information in computer
databases that are accessed through telecommunications, but increasingly these organizations are supplementing their on-line computer
services with the technology of compact discs. The American Theolog-

9. The databases we discuss here are ones the authors have used or investigated;
they are merely suggestive of what is available and we by no means provide a comprehensive coverage. Students should be aware of *Historical Abstracts* and *America: History
and Life* by ABC-Clio; MARC and REMARC, which contain the books catalogued by
the Library of Congress; the Institute for Scientific Information which has produced,
on-line, the *Social Sciences Citation Index* and the *Arts and Humanities Index*.

ical Library Association, for example, has supplied scholars for years with the contents of *Religion Index One*, on-line.[10] The ATLA then collaborated with the H. W. Wilson Company to make this well-used religious index available in a CD-ROM version (the so-called "Wilsondisc"). The ATLA has now produced its own CD-ROM edition entitled "Religion Database on CD-ROM." In both their on-line and CD-ROM expressions, these databases are enormously powerful searching tools. The uninitiated, however, should be made aware of a number of potential pitfalls.

In the first place, all computerized databases must be used with caution because they are limited by the parameters of the database itself.[11] It is an elementary observation, but one that nonetheless needs to be made, that access to the *Religion Index One* database will yield nothing more than what is already in *Religion Index One*. The retrospective coverage of many on-line databases is limited to about ten years. This is the case, for example, with the *Arts and Humanities Citation Index;* in contrast, *America: History and Life* is unusual in its ability to reach back to its origins in 1964. Before using a database, therefore, students must understand the limitations of its retrospective coverage; this is but another reason for insisting upon careful work in traditional bibliographical reference works. In the second place, databases are limited by the interests, insights, skills, and intelligence of the people doing the indexing. They may not in every case be able to identify all the topics that are discussed in the literature they are indexing. On the other hand, the advantages of using these databases outweigh the disadvantages. For example, keyword searches by computer can ferret out information that may not be included in a hard-copy index, these searches are much faster than manual searches, and they are typically more up-to-date than traditional sources. Moreover, they provide the student with either hard-copy printouts or computer files of biblio-

---

10. The ATLA has generated a variety of hard copy bibliographies from its database, including *Liberation Theology, Black Theology and the Third World.*

11. Several articles dealing with databases appeared in the American Historical Association newsletter, *Perspectives:* David Y. Allen, "Computers and the Historian: Computerized Literature Searching, A Do-It-Yourself Activity?" 23, no. 2 (1985): 23-25; Joyce Duncan Falk, "OCLC and RLIN: Research Libraries at the Scholar's Fingertips," 27, no. 5 (1989): 1, 11-13, 17; and on a related topic, see Donald Mabry, "Electronic Mail and Historians," 29, no. 2 (1991): 1, 4-6. The best overall, up-to-date guide is Janice Reiff's *Structuring the Past,* pp. 11-18, 43-52, and the references cited there.

graphical information that can be introduced into the text of a chapter with little effort.

Illustration of both the value and limitation of databases can be drawn from our past use of two excellent tools, the OCLC system and RLIN. OCLC (Online Computer Library Center), like RLIN (Research Libraries Information Network), is a vast library catalogue database drawn from a nationwide network of cooperating research libraries.[12] It not only allows the student to search scores of research libraries at once, but it produces printouts of bibliographical materials and it serves as the basis for an electronically generated interlibrary loan service. The researcher's resources instantly become as large as the database — which is enormous, extending now to over 8,000 libraries in some 26 countries.

There are, however, serious unavoidable limitations in the use of these networks, imposed both by the still vast reservoir of unentered materials, even in the libraries belonging to the networks, and by problems in programming. For example, OCLC is at present unable to print out the run of titles in an academic series. OCLC will provide complete bibliographical information and will identify the locations of individual volumes but will not generate a list of all the volumes in *Corpus Catholicorum,* a major collection of Catholic writers of the sixteenth century (more than fifty volumes, representing an editing process of three quarters of a century). If the title *Corpus Catholicorum* is entered, a reference to the series title, listing the number of volumes in the series, is generated, but the titles of the individual volumes cannot be retrieved. When the database was compiled, the programmers did not think of this particular way of referencing and using the information in the database. Happily, this particular problem is about to be permanently solved, because the entire *Corpus Catholicorum* is being placed on CD-ROM and will be packaged with the latest, most powerful retrieval software.

Another problem centers around the provisional nature of the construction of all databases. Although all new books are being entered daily by the member libraries as the works are accessioned, it is taking some of the large research libraries a long time to enter their entire old catalogue into the database — and they are beginning with the letter

---

12. Our comments provide only the briefest of introductions to these vast resources. We concentrate here, for example, on the search of secondary literature. The data in OCLC and RLIN actually falls into eight categories: books, periodicals, maps, manuscripts, music scores, visual materials, audio recordings, and a variety of data files.

"A" and working toward the letter "Z." If, for example, a researcher attempts to locate Wilhelm Zuylen, *Bartholomaus Keckermann: Sein Leben und Wirken* (Leipzig, 1934), the OCLC may turn up nothing. Several years ago, the database indicated that this book was not to be found anywhere in the country. Nevertheless, it was in fact available through interlibrary loan from UCLA, which is a member library of OCLC. The UCLA library had simply not gotten as far as "Zuylen" in their OCLC inputting effort. This is, of course, a limitation that will disappear totally in time. Efforts at retrospective conversions of materials to machine-readable form are impressive, but some major libraries in the country will probably never belong to any of the networks, and thus the larger holdings nationwide, represented, for example, by the *National Union Catalogue of Pre-1956 Imprints,* will still need to be checked manually. Using a database, therefore, does not make it possible for a researcher to avoid manual work in printed indices: *computerized searches of a database must still be used in conjunction with standard references.*

In recent years, the longstanding differences between OCLC and RLIN have diminished, and either network may now be used with considerable confidence. OCLC is now fully engaged with major research libraries, both OCLC and RLIN include all Library of Congress holdings that are available in machine-readable form, and both support the individual scholars' access through personal computers. But of these two national bibliographic databases, RLIN is currently somewhat larger than OCLC, and its archive and manuscript files are more extensive. RLIN also has several specialized databases, the most important for church historians being the *Eighteenth-Century Short Title Catalog* (which will be discussed in the next chapter).[13] As with most current databases, RLIN will allow records to be searched on any word in a title; it supports Boolean logic to combine or exclude various words, and the program also displays helpful truncation and browse features. Connect time with RLIN, however, can be expensive, averaging between ten and twenty dollars an hour, depending on the type of hookup that is available.

13. RLIN also makes the Medieval and Early Modern Data Bank based at Rutgers University available, but to date this project concentrates on data that can be tabulated, rather than on texts. It does, however, have some value for the theologian or church historian in that it has a gazetteer of Latin and vernacular place names.

In addition to these large networks, most major research libraries may now be accessed through the individual scholar's personal computer, and in this case, the only expense is that of the telephone call (App. II). For example, on the East Coast, on-line services are available at Harvard University (HOLLIS), Boston University (TOMUS), Yale University (ORBIS), Columbia University (CLIO), and many smaller colleges, such as Wellesley; the New York Public Library alone eschews the stuffy acronym, with its CATNYP — "Catalog of the NY Public Library"; in the Midwest, the University of Michigan (MIRLYN) and the University of Minnesota (LUMINA) have on-line services; and in the West, we have the University of California system (MELVYL) and numerous smaller institutions.

Two of the University library on-line services we have used will illustrate the possibilities and some of the disadvantages of telecommunications. MELVYL allows the student access to the 6.5 million titles of the University of California libraries, including the rare book holdings of the Clark Library. The program is unusually easy to use, the response time is very rapid, and directives appear throughout a session for "the fastest and most effective way to search." However, only University of California users can acquire access to some of their services, such as the indexes to recent articles (a password is required, for example, to view "Current Contents"). A major East Coast library offers a second illustration. The Speer Library at Princeton Theological Seminary used the CARLYLE on-line catalog for years, and with this software, one could do a search under the Sprague Collection, an extremely valuable collection of nineteenth-century American sermons and religious pamphlets. It was possible, for example, to retrieve an itemized list of the whole of that collection; alternatively, during a recent project on theological education, a word search, utilizing the single entry "student," resulted in a list from the Sprague Collection with ninety-five titles of interest. The Speer Library recently replaced CARLYLE with NOTIS, and with the latter software, individual items in the Sprague Collection may still be found, but only if the researcher knows the individual author or individual title beforehand. Despite these and similar drawbacks that could be noted, library databases have displaced hard-copy card catalogs to the point that they are now the best single source for developing an initial bibliography of monographs and related books on topics of research.

In addition to networks and individual library databases, there are a few well-organized specializations that are moving toward comprehensive databases of secondary literature (App. III). One of the most impressive projects is found in Patristics. The *Bibliographical Information Base in Patristics* stores information from books and articles in the field, and it currently has an inventory of the contents of more than 300 journals. The retrieval software of this database is designed specifically to serve Patristic scholars in obtaining ready access to summaries of secondary works that are pertinent to their research.

Since each library and network database is structured differently, students should be alert to the need to change searching strategies when they change databases or libraries. The attempts of a rank novice will produce some results with any database, but excellent results will require serious investigation of the searching methods of each discrete database, and often the best results will only be achieved with practice. Students would thus be well advised, especially at the outset of their research, to rely on the expertise of librarians who have had considerable experience in using on-line databases. Once the database has been used to develop an initial bibliographical survey, then one should go on from one's basic list to the more traditional references and continue to fill out the bibliography. Of course, the bibliographical search is not something that happens once and for all at the beginning of one's work on a dissertation. Building a comprehensive bibliography of secondary literature not only takes a lengthy period of time initially, it continues in the addition of monographs, articles, and dissertations that appear during the entire length of one's research.

A useful pattern of research is to begin with a database search, utilizing the resources of either on-line searches or compact discs, first of *Dissertation Abstracts International* and of "Religion Database on CD-ROM," fully aware that these searches will have to be supplemented with a manual investigation of other, more traditional resources. Then one should move on to a resource like *Recently Published Articles*, and finally turn to the most recent issues of major journals in the field.

Scholarly Journals

Students at the doctoral level should not only regularly consult major journals in their field, they should also subscribe to one or more of those journals (Bib. I.C). Those doing advanced work in church history should think seriously of taking *Church History,* the standard and best journal for the study of church history, broadly understood, in this country, or the *Journal of Ecclesiastical History,* which is the British counterpart. Regular consultation of scholarly journals is the only way to maintain a truly current knowledge of articles and monographs in one's field: the standard indices are seldom able to list an article within a year of its publication and the review sections of the journals will frequently offer the first available notice of new books in a field.

The best international church-historical journal is *Revue d'Histoire Ecclésiastique,* which, like *Ephemerides,* is published at Louvain. *Revue d'Histoire Ecclesiastique* appears three times annually in a large volume of about 450 pages. Though written primarily in French, it covers literature of all countries, the majority of articles being in French or in German. It is the bibliographical breadth of the *Revue,* however, that is stunning. It does far more than any other journal with reviewing research, including work in progress at various universities in Europe. It reviews articles and frequently offers critiques; and it reviews a greater number of books than any other journal of church history. It is therefore the standard work, although written in foreign languages, for virtually all scholars working in church history.

In addition to using indices to find articles in one's field, it is a worthwhile practice simply to survey several of the major journals in the discipline by working one's way back in time from the most recent issue. This is the only way to find major articles in a field before they are listed in the standard indices. As in the case of the dissertation search, the journal search provides a helpful sense of the kinds of articles and the styles of research found in various fields of study. One of the most valuable contributions that journals make to scholarship is the bibliographical essay that appears from time to time. Most of the articles that fall under the heading of "bibliographic essay" will identify and analyze the literature in a given field, including monographs, dissertations, and articles, written during the past twenty years or so. Bibliographical essays can also be of significant value when one arrives at one's first teaching position. The specific topics around which lectures are formed can be greatly strengthened by reviewing the recent literature found in these essays. The bibliographic essay can thus save a considerable amount of time; students should remain alert to their value for both research and teaching.

One of the major specialized bibliographies that is made available in a journal is the exhaustive Calvin bibliography published yearly in *Calvin Theological Journal*. The editor of the bibliography is presently collating the various yearly bibliographies into a single cumulative bibliography. A further advantage of this particular bibliography is that approximately ninety percent of the articles and monographs cited are available at the H. Henry Meeter Center for Calvin Studies in Grand Rapids, Michigan, and copies are available from the Center on request. Up-to-date cumulative indices are typically available for most other major periodicals as well. After databases, current periodicals remain the best means of identifying pertinent monographs through their book reviews sections, notices of books received but not reviewed, and publishers' advertisements of new and forthcoming books.

Handbooks, Bibliographical Guides, and General Surveys

The most recent handbook on church history is G. E. Gorman and Lyn Gorman, *Theological and Religious Reference Materials: Systematic Theology and Church History* (Bib. I.D). The organization of this volume leaves much to be desired, but it remains the best, most comprehensive annotated bibliographical guide to research reference tools in church history and theology presently available. A more accessible guide, though covering the broader field of history in general, is the recently published *Reference Sources in History: An Introductory Guide*.

Yet another kind of bibliographical tool is the bibliography of bibliographies, such as the recent volume on women by Patricia Ballou. These are unique tools whose value might not be immediately recognized by the student researcher, but they are a very important genre of reference works. If a scholar wants to find a bibliography on her particular topic, one of the first places that she should look is a bibliography of bibliographies. This advice is particularly germane to the search for primary materials, because even the best, most recent article on any given topic will commonly not cite the scholarly bibliographies that contributed to the location of primary documents. Such bibliographical guides, as helpful as they are to the researcher, tend to remain deeply layered in the research process and hence uncited in the scholar's final published product.

Dictionaries and Encyclopedias

The use of dictionaries and encyclopedias in scholarly work can be a source of trouble and dismay to the uninitiated (Bib. I.E). An initial, necessary distinction must be made between the encyclopedias and topical dictionaries written for the general public and those written by scholars for students in scholarly fields and for other scholars. The former, including such famous and prestigious works as the *Britannica*, *Americana*, *Colliers Encyclopedia* and the *World Almanac* ought to be avoided as conceived on a level below that of graduate scholarship. The latter, some of which follow, are of considerable value and worthy of citation in scholarly studies.

Basic language dictionaries such as *Webster* and *Cassell* are not cited in our bibliography, but are also excluded from the above caveat. Similarly, certain encyclopedias of a more general scope are also capable of being cited in scholarly work: one is the 1911 edition of the *Britannica*, which has signed articles by major scholars of its day, including, for example, a major article on Gnosticism by Adolf von Harnack. It is, of course, out-of-date. The basic rule for the use of dictionaries and encyclopedias in scholarly work is that only those ought to be cited that relate to specialized areas of research — such as dictionaries and encyclopedias of church history, philosophy, theology, and so forth. These specialized works can be divided into several distinct categories.

Linguistic Tools: Dictionaries and Paleographic Aids

The briefest survey of linguistic tools shows that the standard language dictionaries do not always serve the purposes of research (Bib. I.E.1). For example, the language of a medieval Latin source may be illuminated by the definitions in Cassell's *Latin Dictionary,* but particular medieval words or usages might not be found at all in a classical dictionary such as this. Or if the word is present in the classical dictionary, the meaning may not fit the context in the medieval document. In these cases, specialized dictionaries must be consulted, such as Albert Blaise, *Lexicon Latinitatis Medii Aevi* ("A Lexicon of Medieval Latinity") or Charles Du Cange, *Glossarium Mediae et Infimae Latinitatis,* which is a glossary of Middle and Later Latin. As the titles and annotations indicate, many of these dictionaries are written in languages other than English.

Thus, French is needed to use Blaise and Latin is required to use Du Cange. Roy J. Deferrari's superb *A Lexicon of St. Thomas Aquinas* is an English language lexicon limited to Thomas Aquinas's theological and philosophical language that, nevertheless, has broad application for the study of medieval theology. The *Medieval Latin Word-List* is in English; Niermeyer is English-French; while Souter is in English. These, as their titles (given in full in the bibliography) indicate, are very specific lexica that deal with temporally and geographically defined usages. The *Dictionnaire de l'ancienne langue française* is also a case of a very important historically oriented dictionary. It is the French equivalent to the *Oxford English Dictionary,* which is itself a crucial reference book for all scholars working in the English language. For example, the range of meanings of a word in the fifteenth century in French or English can be determined from these dictionaries.

Another example of the specificity of language tools is Lampe, *A Patristic Greek Lexicon.* Patristic Greek usage and vocabulary are somewhat different from classical Greek and extremely different from the *koine* Greek of the New Testament. Separate dictionaries must be used in each of these fields — although the classical and the patristic lexica will serve fairly well for the study of *koine.* The study of NT Greek in seminary is not sufficient preparation for research in Patristics, particularly the patristic Greek of the third century and following.

Paleographical aids must be noted separately as a distinct class of linguistic tool. Late medieval and early modern printed books do not oblige the standard twenty-six-letter modified Roman alphabet of the nineteenth and twentieth centuries. Not only does one find the standard long "s" at the beginning and in the middle of words, the identity of "u" and "v," and the use of "vv" in the place of "w," one also finds an enormous number of abbreviations. Thus, *Xpus* in a Latin text is a Latin version of *Christus,* slightly abbreviated. Similarly, a cross-tailed "p" in a Latin text stands for "per." In addition, vowels and common syllables, like declension endings, are frequently replaced by superscripted dashes and other sigla.

The high cost of parchment and rag paper, together with the need to find an expeditious way to print long books by hand, led medieval copyists to write in shorthand. Early printed books followed the same shorthand patterns. The systems of shorthand were quite intricate, involving some hundred sigla and varying from century to century and country to country. In other words, just knowing Latin does not necessarily qualify a person to read a medieval or early modern document — even one that has been done in a fine hand or set in print. The abbreviations are indexed and defined in such works as Capelli, *Dizionario di Abbreviature Latine,* or Chassant, *Dictionnaire des abbreviations latines.* The abbreviations are offered, first in alphabetical, and then, within the alphabetical listing, in chronological order. Not only is the abbreviation defined, it is also identified in terms of the century or centuries in which it was used with a particular meaning.

Biographical Dictionaries and Encyclopedias

Virtually every country has its own biographical dictionary (Bib. I.E.2). If one knows the birthplace of an individual, one can usually find a good biographical essay in one of the major national biographical dictionaries. The *Dictionary of National Biography* is, of course, the leading reference work for Great Britain. The *Dictionary of American Biography* is a good tool for the United States (but not as good as *DNB* is for Britain). Both of these well-used works are currently being revised, the latter under the title *American National Biography.* The bibliography contains a list of dictionaries for most of the western European nations.

Some libraries now provide a bio-base available on microfiche that indexes several hundred different biographical dictionaries. A project is also presently under way to conflate all major biographical dictionaries and reproduce them on fiche (App. IV.A under Saur). Included in this compilation are American, British, German, Spanish, Portuguese, and Latin American biographies. Saur's "British Biographical Archive," for example, draws upon 324 sources and includes a quarter of a million biographies on 1400 fiche. The value of such compilations is that each of the biographies of the individual being referenced are put together on the same page, resulting in a comparative source that retains all of the details and virtues of each separate bibliography. There are also specialized topical-biographical tools, like the *Dictionary of Scientific Biography.*

Theological and Church-Historical
Dictionaries and Encyclopedias

The note of caution sounded above concerning the use of dictionaries and encyclopedias in general applies in a more specific way to this section of the bibliography (Bib. I.E.4). Some of the works are genuinely scholarly and some are not. Asterisks in the bibliography identify several of the genuinely eminent works. In the main, one-volume dictionaries are not as useful as multivolume works. Similarly, multiauthor dictionaries that do not have signed articles should not, with a few exceptions, be trusted; one notable exception is F. L. Cross's *Oxford Dictionary of the Christian Church.*

Some comments concerning individual works are in order. The *Dictionnaire de théologie catholique* is a work of some thirty volumes (each "volume" is published in two parts). It is also printed in narrow line, double column folio, and is an enormous project. Many of the articles in this dictionary are full-fledged monographs and go on for one hundred to two hundred folio columns. This is a tool that will not be superseded in the foreseeable future. It remains the standard source for medieval church history and the history of doctrine; it is a fine source for the patristic period and for Catholic theology in general. In addition, it should be consulted for topical essays; it contains, for example, an essay that discusses the history of the concept of theology in monographic detail. (This essay and several others have actually been translated into English as monographs.) The *Dictionnaire* is not to be ignored; it is a beginning place for virtually all study of medieval theology. *The New Catholic Encyclopedia* is another excellent resource and should be consulted with *Dictionnaire,* particularly for bibliographical references, inasmuch as it is a more recent work and will tend to cite major English-language monographs.

The New Schaff-Herzog Encyclopedia of Religious Knowledge is also a fine tool, but it does not really replace the *Realencyklopädie für protestantische Theologie und Kirche.* Haag, *La France Protestante,* is also an older but nonsuperseded reference work; it contains biographies of French Protestants from the Reformation and the seventeenth and eighteenth centuries. Other specialized biographical and topical works that should be singled out for mention are: the *Encyclopedia of Philosophy,* the *Encyclopaedia of Religion and Ethics,* and the *Encyclopédie des Sciences religieuses.* All of these works should be noted as potential sources of data and bibliography in research. The shorter, one-volume dictionaries tend to exclude (or roughly duplicate) one another, and it is seldom useful to consult more than one of them. But one ought to survey as many of the longer multivolume pieces on a subject as possible.

There are several important issues in the method of research that bear directly on the use of biographical and topical dictionaries and encyclopedias. Particularly in past ages, individuals have been regularly known by different names, often because of references to them occurring in different languages. The medieval theologian named Hervaeus Natalis, for example, was also called Hervé Nédellec and Hervaeus Britto. A careless reader might conclude that the three names indicate three different people. The fact is that Hervé was a French theologian who was known in Latin as Hervaeus Natalis or Hervaeus Britto.

Knowledge of such variations of names is crucial to the construction of a bibliography. There is at least one extant bibliography on the study of seventeenth-century Protestantism that lists the early twentieth-century work (c. 1908) of Emil Weber separately from the work of Hans Emil Weber, written after 1920 — leading several students to conclude that there were two different Webers, perhaps father and son, engaged in related research. The fact is that Emil and Hans Emil are the same person. Such problems of identity continue right up to the present. Virtually no library in the country has a main catalogue reference to Emil Brunner: he is catalogued, not as he wrote, but as he was born, Heinrich Emil Brunner. The correct attributions for anonymous and pseudonymous works will be found in the numerous specialized works that have painstakingly traced these books to their source (Bib. I.E.3).

Along the same lines, we have to recognize that our present-day convention of translating everything but the name of an author was not the typical usage of the Middle Ages or of the sixteenth and seventeenth centuries: translators and even the thinkers themselves sought out foreign-language translations and equivalents of their names. It was even typical of writers in the age of the Renaissance to translate their names into Latin or Greek: thus the rather lowly sounding German theologians Buchmann, Goldschmied, and Schwartzerd became Bibliander, Aurifaber, and Melanchthon. The easiest way to identify the various names of a person or various spellings of a person's name is to look in a good specialized dictionary of the period.

Recognize from the beginning of your work that the English version of a medieval thinker's name, like Giles of Rome or Albert the Great, will not be found in medieval sources or in contemporary resources written in other languages: there one would find Aegidius Romanus (sometimes

Aegidius de Columna) and Albertus Magnus. In order to find out the Latin form of a medieval thinker's name, one could look in The *New Catholic Encyclopedia*. Then, knowing the individual's name in other forms, one could search various major research tools with some confidence of finding references to the individual. In other words, all forms of a name must be searched — Giles of Rome, Aegidius Romanus and Aegidius de Columna, or Nicholas of Cusa, Nikolaus von Cues, Nicholas of Cues, and Nicholaus Cusanus. Some library catalogues will index the latter under "Cusanus, Nicholaus," others under "Cues, Nicholas of," and so forth.

Finally, some comment is necessary concerning hierarchies of value and use in the consultation of biographical dictionaries and ency-clopedias, and topical, theological, and church-historical dictionaries and encyclopedias. Some of these works are oriented toward very specific tasks and should be consulted on the basis of certain kinds of initial information about an individual. In the case of the various national biographies, the obvious initial information is the country of a person's birth or primary historical residence. A search for information concerning American and British thinkers would naturally begin with the *Dictionary of American Biography* for America and *Dictionary of National Biography* for Britain. Details about the life of a German figure would be found in *Allgemeines deutsches Biographie,* and so forth.

If, however, the figure in question can be identified as a relatively significant Protestant theologian, the biographical search process can begin with the *Realencyclopädie für protestantische Theologie und Kirche* and its English-language equivalent, *The New Schaff-Herzog Encyclopedia* or, in the case of more recent European thinkers, with *Religion in Geschichte und Gegenwart.* Both the *Realencyklopädie* and *Schaff-Herzog* are excellent resources, despite their age. Many of the articles in the original *Realencyklopädie* were written by major scholars of the last cen-tury and have not yet been superseded. *The New Schaff-Herzog* is a translation of the *Realencyclopädie* which both expands and reduces the original. On the one hand it augments the encyclopedia with British and American materials. On the other hand it deletes large sections, typically theological detail and citation of old sources, from some of the major articles that were in the original German. *The New Schaff-Herzog,* then, does not render use of the *Realencyclopädie* unnecessary for English-speaking scholars: major articles in *The New Schaff-Herzog,* particularly those dealing with the theology of the European Reformation or with the development of Protestant theology on the continent, are typically abbreviated, sometimes with problematic results. In the hierarchy of value and use, the *Realencyklopädie* precedes the *New Schaff-Herzog* for the continental European references, while *Religion in Geschichte und Gegenwart* precedes both, particularly on recent topics or on topics that have undergone historiographical revision since the time of the earlier encyclopedias.

If reference to a Protestant theologian cannot be found in any of these sources, a series of questions narrowing the search ought to be asked: "Should the person be discussed in a national biographical dictionary? If not, would this individual be discussed in some other kind of biographical dictionary, that is, a dictionary with a different set of organizational limits? Given the parameters of the search, what dictionary is useful?" If the research is concerned with a sixteenth-, seventeenth- or early eighteenth-century author, then Jocher is very useful. Jocher was first issued in 1750 and consists of one full encyclopedia and a fragmentary second encyclopedia: there is a complete alphabet from the mid-eighteenth century and an added set of volumes that reach the letter "S" dating from the late nineteenth century. The eighteenth-century printing of Jocher is a very important resource because what many people viewed as significant in 1750 was no longer viewed as important in the late nineteenth and early twentieth centuries when the *Realencyclopädie* (1896) and *New Schaff-Herzog* (1908) were published. From the point of view of critical historical method, Jocher stands lower on the hierarchy than the other encyclopedias: searches ought to begin with the best sources and note the relevant materials in those sources, although the most information may eventually derive from a source that is lower on the list.

In Roman Catholic studies, the first place that one might want to look is *The New Catholic Encyclopedia*, or if one's French is good, *Dictionnaire de théologie catholique*. If the person is not found in either of these places, then the search might proceed to the *Dictionnaire de spiritualité* or the *Dictionnaire apologetique*. Failing in all of these places, the process can continue with works like Hurter's *Nomenclator litterarius theologiae catholicae*, which is poorly organized, uncritical, and difficult to use, but is also a gold mine of information.

HISTORICAL ATLASES AND GUIDES TO HISTORICAL GEOGRAPHY

One of the things that a person learns very quickly in studying history is that the political geography of the world has changed (Bib. I.F). It changes constantly. The map of Europe and the map of Asia were very different even five years ago. Boundaries have shifted, countries have appeared and disappeared, and place names have changed as the vernacular of various nations has replaced Latin. Several of the scenes in Shakespeare's *Twelfth Night* take place in the palace of the Duke of Illyria. Many of those who enjoy the play in the twentieth century — including some of the benighted authors of program notes — have assumed that Illyria is an imaginary place, simply because it is no longer on the map. Such program notes would have been quite distressing to the sixteenth-century Lutheran theologian Matthias Flacius Illyricus, who was born and reared in the country in question — known until recently as Yugoslavia. Similarly, the River Ister was an important river in the history of Europe, but the student will not find it on any European map because now it is called the Danube. These and other Latin place names can be identified using Theodor Graesse's *Orbis Latinus,* which is the definitive dictionary of Latin place names. *Webster's Geographical Dictionary* can serve a similar purpose in addition to being a source for other details concerning the countries of the world.

These tools are important for the identification of the places of publication of older books. Quite a few seventeenth-century theological books were published in Trajecti Ad Rhenum, present-day Utrecht; a proper citation would indicate Utrecht as the place of publication. Not only is it important that the citation be formally correct, it is also significant to most research to identify major centers of publication and the places of publication of the works of particular authors: this kind of data often has intellectual and political significance, such as the publication, in 1582, of the "Rheims" translation of the New Testament into English at Rheims in France and the publication of Socinian works in the seventeenth century in Amsterdam.

By the same token, if one wishes to find out the location and geographical features of the Frankish kingdoms of Neustria and Austrasia, one would obviously not look at the most recent *Rand McNally Atlas*. A historical atlas must be consulted. The works of Hartmann, McEvedy, and Kinder are noteworthy. Hartmann offers a specifically church-historical perspective; McEvedy is especially useful for visualization of economic and demographic issues; Kinder is significant for its worldwide scale.

4. *Research in Primary Sources and the Use of Text Databases and Materials in Microform*

A research topic cannot be defended solely on the grounds that it has received insufficient attention in the secondary literature; at this early stage of research, such an argument for the topic's viability is only half convincing. Every topic must also be defended by showing that it can be adequately grounded in primary sources. Therefore, while a student must have a sufficient acquaintance with the general contours of his or her field of study to defend the preliminary viability of the topic, a time will come when it is necessary to turn to primary documents. Too much time spent in acquiring background material can be dangerous, for as one experienced mentor put it, "you may become hypnotized by a sense of your own ignorance."[1] Kitson Clark offers good advice for those who may begin to feel depressed or overwhelmed by the thought that they will never know enough about their topic: "You must, if you are working on secondary authorities, turn at once to work on primary evidence, and if you are working on primary evidence, you must start to write and risk the dangers of ignorance." The wise research student is conscious of the fact that one's work is always done in ignorance of much that one ought to have known.[2]

While the distinction between primary and secondary sources

---

1. G. Kitson Clark, *Guide for Research Students Working on Historical Subjects,* 2nd ed. (Cambridge: Cambridge University Press, 1968), p. 17.
2. Kitson Clark, *Guide for Research Students,* p. 18.

cannot be rigidly maintained, we turn in this chapter to a more or less chronological treatment of the reference tools of church history and historical theology with a greater focus on primary research. Here we will discuss the use of the new text databases and the new storage techniques in microform for locating and searching primary source materials. We begin, however, with a brief survey of standard reference works for primary research. Students who acquire a thorough understanding of the use of traditional resources, such as specialized handbooks and concordances, will work with greater confidence and hence benefit most from the newer methods of searching and retrieval.

CHURCH HISTORY: BY PERIOD

Beyond the important general sources mentioned in the preceding chapter, there are numerous specialized bibliographies that cover more limited time frames and topics. Typically, these works do not offer much biographical information, but they do provide very detailed bibliographical material. Researchers need to identify the specialized bibliographies that pertain directly to their field of research. The listing offered in our bibliography is far from complete but it does provide an overview of the most important works of historical bibliography. These and other specialized bibliographies can be found in the bibliography section of most libraries and in what ought to be the most obvious source: the subject catalog of major research libraries.

Early Church

"Patristics" is the term given to the study of the church fathers of the first five centuries. It is one of the best-organized fields of research in the whole of church history — with most of the documents available in good editions and translations and with a vast array of monographic and periodical literature available to the student or researcher. The best and most expeditious access into this field is through the standard manuals of "Patrology" which offer, usually by period, a series of biographical, topical, and bibliographical studies of all of the writers of the early church.

By far the most valuable patrology in English is Johannes Quasten's work, now in four volumes (Bib. II.A.1). The fourth volume is a recent addition to the set that completes its survey of the patristic era by discussing the fourth century and St. Augustine. It is an unusually valuable work because of its superb organization. It offers basic information on the life and work of an individual, provides a comprehensive listing of extant editions and translations, and then discusses the various doctrines that the person wrote on, with relatively up-to-date bibliographies. Fulbert Cayre's *Manual of Patrology* is distinctive not only because it extends the scope of patrology through the sixteenth century and into the modern period, but because it focuses on the history of spirituality.

The recent completion of a massive scholarly endeavor deserves special attention. The *Encyclopedia of the Early Church* represents the work of more than 150 patristic scholars from some seventeen countries, and it reflects a truly ecumenical range of Christian traditions. This work summarizes several recent decades of patristic scholarship on a truly comprehensive scale and must be used as a guide for anyone seeking a way into the field for the first time.

The bibliography lists a number of tools that function much like a concordance of the Bible. André Benoit provides us with a list of biblical references and allusions in the fathers through Origen (Bib. II.A.3). This work will be used primarily to study the fathers' use of Scripture, but because the biblical references in the fathers are so pervasive, it will serve as a kind of concordance as well. Edgar Goodspeed does something a little different in his *Index Patristica:* the "index" is a concordance of words that are found in the Apostolic Fathers with every word in this body of literature listed in Greek. There is nothing available in traditional sources that accomplishes the same thing for the entire body of patristic literature, but the CD-ROM project entitled *Thesaurus Linguae Graecae* (discussed below) offers us a far more powerful searching tool than the traditional concordance.

Students should be especially alert to the value of both the contents of and the indices to the major series edited by Jacques-Paul Migne, the *Patrologia Latina* and the *Patrologia Graeca*. The *Patrologia Latina* extends from the earliest church writings in Latin up to the death of Innocent III in 1216. 1216 is a significant terminal point because it closes the *Patrologia* at the beginning of the great era of scholasticism: the *Patrologia* does not contain all of the large systems written in the thirteenth century, the *Sentence* commentaries and *Summas*. The *Patrologia*

Graeca goes from earliest times up to the eighth or ninth century. Both sets, but particularly the Latin set, are very well indexed (at least for their day): the sets are indexed by doctrine, by title, by century, by author, and by Scripture reference. The index will indicate, for example, who wrote treatises on Christology in the fifth century.

Another feature of the *Patrologia Graeca* worth noting is that it contains a Latin translation of the whole Greek patrology on a facing column. Similarly, *Sources chrétiennes* offers a French translation on the facing page. Both are very useful for purposes of interpretation as well as translation: the Latin translation, in particular, provides a guide to the technical theological understanding of the language of the Greek fathers by Western writers.

The Medieval Church

Two general resources that all researchers in medieval studies must be familiar with are Louis Paetow's *A Guide to the Study of Medieval History* and its sequel, Gray Cowan Boyce's *Literature of Medieval History, 1930-1975*; both are superb references works for all topics in medieval studies (Bib. II.B.2). Following them is a list of various bibliographies, some older and some newer but all very important in particular fields. For example, Farrar and Evans's *Bibliography of English Translations from Medieval Sources* is an exhaustive effort, continued in Mary Anne Ferguson, *Bibliography of English Translations from Medieval Sources, 1943-1967*. Students are often surprised to discover how much material is available in translation and how many series of translated sources are readily available. On the other hand, numerous critical tools remain untranslated and are indispensable. For example, Manitius, *Geschichte der Lateinischen Literatur des Mittelalters* is old but it has never been superseded.

Not all of the resources in this bibliography will be used regularly. We have included a number of highly specialized entries, for example, Berkhout and Russell, *Medieval Heresies: A Bibliography 1960-1979*; and Cosenza's unparalleled *Biographical and Bibliographical Dictionary of the Italian Humanists and of the World of Classical Scholarship in Italy, 1300-1800*. A well-catalogued library will put virtually all of the books on the same subject very close to one another. For example, there is a whole section in the reference room of major libraries that gathers together

bibliographies of books printed in the sixteenth century. One will find
large subject-area bibliographies, and extremely narrowly defined bibliographies, such as bibliographies of the publications of individual
printers. The six-volume *Bibliography of the Plantin Press of Antwerp
1555-1589*, published in Amsterdam in 1980, is particularly valuable
because it contains lengthy descriptions of each book printed by this
major Renaissance press. This kind of resource is located primarily by
shelf reading the bibliography section of a major research library in
one's particular area of specialization. Some libraries will make a shelf
list available on request, and some online catalogs, such as INNOPAC
of Wellesley College, actually allow one to browse the books shelved
near the one originally requested, on screen.

Another source offering a minimal amount of bibliographical information, but unparalleled in its specific frame of reference, is comprised of the two works by Stegmüller, the *Repertorium Biblicum* and
the *Repertorium Commentariorum* (Bib. II.B.4). Both works indicate in
exhaustive detail what various authors wrote and where the manuscript
sources can be located. Both are alphabetically arranged by author.
Stegmüller lists all known editions and locations of virtually every Bible
commentary and every commentary on Lombard's *Sentences* written in
the Middle Ages. In addition, the volume lists holdings of libraries all
around the world: although Stegmüller lived and worked in Würzburg
he records items as distant from him as McGill University in Montréal
or Harvard or Yale. Students need to begin, very rapidly, to identify the
specific sources and tools, including the specialized bibliographies, relevant to their narrow research fields.

Many of the works cited in our bibliography, however, will not be
chronologically defined. For example, under the section on the Reformation and Post-Reformation (Bib. II.C.1), we find the *Catalogue
général des livres imprimés de la Bibliothèque Nationale,* the general catalog of printed books in the Bibliothèque Nationale of France. This
work extends to 231 volumes. It is a major source for bibliographical
information about older authors and their work but, unlike a lot of
catalogues, including the *National Union Catalog,* it does not simply list
books: it describes them at length. Under "Thomas Aquinas," for example, it will list sixteenth-, seventeenth- and eighteenth-century editions of the complete works of Thomas Aquinas, and then identifies the
contents of each volume of each of those sets of Thomas Aquinas's
works. The work thus goes considerably beyond just a primary biblio-

graphical reference. It is a detailed description of the individual volumes and sets of volumes that are available.

Monographic series need to be noted separately not only because occasionally a library will fail to catalog monographic literature by author, but also because one can frequently scan the list of titles in a series and find useful works that might otherwise have been missed in a bibliographical search (Bib. II.B.5). When a series is catalogued or shelved as a set, it is frequently worthwhile to examine the set as a whole. For example, the major series on Reformation studies published by Neukirchener Verlag contains several groupings of volumes on related topics.

An extended example of how one might use such resources may be valuable. One could research the works of medieval doctors in print in the sixteenth century by extracting relevant information from Stegmüller and then moving onto the catalog of the *Bibliothèque Nationale* and its supplement; from there one would look at the *Catalogue of Books Printed on the Continent of Europe, 1501-1600 in Cambridge Libraries* and the Bodleian catalog from Oxford, *Catalogus librorum impressorum Bibliothecae Bodleianae in Academia Oxoniensi.* Next, one might examine Graesse's *Trésor* for other listings of the same books, and after that the British Museum catalog. Each of these catalogues was compiled with different resources at its disposal and each has a different scope. A composite list drawn from the whole group of catalogues will show whether there was any one city, university, or printer that specialized in editions of a particular theologian or if there is a concentration of publication of scholastic theology in any one place. Such information is useful historically, and in fact may provide the basis for an article or book.

REFORMATION AND POST-REFORMATION

The vast range and extent of the secondary literature on the Reformation means that students of this period face a serious obstacle at the very outset (Bib. II.C.1). On the general level, *Archiv für Reformationsgeschichte* is an important resource, and Bainton's brief bibliography is a possible place to begin; more specialized are Bourilly and the *Calvin Theological Journal*'s annual Calvin Bibliography mentioned earlier. Of course, with Luther, Calvin, and other major figures of the

Reformation, one should go directly to the primary specialized bibliographies. In addition to the *Calvin Theological Journal* and Niesel, *Calvin-Bibliographie,* and in addition to the *Lutherjahrbuch* and Schottenloher's *Bibliographie zur Deutschen Geschichte im Zeitalter der Glaubensspaltung, 1517-1558* (a limited early German Reformation resource), students will soon need to become familiar with the standard editions of the primary sources; in the case of Calvin, the *Corpus Reformatorum* and the new *Ioannis Calvini Opera Omnia denno recognita,* and in the case of Luther, the Weimar edition of his collected works. Recent microform editions of primary sources, discussed below, provide ease of access to the works of the minor as well as the major figures of the Reformation, as do the finding guides that are provided by the libraries that hold major collections.

Sixteenth- through Eighteenth-Century British Sources

Under "Modern British Sources" we have placed the *British Library General Catalogue of Printed Books to 1975,* a critically important resource for anyone working in English church history (Bib. III.C). The same point can be made concerning the *National Union Catalog of Pre-1956 Imprints,* a source for books in the United States that in some ways parallels the *British Library General Catalogue* (Bib. IV.D.1). The *National Union Catalog* cites every printed book available in this country in all of the libraries belonging to the National Union and notes, in abbreviated form, the libraries in which the source may be found. It is available both on microfiche and in hard copy and is a basic research tool for materials published prior to 1956; it is so extensive that it almost takes on the character of a primary source. The importance of this reference work for research is indicated by the fact that bibliographies have been compiled from it and published separately.[3] The *British Library General Catalogue* cites all holdings of the British Museum (now known as the British Library). Since many of the sources that were published in England were simultaneously published in this country and since both catalogues list all holdings, regardless of place of publi-

---

3. For example, we find *Freemasons and Freemasonry: A Bibliography Extracted from Volume 184 of "The National Union Catalog, Pre-1956 Imprints"* (London: Mansell Publishing, 1973). With some added material, this bibliography ran to about 5,000 items.

cation, these catalogues ought to be used in virtually all areas of research — they are not, in other words, specific to any particular country.

More recent holdings in the National Union libraries can be identified by reference to the ongoing, constantly updated Library of Congress/National Union project with its annual supplements. Both this set and the pre-1956 imprint catalogue can be used effectively in tandem with the *American Library Directory* (Bib. VI), a listing of all U.S. libraries, alphabetized by state and city. It is refined to the point of identifying assistant librarians for special collections in virtually all major libraries.

One way to obtain a book is to look it up in the *National Union Catalog*, find where it is located, and then if it cannot be obtained through normal interlibrary loan procedures, write to the particular library. Frequently, for example, rare books have been microfilmed and the location of the film will be listed either in the *National Register of Microform Masters* or in the *National Union Catalog of Pre-1956 Imprints* (App. IV.A). The address of the library and of the librarian most likely to be of assistance will be found in the *American Library Directory*. Many libraries are willing to provide single copies of extant microfilms at a minimal cost to researchers. A great many rare books that are crucial for historical and theological research in the sixteenth through the eighteenth centuries will be readily located through the *National Union Catalog*.

As in every field, however, there are more specialized, technical bibliographies that must be consulted. Pollard and Redgrave is far more extensive in its listings than the British Library catalogue: Pollard and Redgrave provides a "short title" for all English books — that is, all books printed in any language in England and all books printed anywhere in English from the beginning of printing to 1640 (Bib. III.C). The student of early modern England must use Pollard and Redgrave, and for the second half of the seventeenth century, its sequel, Donald Wing's *Short-Title Catalogue of Books Printed in England, Scotland, Ireland, Wales and British America and of English Books Printed in Other Countries 1641-1700*. Pollard and Redgrave, and Wing, will remain essential tools until the computerized version of the database, currently in progress, is completed.[4]

Students of eighteenth-century church history and theology until

4. Currently the titles in Wing are available in the OCLC database, but the North American ESTC project will update Wing substantially.

very recently were dependent on the catalogs to major libraries and the more specialized guides to unique collections, like the *Catalogue of Dr. Williams's Library*, for English Nonconformists. General guides to the literature of the century such as Stanley Pargellis and D. J. Medley were helpful, and significant strides in comprehensive listings were made by F. J. G. Robinson et al. in their *Eighteenth-Century British Books: An Author Union Catalog* (5 vols.). These single and multivolume works have now been superseded by the *Eighteenth-Century Short Title Catalog* project, discussed below.

American Church History

Just as specialized bibliographies are needed to supplement the major catalogs in British sources, students of American church history will not be satisfied with *The National Union Catalog of Pre-1956 Imprints*. All scholars who work in colonial American history will be acquainted with Charles Evans's *American Bibliography* and the supplements by Roger Bristol (Bib. IV.D.1). The work of Evans and Bristol is continued into the nineteenth century by the multivolume work of Shaw and Shoemaker, under the same title. One will, however, eventually turn to even more specialized bibliographies. If, for example, the topic is the American Revolution, in the card catalog of every major research library, under the heading "American Revolution," one will find Thomas R. Adams's *American Independence: A Bibliographical Study of American Political Pamphlets*. The term "pamphlet" in eighteenth-century parlance was understood to include printed sermons, and hence the use of Adams is one convenient way of obtaining information on the political engagement of the American pulpit.

In American church history, studies in the past have often been confined to denominations, and there are numerous tools that will guide one into the literature of specific religious bodies (Bib. IV.D.2). Particularly notable in this regard are the guides by John Tracy Ellis and Robert Trisco on American Catholic history, and the massive "register" of Baptist source materials compiled by Edward Starr. Just as with bibliographies that deal primarily with secondary sources in a specialized topic area, there are specialized guides that will lead one into primary source materials, as, for example, we find in the research bibliographies for Black Studies and the history of Evangelicals in America.

Garland Publishing Incorporated has recently undertaken a significant publishing endeavor in order to preserve and make more readily available a wide range of nineteenth- and twentieth-century American religious materials. Protestant source materials are organized into a small number of specific categories. The series of reprints, for example, entitled "Women in American Protestant Religion, 1800-1930" runs to thirty-six volumes. Facsimile reproductions of books on the topics of Fundamentalism, and other series on the Pentecostal and Holiness movements, each extend to more than forty volumes, with some of the individual volumes containing numerous rare tracts and pamphlets. Experts in each of the areas covered by the series provide important bibliographical and contextual guidance on the most recent scholarship.

COMPUTERIZED DATABASES AND PRIMARY RESEARCH

To this point in the present chapter, we have been examining traditional guides to resources. Three interdisciplinary collaborative efforts, two of which are a little more than a decade old, and a third which is even more recent, have already transformed the way church historians and theologians study the past. The first pertains to the early history of the church, the second to the Middle Ages, and the last to the modern period, and each of these major undertakings offers the student unprecedented ease of search and stunning breadth of bibliographical sweep. These projects are so revolutionary in their implications for research that they each deserve a brief introduction.[5]

The Thesaurus Linguae Graecae (TLG) project has collected and entered into a computer the standard scholarly editions of all Greek authors who wrote from the time of Homer (ca. 750 B.C.) to A.D. 600.[6] This massive database comprises some 60 million words representing more than 6,000 works by 587 authors, making it one of the largest collections of machine-readable texts in the world (App. III). The first phase of the TLG project, covering the period up to A.D. 600, is complete;

5. See the Appendix for information concerning how to contact the centers for these projects.
6. John J. Hughes, "From Homer to Hesychius — The Thesaurus Linguae Graecae Project," *Bits & Bytes Review* 1, no. 7 (1987): 1; *Thesaurus Linguae Graecae Newsletter* no. 13 (May 1988).

the second phase is currently under way and will extend to the year 1453, providing even greater access to the literature of the Eastern church. The works of all of the Greek fathers of the early church may now be examined and compared in ways heretofore thought impossible. All of the occurrences of a word or a phrase or a combination of words and phrases may be located in minutes.

The Thesaurus is the lexicographer's dream come true, but it offers perhaps even greater potential for the church historian. Studies of theological terms and phrases in the large corpus of the works of Athanasius, the Cappadocian fathers, or Eusebius of Caesarea will undoubtedly bring many new insights to light. For example, a search of all references to women would reveal the precise usage and intent of the fathers, and examination of terms related to ascetic practices will give us new insights into the spiritual disciplines. Study of early Christian usage with respect to the Romans and the state should result in clearer understanding of church-state relations. Comparative studies will be equally useful; the comparison of Christian and pagan authors may show new ways in which the early Christians related to the surrounding culture.

The miniaturization that is made possible by technology in microform and compact discs offers scholars convenience that is second in importance only to the searching power of the computer. The Thesaurus Linguae Graecae currently provides access to 6,459 separate Greek works in their entirety on a single compact disc. The TLG does provide individual searches for scholars, though the disc itself may be obtained by institutions willing to agree to licensing stipulations. Scholars will still find Migne's *Patrologia* useful, but it will be only a matter of time before the new medium will force such traditional sources, when used in isolation, into obsolescence. However, when the Thesaurus is used in conjunction with the *Bibliographical Information Base in Patristics* for secondary literature (see chapter 3, above), the ease of access to the entire field of Patristics, including both primary and secondary sources, is perhaps without parallel in any other specialization to date.

Chadwyck-Healey Inc., a major supplier of scholarly source materials in microform, has provided for the Western, Latin Church, what the Thesaurus Linguae Graecae accomplished for the early church and Eastern Orthodoxy. It is currently publishing the *Patrologia Latina Database* on both CD-ROM and magnetic tape. The project makes the complete edition of Migne's *Patrologia Latina* available, including text, notes, prefatory material, and indices. The original edition of 221 volumes includes all major and minor Latin fathers from Tertullian in A.D. 200 through Pope Innocent III. The new CD-ROM version, however, while concluding in the early thirteenth century, is so massive that it is produced on five compact discs and is priced beyond the range of the individual scholar's pocketbook.

As with the *Thesaurus Linguae Graecae*, the retrieval software of the *Patrologia Latina* revolutionizes research through the use of Boolean searches, as well as single word, phrase, and proximity searches.[7] Since the corpus of individual authors may be isolated, new studies of aspects of a single author's thought will proliferate, and with the possibility of word studies, as well as concepts related to phrases, newly conceived projects on subjects that span a wide range of Western authors (from Augustine to Boethius to Alcuin to Anselm) will yield a tremendous number of new rescarch topics. Scholarship on such pivotal theological terms as nature and grace, virtue, the soul and the spirit, Christ and the Trinity can now be extended over a much greater chronological sweep with a precision heretofore impossible. In addition, Scripture references, phrases, and even vague allusions can be traced with tremendous speed and accuracy.

In the study of modern church history, no collaborative project has rivaled that of the *Eighteenth-Century Short Title Catalog* (ESTC) in terms of scope and complexity. This project has catalogued on computer approximately a quarter of a million titles of eighteenth-century books, sermons, pamphlets, and ephemera.[8] The ESTC differs from the preceding endeavors in that it does not provide the actual texts of a document, but only a listing of the title and the library in which it can be found. Nevertheless, nearly 1,000 libraries worldwide have contributed records to the ESTC file, making it the largest single retrospective cataloging operation ever undertaken. This computer-based bibliography

---

7. The publisher has used the well-established Text Encoding Initiative version of Standard Generalized Markup Language. Such care, while expensive and time-consuming, will undoubtedly guarantee the long-term scholarly durability of the project.

8. It will eventually reach its projected total of 400,000 imprints, but since many of the titles to be added are editions and variant printings, the vast majority of works are currently available; see Henry L. Snyder, "A Major New Bibliographical Tool for Scholars," *The Clark Newsletter: Bulletin of the UCLA Center for 17th and 18th Century Studies,* no. 13 (Fall 1987): 4; and *Factotum: Newsletter of the XVIIIth Century STC,* occasional paper 5, March 1987.

puts incredible searching power at the fingertips of the historian; in addition to locating all of the published works of individual authors, it is possible to search any word or combination of words in a title. Important contemporary topics such as toleration, secularization, religious pluralism, and spirituality can now be examined in detail, exhaustively tracing their roots in the early modern period. Most of the first editions of books and pamphlets have already been recorded; when the catalog is complete with approximately half a million items, between a third and a half of the entries will be different editions of the same works.[9]

A current research project on the pulpit in late eighteenth-century British politics provides three illustrations of the use of the ESTC. In a matter of seconds one learns that the output of Anglican sermons three years into the French Revolution (1792) was almost double the number of sermons published at the height of the American Revolution (1778). A very small investment of time thereby yields a valuable comparative datum that may lead to a working hypothesis concerning the influence of the pulpit in the age of revolution. But since the ESTC lists all of the libraries in which a given document is located, one of its greatest values lies in its noting the physical location of documents. In thirty minutes at a computer terminal, it was possible to search sixteen major research libraries spread throughout the United States and Great Britain for sermons preached during the opening year of the French Revolution. The bulk of the sermons were predictably found in the British Library and Cambridge University Library, but the search revealed unique copies of sermons that can be obtained nowhere but at the Huntington Library, Exeter Central Library, Birmingham Public Library, and Liverpool University Library. The ESTC thereby allows one to make travel plans for research abroad with the confidence that one's efforts will not be needlessly reduplicated in North American libraries.

The greatest use of the ESTC, however, lies in its providing a nearly complete bibliography of all published works on a given topic. Within a few hours, one can obtain a complete list of all sermons printed in

9. That in its own right is a valuable asset because it indicates the number of times a text was published in a century and, by extension, something about the influence or importance of the book. Since it is very difficult to get accurate numbers on press runs of old books, often the best information that we have is the number of editions. Several editions or several press runs with different imprint pages can indicate the historical significance of a book.

Great Britain during the American Revolution (the years 1774-1783 yield 1,259 titles) and the French Revolution (the years 1789-1798 yield 2,316 titles). Using traditional techniques for this task would have consumed four to six months of full-time research, and the expense would have been prohibitive for most scholars.[10] As noted in the preceding chapter, through the Research Library Information Network we have on-line access to *The Eighteenth-Century Short Title Catalog,* both in major research libraries and through desktop personal computers. The ESTC is also available on CD-ROM.

The ESTC is currently the most powerful bibliographical tool for every subject area in English from 1700-1800, and the project continues to expand. Through major funding from the National Endowment for the Humanities, ESTC of North America is presently entering all of the titles from Pollard and Redgrave and Wing in the computer, and in the process, it is adding the most recent information on the location of all of these sources. In addition, many books in the Oxford and Cambridge College libraries are being added to this central catalog for the first time. This means that every title in English from the beginning of printing to the year 1800 will soon be available to the researcher at a desktop computer.[11]

Because of the wide geographical dispersion of sources, in the past a scholar was physically limited to the collections of a relatively small number of major libraries. Commonly, the scholar who cast the widest net commanded the greatest authority. But a library's holdings are ordinarily established on the haphazard basis of the availability of primary sources, not on the rational grounds of collecting all the sources pertaining to an individual scholar's narrow interests. Thus even a tolerably complete search would sometimes result in serious lacunae; and since the process of interpretation begins with the selection of sources, we cannot construe the old approach of examining collection after collection as genuinely critical. Today, for the first time in history, thanks to the efforts of the scholars working on the Thesaurus Linguae Graecae, the Patrologia Latina Database, and *The Eighteenth-Century Short Title*

---

10. For a comparable project, see Peter Hogg, "The Abolition of the Slave Trade: A Bibliographer Looks at the ESTC," pp. 93-104 in M. Crump and M. Harris, eds., *Searching the Eighteenth Century* (London: The British Library, 1983).

11. To keep abreast of these developments, students may subscribe to the ESTC newsletter, entitled *Factotum.* For the address, see the Appendix, below.

Catalog, the researcher enjoys the possibility of perusing all the extant literature in a field. Where the bulk of sources is too great, samples can be chosen on rational grounds of selection rather than simply one's ability to travel the distance. In this case, the method is thus genuinely critical and not dependent on haphazard collecting.

THE NEW SOURCES IN MICROFORM

In order to provide some sense of the range of materials now available in microform (including microfilm, microfiche, and microdot cards), we will survey in rough chronological order several pertinent collections of the more important publishers.[12] This overview is by no means intended to be comprehensive, but rather illustrative of the types of collections that support church historical and theological research (see App. IV.A for further details). The corpus of ancient texts, while vast, is sufficiently limited that traditional scholarly editions, combined with the new medium of CD-ROM, make microform editions less necessary (although many rare texts have already been microfilmed). The same, however, cannot be said of the medieval period.

Three British firms in particular have concentrated some effort on the Western world before the Reformation. World Microfilms specializes in microfilming medieval manuscripts. The manuscript collections of Trinity College, Cambridge; Lincoln Cathedral Library; and Lambeth Palace Library are available, including many biblical, patristic, and theological studies. Medieval and Renaissance manuscript collections at six Oxford colleges and at Trinity College, Dublin, have been filmed.[13] Microform Academic Publishers has a large collection of both printed and manuscript materials on British history, including, for example, the Holkham illuminated manuscripts of the fourteenth and fifteenth centuries. Harvester Press has filmed literary and historical manuscripts in the Cotton Collection in the British Library. The church court records of Ely and Chichester (1400-1660) are on film, and Harvester has the

12. For a good, brief introduction to the topic of microform materials in history, see Frank Freidel, ed., with Richard K. Showman, *Harvard Guide to American History,* rev. ed., 2 vols. (Cambridge, Mass.: Belknap Press, 1974), vol. 1, pp. 109-12.
13. They have also copied many seventeenth-nineteenth century Anglican materials, for example, bishops' visitation returns, and the archives of the Society for Promoting Christian Knowledge.

most important items from the Tanner Collection in the Bodleian Library on Church and State from 1550 to 1700. Finally, Primary Source Media, formerly Research Publications of Woodbridge, Connecticut, has recently added the medieval manuscript collections of Pembroke College, Cambridge, to an already impressive list of manuscript collections from St. John's College, Oxford, the Society of Antiquaries, London, and literary manuscripts, chronicles, and documents from Cambridge University Library.

With the advent of printing in the late fifteenth century, the bulk of available source material becomes daunting, and yet enormous strides in microfilming documents have recently been made. Between the Center for Reformation Research in St. Louis, Missouri, and Inter Documentation Company of Leiden, the Netherlands, one can find in microform virtually every significant document of the Protestant Reformation. Inter Documentation Company has major microfiche collections on Reformed Protestantism, sixteenth-century pamphlets in German and Latin (1501-30), the Radical Reformation, and Dutch Protestants (ca. 1486-1684), religion in Latin America, and massive missionary society publications. To give an idea of the magnitude of these collections, the German and Latin pamphlet series alone comprise approximately 5,000 separate documents. Migne's *Patrologiae Cursus Completus* (Latin and Greek combined extending to 432 vols.) is also on fiche. These are well-produced reproductions, but they are quite expensive; individual items, however, may be purchased separately.

The Center for Reformation Research has approximately 10,000 manuscript and printed sources on microform pertaining to the Reformation. The finding guide that describes these materials runs to eight volumes. Since the Center was designed to serve the academic community, individual reels of microfilm are available on interlibrary loan, and students will find that copies can be made much less expensively than those provided by Inter Documentation Company. University Microfilms International may be thought of as the English counterpart to Inter Documentation Company, and it has served the scholarship of the English Reformation very well indeed. UMI has microfilmed virtually every pamphlet and book found in the Short Title Catalogs of Pollard and Redgrave (through the year 1640), and many in Wing (through 1700). The importance of this fact for the research student can hardly be overstated because it means that the entire corpus of English literature from the period of the Reformation through the early modern period is presently available on film at major research libraries, and for those items that are not immediately available, through inter-library loan. One has at one's fingertips — in Los Angeles, Riverside, or Irvine, California (!) — a better library of British materials on any subject than at Oxford or Cambridge or the British Museum. All that is lacking — from an aesthetic point of view, a considerable loss — is the ethos of the old-world setting and the aroma of the old books.

As one would expect, the number of titles for the eighteenth century increases over the earlier centuries at an exponential rate, and yet many of the items in the *Eighteenth-Century Short Title Catalog* are currently available on 35mm microfilm. The Early American Imprint Series that reproduces most of the publications of seventeenth- and eighteenth-century colonial America on microfiche is an old series that has long served students well.[14] Currently, however, Primary Source Media is well into the process of microfilming every substantial title in the ESTC, and guides to the project are available from the publisher. The on-line version of the ESTC, which is constantly updated, and the CD-ROM provide the exact reel number of every item that has been microfilmed to date. When combined and completed, the two publishing ventures of UMI and Primary Source Media will provide access to every important book or pamphlet published in English from the beginning of printing in 1475 through 1800.

The other major project of this kind is the *Nineteenth-Century Short Title Catalog,* which currently only goes through 1870. It is more massive in size than the other projects, simply because of the bulk of material that is available. Some sense of the vastness of the project can be gathered from the first series, which runs only from 1800 through 1815 and which by itself lists as many titles as those for the whole of the eighteenth century. Some of this material is being put on film, but the choice of materials must be more selective: Chadwyck-Healey is filming major works within clearly defined subject areas, including one on "Beliefs and Religion." Lost Cause Press also has major microform collections on nineteenth-century American literature and history (over 4,000 vols.), the anti-slavery collection from the Oberlin College Library, and theology and church history collections for Britain, the United

---

14. Readex Film Products is responsible for the Early American Imprint Series. It is also the major supplier of Early American Newspapers (1704-1820) on microfilm.

States, and Canada (a basic library of about 2,000 vols.). They do not, however, sell individual reels.[15]

Several additional publishing ventures that bear upon modern church history and theology deserve mention. Since it began microfilming in 1952, the Historical Commission of the Southern Baptist Convention's holdings have grown to more than 14,000,000 pages of text to date, drawing on printed and manuscript Baptist materials in North and South America, England, continental Europe, Africa, and Russia. Seventeenth- and eighteenth-century English Baptist materials from the British Library, the Bodleian Library, and the Angus Library at Regent's Park College, Oxford, comprise 2,400 additional items. The Commission, as with Inter Documentation Company and UMI, accepts requests for the filming of specific documents that have not been filmed before. Inter Documentation Company is also in the process of producing on approximately 500 microfiche a vast collection of Methodist documents, and calling it "one of the largest and most comprehensive microform projects ever to have been released in the field of church history."[16]

Students should be aware of the fact that just as scholars have compiled bibliographies of secondary literature in specialized fields, there now exist large collections of primary materials in microform in a number of specialized fields of study. Two areas illustrate such works particularly well: women's studies and newspapers and religious periodicals. Primary Source Media's History of Women collection alone comprises 3,000,000 pages of pamphlets, manuscripts, and periodicals. Other reference works, already mentioned, have been utilized in a special way for those interested in women's studies. For example, Hilda Smith and Susan Cardinale have compiled *Women and the Literature of the Seventeenth Century: An Annotated Bibliography based on Wing's Short Title Catalog* (Bib. III.C). Newspapers have demanded the special attention of archivists and librarians,

---

15. Primary Source Media has also done a lot with source materials in American church history. The company is copying Joseph Sabin's *Bibliotheca Americana* on microfiche, a collection now running to more than 600 volumes. Primary Source Media has filmed the records of the Moravian Mission among the Indians of North America, and they have a microfilm collection of Social Problems and the American Churches. General Microfilm Company should also be mentioned in this regard. This company has small microfilm and microfiche collections on the Shakers in America, the Jesuits in New France, and a collection of written directories from the Catholic Church (1857-72).

16. The projected completion date is the late 1990s.

in part because of their fragile character, especially in the nineteenth century, and in part because the early numbers (seventeenth and early eighteenth centuries) are so rare. Primary Source Media has filmed Charles Burney's large collection of English newspapers, 1662-1820.[17] This collection of "Early English Newspapers" brings an unprecedented number of English provincial papers together in one place, and most major research libraries subscribe to this series. Thus, for any given year, the microfilm collection offers the scholar a geographical sweep of public opinion that rivals the holdings of the British Library's newspaper collection at Colindale. In American studies, a great many nineteenth-century religious periodicals that are essential for the history of the period are now available through University Microfilms International. In addition, World Microfilms has a number of nineteenth- and twentieth-century Quaker and Methodist periodicals.[18]

The strategic implications of some of these collections for new research projects should be readily grasped. The history of nineteenth-century primary, secondary, and college education, for example, cannot be understood apart from the contribution of Protestant Evangelicals, and the vast collection of religious periodicals now available in microform will greatly facilitate research in this field. One recent study utilized the medium of microfilm to examine the English provincial press, that is, English newspapers outside of London. Some twenty newspapers for a six-month period of the American Revolution were examined without having to visit a single archive in Great Britain. This small sample provided more information than any other work that had been done to date on the provincial press in England, and it challenged long-held assumptions about the popularity of the war, simply because a wide variety of local papers were available in the same medium and all at the same place.

Broadly speaking, the English provincial press in the eighteenth

17. The company provides guides for this specific collection, but for guidance in the broader area of newspapers students should consult regularly updated *Newspapers in Microform: Domestic* for papers published in the United States, and *Newspapers in Microform: Foreign Countries* for those abroad.

18. OCLC is currently cataloging holdings for U.S. newspapers dating back to the beginning of printing in this country. The United States Newspaper Program Union List is available online, through OCLC, and in microfiche. Projects like the CD-ROM Subject Index to Pre-1800 British Periodicals undertaken by James Tierney and supported by Primary Source Media will transform the efficiency of the researcher. *The Clark Newsletter: Bulletin of the UCLA Center for 17th and 18th-Century Studies* 20 (Spring 1991): 10.

century has not been read closely by modern historians, and this generalization may apply to other Western countries as well. Yet many important questions regarding religion and public opinion remain to be answered. For example, the question of the relationship between the religious content and influence of the press, on the one hand, and popular forms of religious expression, such as the printed sermon, on the other, is begging to be addressed. A detailed comparative examination of the two should shed light on the highly debated issue of the secularization of the West, and help illumine the question, not only of the timing of "de-Christianization," but the mechanisms of this phenomenon as well. Such illustrations suggest that new projects for dissertations can be generated almost strictly on the basis of the availability of new source materials on microfilm. In other words, new topics can occasionally be defended simply on the grounds of the comprehensiveness of materials available to us for the first time on microform, or available because of microform reproduction, in one place in a previously unimaginable concentration. Thus, any university library in possession of the complete Early English Book series (1475-1640; 1641-1700) and of the various IDC sixteenth- and seventeenth-century microfiche series will rival and exceed the holdings of rare book rooms in old, established universities. Similarly, attentive use of the microform holdings of the Center for Reformation Research and of the ATLA Preservation Filming in Religion project can provide resources for otherwise unmanageable projects.

The microfilming of source materials has not been limited to the reproduction of printed materials alone; major archives of manuscript material are now being put on microfilm or microfiche.[19] For example, the Genealogical Society of Utah holds over one and a half million reels of microfilm, making their collection of filmed manuscripts the largest in the world (App. IV.B). Many of these records are in the form of vital statistics (birth and baptismal registers), but there are numerous church records from a wide variety of denominations as well, including records of parish vestries, church wardens, and some Sunday school records.[20]

---

19. All kinds of guides to microform collections of archival material, ranging from national to local records, are available. For a brief introduction, see Freidel, *Harvard Guide to American History*, vol. 1, pp. 111-12.

20. See Arlene Eakle, et al., comp., *Descriptive Inventory of the English Collection* (App. IV.B). In the last decade, the New York collection, large to begin with, has increased threefold.

The microfilm archives are thus of tremendous value for anyone interested in the various ways in which quantitative techniques may be applied to church history, and they have value for the denominational historian as well. It seems to be increasingly evident that the historian who neglects the availability of these new techniques of searching and new sources of historical information will do so to his or her own great harm.

RESEARCH IN ARCHIVES

As indicated previously, the contemporary florescence of microform and CD-ROM resources must not be allowed to obscure the continued importance of great libraries and archives to certain kinds of research projects. Not only is there a high aesthetic factor involved in the use of original sources in their original form — such as the correspondence of Abraham Lincoln, the handwritten minutes of the Consistory of Geneva, or a late medieval manuscript or printed book — there is also the fact that many such resources are not now and may never be placed on CD-ROM or made available in microform. And, even when such a source is given in electronic format, such issues as the correct reading of a sixteenth-century hand, the proper understanding of marginalia, and so forth, can only be resolved from the original.

In some ways, research that utilizes unpublished manuscripts differs only marginally from that involving published books, especially when the books are dated before 1800 and hence considered rare (Bib. III.F; IV.G).[21] Manuscripts, for example, are often very delicate and must be handled with the same care as rare books and pamphlets. On the other hand, individual manuscripts of sermons, diaries, and correspondence are almost without exception unique, and thus irreplaceable. This places an even greater burden of care on the person who wishes to examine them. Each archive that contains manuscript materials has its own conventions and set of protocols; each has its idiosyncrasies that the student can only navigate by great patience and experience. It is thus difficult to make general rules that apply to all circumstances alike, but

21. An excellent book for recent works on searching archives is Ronald H. Fritze, Brian E. Coutts, and Louis A. Vyhnanek. *Reference Sources in History: An Introductory Guide* (Santa Barbara: ABC-Clio, 1990); see chapter 13, pp. 245-71.

there are a few stipulations that are universally applicable and should be strictly observed.

Research that involves manuscripts requires that students pay particularly close attention to the various printed guides that accompany the collection. In fact, it is highly advisable to study the guides to manuscript collections even before seeking permission to examine the collection, and the same applies to the introductory guides for readers provided by almost every major research library. We have known students who have failed to prepare themselves for research and then proceed to waste the time of librarians who have much more important things to do than tutor lazy students. Admittance to research libraries is commonly gained only by permission, and an obnoxious research student reflects ill, not only upon themselves, but upon the school they represent and upon their primary supervisor. If one's inconsiderate behavior contributes to difficulty for future applicants who request the privilege of access to manuscripts and rare books, they have not only hurt themselves, but they have, as one veteran put it, committed a "serious offence" against scholarship.[22]

If the first step of careful preparation is neglected, the result may be utter bewilderment and days of lost time. This advice is readily confirmed by the experience of many beginning students, and a few experienced ones as well, when they encounter new situations and fail to make the necessary adjustments. The Public Record Office in the United Kingdom offers a useful illustration of the point.[23] This repository is, as the name implies, a record office; that is to say, it is not a library nor are its holdings organized in a fashion that the uninitiated will recognize, much less fathom. Directories list classes of papers by government department, and this in itself can be daunting, because the system of classification necessitates some knowledge of the history and functioning of the British government. The beginner is frustrated further by the vastness of the collections and, until very recently, their division into two entirely separate locations. Though research on a single topic may necessitate the use of papers under the classification R.G. (for

22. Kitson Clark, *Guide for Research Students,* p. 25.
23. See the excellent article by Geraldine Beech, "Historical Research in the Public Record Office, London," *Perspectives* (the American Historical Association Newsletter) 29, no. 9 (December 1991): 13-14, 16. The basic finding guide, available in microfiche, is the *Public Record Office Current Guide.*

Registrar General) and H.O. (for Home Office), for many years the former were located at the P.R.O., Chancery Lane, in central London, and the latter were at the new facility in Kew, Surrey. After the energy expended to learn such things and the inevitable accompanying discouragement, there is some consolation in having an excuse to travel to Kew and visit not only the archive, but the world famous gardens as well. Happily, the new facilities at Kew are modernized and the time to requisition documents is now much less than it used to be at Chancery Lane.

The specific method by which manuscripts are requisitioned differs from library to library; the Students' Room at the British Library differs from the Rare Book Rooms in the University Library, Cambridge, and they are as different from each other as the Bodleian Library at Oxford is from the John Rylands University Library at Manchester. In some settings, such as Dr. Williams's Library in London, the atmosphere is relaxed and the staff unusually helpful; in other settings, the ambiance may be depressing and the assistance unfriendly, possibly even hostile. Manuscripts are normally paged with a definite limit to the number of documents that one can examine at once, and the waiting period will vary between twenty minutes to two or more hours. In every case, proof of one's serious intent as a scholar is required, and the use of ink in any form is absolutely forbidden.

Students should first familiarize themselves with the general guides that provide broad overviews at the national level, and then proceed to the guides of specific archives and libraries. For example, chapters 5 and 6 of the *Harvard Guide to American History* on public documents and unpublished sources works at the most general level, and will provide a good initial orientation for students working in American history.[24] We have listed several *Guides* under "Archives and Manuscripts" in the bibliography (Bib. III.F; IV.G) that are important resources for Americanists, such as the *National Union Catalog of Manuscript Collections,* and Hamer's *Guide to Archives and Manuscripts in the United States.* For the United Kingdom, the second edition of Janet Foster and Julia Sheppard's *British Archives: A Guide to Archive Resources in the United Kingdom* should be examined. The Historical Manuscripts Commission in Britain (located next to the Public Record Office in

---

24. See also the brief but helpful discussion of foreign archives on pp. 100-105 of vol. 1.

Chancery Lane), publishes guides for a large number of manuscript collections. A good brief overview of the main research centers in the UK is found in G. Kitson Clark and G. R. Elton, *Guide to Research Facilities in History,* which directs one to the rare book and manuscript collections of major university libraries and libraries in the neighborhoods of the universities. A small publication entitled *Record Repositories in Great Britain* is available from Her Majesty's Stationery Office in London; it is an extremely helpful brief guide for students requiring information on the addresses, services, and holdings of local record offices.

In the search for pertinent manuscript materials for research, we are no longer limited to hard-copy guides. In the previous chapter we have alluded to the fact that RLIN can facilitate research in archives as well as in printed sources. Likewise, OCLC must not be thought of as useful only for secondary literature. In addition, every major research library will supply guides for its manuscript collections. *Medieval and Renaissance Studies: A Location Guide* from the North Carolina University Library is noted in our Bibliography as a random sample of a guide to manuscript holdings, and we have supplied several listings for the Huntington library to further illustrate the point. The John Rylands University Library of Manchester has a small booklet entitled "Theology and Church History: A Guide to Research Resources," with separate sections on "Aids to Research," "Manuscripts and Archives," "Printed Books," and "Microforms."[25] Dr. Williams's Library provides similar guidance with its "Guide to the Manuscripts."

Students should not overlook the fact that a considerable amount of research can be carried on by mail. There seems to be simply no end to the kind of materials that can be obtained on written request — from printed books that can be microfilmed to xerographic copies of rare archival materials. When requesting copied materials, it is usually advisable, from the standpoint of expense, to request the materials on 35 mm positive film. Normally, archivists will not allow unpublished manuscripts to be xeroxed, although we have obtained the correspondence of several leading eighteen-century figures in this medium, via the Royal Mail. Additionally, if the needed materials cannot be obtained by post,

---

25. In addition, there are more specialized guides for the John Rylands Library: for example, "Methodist Archives; Catalogues, Handlists, Bibliographies and Some Important Reference Works."

or if the situation demands research in its own right, it is entirely possible to contact local researchers who will do the research for you. In one small part of a much larger project, for example, it became necessary to obtain occupational information from a number of Anglican baptismal registers in Bristol, England. A letter of inquiry to the librarian at the Bristol Central Library resulted in a list of several local researchers. Armed with the names and addresses of these local historians, it was not a great deal of trouble to make the necessary arrangements for the work to be done. The expense, of course, was much less than the cost of travel to Bristol, though there was a commensurate loss in pleasure.

Students should always be alert to the desirability of innovative approaches in obtaining necessary information, and they should let nothing stand in the way of acquiring the sources they need. The complaint, sometimes heard, that the needed materials were unavailable, is not a legitimate excuse. Several different sources, for example, can often be used in conjunction to find a reference. One can start with a bibliographical source for a particular century and then find out that the individual being researched has written something of significance. Depending on when and where it was published, there may very well be a particular collection of materials that makes it readily available. Or if that is not the case (i.e., if an older source is not found either in the Early English Books microfilm series or in fiche sets from Interdocumentation Company), then the next step may be to go to the *National Union Catalog of Pre-1956 Imprints* or to the *National Register of Microform Masters* and see whether a copy of the documents exists in some other place. Good research technique is not just a matter of knowing individual sources; it is a matter of knowing how to move between the various sources in order to locate suitable resources for oneself.

Finally, it is essential that students recognize from the beginning the need to have hands-on access to their entire bibliography — either in the form of careful notes or in the form of hard copy. A scholar's library will contain, in addition to books and journals, xerographic and microform copies of articles and documents. That is one reason why students should consider purchasing a microfilm or microfiche reader. Typically, scholars will have a considerable library of secondary literature on hand as well. After having worked through periodical indices, a researcher will often make xerographic copies of every article that has a direct bearing on his or her topic and have them filed in a coherent order, coordinated with their research bibliography. Then, as one works through the bibliography for one's dissertation or monograph, one has almost instantaneous hands-on access to virtually every needed source, except, of course, the really rare things that can be found only in a specialized library. In some cases, depending on the importance of the source, even rare materials, in the form of xerographic or microform copies, will be immediately at hand.

5. The Practice of Research and the Craft of Writing

As the scholar moves further into research, the various stages of a proper method of investigation blend with one another. After a decade of research and writing, one will not spend a lot of time identifying the topic. One's area of specialization and its subthemes become so familiar that the nature and extent of future research projects are easily anticipated. In addition, the work of gathering materials merges with the tasks of writing and outlining. Assuming a broad continuum in one's general area of research, materials that have been gathered in the course of previous projects are added to a basic research bibliography while, at the same time, the focus of research is changed slightly to adapt to new projects. There is, moreover, no hard-and-fast rule for drafting an outline or developing a pattern of approach: researchers must think about all aspects of their work continuously, even though they tend to move from a gathering and an evaluating stage to a collating stage and finally to the work of writing and redrafting.

Thus, as we conceptualize a thesis or dissertation, our thoughts naturally range over the entire project, from beginning to end. Nevertheless, at the outset of research, once a topic is selected, we must begin by gathering materials and arranging them on the basis of a preliminary outline. Earlier chapters have provided a survey of scholarly tools that enable the researcher to take the first step of acquiring a working knowledge of the bibliography that pertains to his or her specialization. It may be intimidating, but it is nonetheless true, that research students are responsible for being aware of everything that has been written in their field up to the point of their own approach to the topic. Eventually, they will master the entire bibliography of a field, as represented by the most recent and/or the best writings in their specialization. This mastery, however, is not accomplished by simply multiplying references; the basic bibliographical task always involves a process of sifting and evaluation. We turn in this chapter, therefore, to examine basic techniques and skills in research and writing.[1]

EVALUATING RESOURCES AND MATERIALS

Students need to cultivate the ability to identify the important books and articles on a topic and distinguish them from the unimportant ones. Once the basic bibliographic search is completed, we move toward a process of increasing selectivity. Books that are written at a popular level, or are not documented well, or are not respected in the field, should be identified and set aside. Age can say a lot about the strength of a work, particularly with respect to its bibliographical apparatus. But one cannot simply presume that the older book or dissertation is weak; each must be examined on its own merits.

We have already discussed hierarchies of value in the use of reference works such as encyclopedias and dictionaries. The same general rule applies to journal articles. The best, most recent articles will often add additional bibliographical material that will lead one into the subject in more detail, and thus it is always helpful to work from the most recent articles backward. It is also desirable to start with the most important journals, a datum that is sometimes determined by the breadth of the journal's coverage. The journal *Church History* would commonly possess a higher priority than *Methodist History* (unless, of course, one's topic was specifically Methodist history). Articles on Methodism in *Church History* (if the authors have done their work) will undoubtedly refer to articles in the denominational magazine. Research

---

1. Many standard texts examine basic research skills and techniques. Two of the best are Norman F. Cantor and Richard I. Schneider, *How to Study History* (New York, 1967), and especially Jacques Barzun and Henry F. Graff, *The Modern Researcher*, 5th ed. (Fort Worth, 1985). We will not dwell in this chapter on basic writing skills, but students are advised to read, and reread, William Strunk, Jr., and E. B. White, *The Elements of Style*, 3rd ed. (New York, 1979); and William Zinsser, *On Writing Well: An Informal Guide to Writing Nonfiction*, 2nd ed. (New York, 1980).

students should start as broadly as possible with the more authoritative journals and then work their way back, both in time and in detail, as that will save considerable effort along the way.

One should also be alert to the distinction between archival and antiquarian work on the one hand, and critical scholarship on the other. For example, journals like *Notes and Queries* contain edited primary texts but very little scholarly apparatus or critical interaction. In this regard as well, the distinction between primary and secondary sources must always be kept in mind, a distinction that depends a great deal on the intention behind the creation of the evidence and the use to which the evidence is put. We have argued that Williston Walker's *History of the Christian Church* is a good example of a secondary, or in fact even a tertiary source, granting that it does not deal directly with the materials of history and in many places itself is based on what we would call secondary sources. But if one is studying the life and thought of Williston Walker, then it is no longer a secondary source. It is a document that needs to be dealt with differently, in light of the fact that one is going to it, not for the information that it was designed to convey, but for information about the mind of Williston Walker and his various redactors.

Students should also be aware of the distinction between the critical editions of documents that we have come to expect in the late twentieth century, and earlier edited works. Critical editions commonly contain an elaborate editorial apparatus that explains in precise terms the degree of liberty that was taken in collecting, compiling, and editing the documents. Many older edited works, however, especially of diaries, correspondence, speeches, and sermons, leave out entire documents or parts of documents, and sometimes they conflate documents in such a way that the chronology is confused, or even misleadingly altered. We thus distinguish between denominational and antiquarian journals that often contain primary sources, and major journals that seldom do, and we use these sources differently. Research students will also gradually develop a sense of which journals are refereed by specialists, and this knowledge will help place a journal in an implicit hierarchy of authority. Some journals will almost always accept an article, while others require the review of two or even three scholars in the field, and the latter commonly reject more articles than they accept. In time, a person will gradually acquire a sense of which are the careful scholarly journals and which articles are definitive in their field.

TAKING NOTES

The specific method of note taking will inevitably be tailored to the individual and to the precise requirements of his or her own research project, but certain general guidelines can be laid down. The cardinal rule is always to record notes in exactly the same way. One may use blank sheets of paper cut to the size of file cards, or use 6 × 9 narrow-lined loose-leaf paper which goes into standard one-inch and two-inch notebooks. The important thing is to be consistent and to record information with exceeding care. With any system that is adopted, and with any medium that is utilized, the materials that one chooses must be susceptible to conflation. The consistent use of one size sheet of paper allows notes taken for one project to be conflated with notes for another. For example, a sheet taken out of one's church history lectures should ideally be able to fit directly into research on a book. The same principle applies even with the use of laptop computers and databases (see the discussion below).

Never put more than a paragraph or a single idea on one sheet, and never work on the backs of pages. A good reason for using standard paper or paper cut to size and not the commercial 5 × 8 index cards is that with the latter, the bulk of paper soon becomes too great. Index cards are probably three times as thick as twenty weight plain bond. It is also a great deal less expensive to use standard blank or lined paper, and there is an important psychological rationale to this technique as well. If notes are to be collated, it means that there must be no more than one basic idea or paragraph on each piece of paper. Those who use index cards, however, will be inclined not to waste them. Scholars should be willing to waste paper, and if they must err, they should err on the side of using an excess of paper, because it will enable them to avoid the time-consuming task of using scissors and paste and cutting up the note card. Ideally, paragraphs written one year should be able to be inserted between paragraphs of materials that were recorded in other years, or at another stage of research. This is also the reason for using paper that is no larger than 5 × 8 or 6 × 9, and it is the reason for not working on the back of notes.

Some scholars utilize a footnote apparatus on each page. Others use a slug with the author's last name and short title in the upper left-hand corner. Still other scholars, however, use separate file cards, usually 3 × 5, for complete bibliographical information — author, title, place of publication, publisher, date — and file them separately. Cultivating the habit of taking bibliographical information down in proper bibliographical form is essential, with the last name first, then the first name in as full a form as possible, the title, and so on. A strict regime developed in the initial stages of research will serve one well when the final stages of the bibliography and dissertation or thesis are reached. The very first thing to record on the individual sheet of note paper is the author and a short title of the book or article that can take one back to the full reference. If this is conscientiously done on each sheet, the painful and discouraging task of being forced to redo one's work can be avoided.

The distinction between an accurate quotation from a work, a paraphrase of a work, and one's own analysis is crucial. At the very outset of an encounter with a document, the question should be put, "Is this worthy to be quoted in full or not?" The usual answer should be "Not," in that the number of absolutely memorable quotations is few. Then as one studies the document and begins to take notes, it is useful to ask, "Am I best served with a paraphrase, an analysis, or both?" and "To what extent am I borrowing the phraseology of the source?" Notes must make the answer to these questions very clear, because a year from the time the note is recorded, it may be impossible to recall whether the words are the student's own, or whether they are those of the source.

Generally, fewer notes are taken on secondary sources than on primary ones since the principal arguments and main conclusions of secondary sources, such as articles in the field, should already be very familiar. While taking notes, whether from primary or secondary sources, one is required to use discipline to avoid a pattern of passivity. It is a great temptation to put off creative writing until a segment of research is completed, but the temptation should be resisted by requiring oneself to record any insights that have arisen in the course of research. These insights often become the nucleus of a thesis, or part of an introduction or a conclusion, when the project matures to the point of serious writing.

In addition to the temptation to be passive in research, there is also a tendency to overquote material. Beginning students often feel an internal pressure to get the whole text in hand and get it right, but they should steel themselves to put the matter in their own words, being careful, as already noted, to record what level of generalization they have already adopted. Inevitably, the day will come when a needed quotation is missing, and the only alternative will be to go back to a document and pull something out. But slovenly habits that necessitate such retracing of one's work should be noted and avoided. Part of the skill of research involves developing the ability to interact analytically with a document rather than simply reproduce it. The task of the historian is not to reproduce some old document; that is the work of the antiquarian; rather, it is a matter of discovering what is really important in the evidence and eliciting a few supporting phrases or quotations. If there is a document-specific or period-specific or topic-specific technical vocabulary in the document, one needs to understand it and reflect that understanding in the way one handles it. In this case it may be that the vocabulary in the document will need to be reproduced very closely. But by and large, the main endeavor will involve analyzing the evidence and critically dealing with the content of the document. Even at this first stage of research, students should move toward an informed dialogue with the primary evidence and the secondary authorities.

COLLATING NOTES: THE PRELIMINARY OUTLINE

Besides attending to insights that arise in the very process of research, one should constantly be giving thought to how the material will be ordered. While engaging in basic research, reading the so-called "primary" and "secondary" materials, historians and theologians should be thinking all the time, "How does this fit together?" The preliminary outline for both individual chapters and the entire dissertation arises from at least three places. First, the initial consideration of the boundaries of the topic offers some guidance. Second, the outline emerges from the materials themselves and what they provide concerning their chronological or logical flow. Third (and less importantly), the outline arises from secondary sources and other people's opinions about the materials. The last is the least satisfactory place to obtain an outline, although it is going to have some value and influence, particularly since we are entering a discussion about the material that has been going on for some time.

In the beginning stages of research, it is highly desirable to make a clear decision about the best kind of outline to adopt and its suitability to the materials. Is it a chronological/ historical outline? Is it a logical/topical outline? Or does it combine patterns? One may opt for a primarily logical model and then, within the topic and its subsections, proceed chronologically. Or one may choose a logical model and simply move systematically through the topics. On the other hand, a predominantly chronological model may well be best, with logical sections in it. The outline may also be arranged in a third pattern: it may arise from the argument that has been joined with previous scholars. If one chooses the third pattern, then research becomes pieces of evidence for and against a case. In most scholarly work, at some point, these three forms are combined or converge. The one question that must be asked at the very beginning is, "How is this material best organized?" In some fields, such as the history of philosophy or intellectual history, a purely chronological pattern does not often work, granting that (to disagree with some famous general) history is not just "one damn thing after another." A simple attempt to move from a document written in 1595 to a document written in 1596 to a document written in 1597 will almost certainly fail. The important line of investigation may lead from the document written in 1597 and then to its antecedent in 1596 along with other documents written in close proximity, and finally to a heretofore unappreciated author who wrote several years later. In intellectual history and theology, chronology is not necessarily the best way to proceed, although one must always be sensitive to it, granting that influences normally happen in roughly chronological order.

The first outline is necessarily preliminary because in the process of working on additional documents and further secondary materials, and even while writing the essay, one's sense of the shape of the project is going to change, sometimes more and sometimes less substantially. The outline is a kind of skeleton statement of a working hypothesis. The hypothesis is about how the materials fit together, and it can, and indeed should, be changed even up to the very end of the project. As a method for structuring complex material, the outline is absolutely essential, but the importance of one particular form of the outline should not be overestimated. A carefully thought through, preliminary outline, however, must be in place at the beginning of one's work because the outline gives shape and direction to one's entire effort. It will also provide the basis for discussion with one's primary mentor.

As the outline develops and expands, one is then in a position to organize notes around the outline as the research proceeds. Every note card should reserve the upper right hand corner for a slug that indicates the part of the outline into which the material fits. In the very first stages of research this may be little more than an informed guess, and one should not expect too much certainty about the placement of some bits of material until the research has progressed some distance. But the process should be started as soon as possible. When the outline reaches a more complete form, one should go back through all of the cards, entering on them the location in the outline with Roman and Arabic numerals. This process will undoubtedly be repeated for each chapter. The last step involves taking the whole stack of note cards and organizing them according to the outline. One is then in a position to begin writing. The steps in this process are essential, since it is really the only way to control vast amounts of material. There are, however, several possible variations to the pattern. For example, one may expand the outline onto individual sheets and write the heading of the outline on these sheets without anything else on the paper. Then collate the materials behind those sheets, and gradually the sheets become the place where one writes down an introductory paragraph to that particular section, or a transition from the previous section. When writing chapters that extend to forty or fifty pages in length, one simply has to have a method for connecting the complex materials of research coherently to the overall project of the dissertation. The skillful use of a well-conceptualized outline, in turn, is the only convincing way to relate a thesis to its supporting data.

SURVEY OF SECONDARY LITERATURE AND PARADIGMS: WRITING THE FIRST PARAGRAPH

In the introduction of any topic, questions of secondary literature and paradigms arise, and they bear directly on how the first paragraph should be written. The most compelling way of writing a first paragraph is to commence the argument by engaging with other writers in the field. Once the outline is in place and the note cards are collated, a person should have a good grasp of the larger meaning of the topic and its overall shape. By this time one will also have a preliminary sense of the way the thesis fills a gap in the literature and the precise nature and location of the disagreements that have arisen in the course of research with what other people have said about the topic. These considerations yield up the material for a very sound first paragraph of a scholarly article, or the entire first chapter of a dissertation. The first paragraph should lay out the secondary literature in an analytical form. The case, of course, will be argued on the basis of one's own firsthand acquaintance with primary source materials, but while these materials are implicitly present in the opening paragraphs, they are not displayed in detail at this point.

The history of scholarship should be ordered paradigmatically. At a certain stage in research, leading toward the first paragraph or chapter, one should be able to say that certain lines of scholarly argument can be identified and separated. Certain authors fall into place with one line of argumentation or method and other authors with another. The first paragraph or chapter will show that there are several different ways of looking at this material. Having established that there are numerous different treatments of the material in the past, one proceeds to say how these different approaches disagree, which ones have particular insights, and which ones miss issues. After the entire paradigm of previous research is surveyed, one can say, "Granting that scholars have seen this group of issues but have missed these other questions individually, we now have something further to say about this, which moves us off in another direction covering the areas that have been missed." The thesis of the article or dissertation thereby arises directly from critical engagement with the history of scholarship and the knowledge of new or differently construed primary evidence.

Constructed in this fashion, the first paragraph accomplishes a whole series of different important effects. Effect number one is that it crystallizes in the student's mind her own purposes for writing and the distinctive character of her own approach. Previously, it is entirely possible that she may not have fully recognized the value of her own research and its place in the history of scholarship, since to that point she had not articulated it in detail. Secondly, in terms of persuasiveness, this paragraph or chapter proves to the reader that the author knows the material. When submitting a dissertation to a committee, or an article to a journal, or a book to a publisher, beginning scholars face the difficult task of convincing critical readers that what they are saying needs to be said. Those readers, if well chosen, will know the literature and will know the field. The longer it takes one to convince the referee, the less likely it is that the essay will be acceptable. If, however, readers are convinced in the first paragraph of an article that the author understands the literature in the field, that he or she has seen a gap in it, and that there is something important that can be said to fill the gap, then one can be assured of the acceptance of an essay or article. If one expertly surveys the literature in the first sections of the first chapter of a dissertation, one can be assured, most probably, that both internal and external readers will approve it. The paradigm of past scholarship demonstrates that the student has not only exhaustively covered previous research in a specific area, but the compelling way that this material is ordered suggests that the author possesses a commanding knowledge of the field. Scholarly authority is firmly established both on the grounds of comprehending an area of research and on the basis of the intellectual power that orders the material.

Once the first paragraph or paragraphs are completed, one not only has a good introduction to the essay or dissertation, but the beginning of a sound methodology for writing — namely, rigorous discussion with secondary materials in the text of the essay. The body of the essay or chapter should recognize the secondary literature specifically; one should not have to go to the footnotes to locate dialogue with other scholars. This discussion with other authorities arises directly from the introductory paragraph where the issues are set up initially, and this, once again, demonstrates a student's competence throughout the essay. But it does something even more than that. It proves a scholar's own grasp of the material by forcing him or her to enter into conversation with other people who have written about the topic. This needs to be consciously done. The initial survey of scholarship introduces the topic and the issues surrounding it, but the discussion with other authorities is something that must be carried on through the entire project. Otherwise a student may end up writing a monologue that does not necessarily add anything to the history of scholarship.

Authors commonly agree that the first paragraph or two are the most difficult part of any project to write (for each chapter or for each article). It is conceptually the most difficult part of writing because the whole project must be held in mind at once and, at the same time, the discrete parts of the work must be described and an effort made to order them in a compelling way. One may have completed one's research, come to write the first paragraph, and be seized with a tremendous case of writer's block. Recognizing the conceptual difficulty of constructing the first paragraph may help, and it is also an aid to composition to gather together in one place the insights written out during the process of research and see how they may bear upon the introductory sentences. If progress is seriously stymied for any length of time, it may be best to pass over the first paragraph and begin writing out the evidence that supports the thesis. Once the various parts of the argument are written, one will often return to the first paragraph with greater clarity.

Writing the First Chapter

As one begins to write the first chapter, research notes are folded into the discussion with the secondary sources. We begin to draw together in one place the discrete units that become the basis of paragraphs. Most of the time, the order of writing will follow the subsections of the tentative outline. It may, of course, be desirable to rearrange the outline a bit after the introduction is finished. Then we proceed to write through the outline, usually starting with the first subtopic. As one progresses, the bits of information on note cards (or whatever medium employed) are rewritten and put into decent English. By this point one should have a sense of how these single pieces of research can best be fit together, either through the logical or historical connections between them, or by means of the arguments that are joined with other scholars.

Students who have undertaken advanced research are sometimes overwhelmed by the thought, "How do I write a book?" The answer is, "You do not." Nobody writes a book. All scholars do is write little pieces of a book, and they keep on writing little pieces with some sense of the whole given by the outline. Finally, after writing a whole series of small sections, they assemble them into a cohesive whole and make a book. The object is to take a discrete portion of research or writing at a time, engage it rigorously in the light of one's sense of the whole, then move off that topic and do more. If a student writes one subsection every week or every two weeks, then in a year or so the result is a book-length manuscript. The task involves moving through the discrete elements, never losing sight of the larger whole, and hopefully allowing those smaller units of information to shape and alter the project in the process.

As they progress through the various chapters, research students should give conscious attention not only to the substance but to the tone of their work, and to what they are attempting to prove and why. Their work should be primarily constructive rather than destructive, though in most fields there will undoubtedly be some underbrush that needs to be cleared away. Attacking previous authorities, however, is often needless, tendentious, or captious and, as one experienced teacher put it, such attacks are "both irritating and boring to read," to say nothing of being a waste of space.[2] Undue criticism of past scholarship, besides being ungracious and distasteful, is a certain sign of vanity, a quality that young scholars in particular should seek to avoid.

WRITING THE LAST PARAGRAPH

When one has finished writing the body of a chapter or article, the last paragraph should generally understate the importance of one's discoveries. Modesty in conclusions is the best rule. At the end of a long, costly research project, students are characteristically enthusiastic about their accomplishments; we may be tempted to think that we have determined the field for ages to come or broken significant new ground. Such enthusiasm commonly leads one to conclude more than one has actually proven. On the first attempt, therefore, one should exercise restraint and put the question "What are the minimal conclusions that I can draw from this?" Understatement is an art, but it is an art well worth cultivating.

Secondly, while framing the last paragraph, ask specifically, "Exactly what did I argue in the essay?" Never draw conclusions for a larger field than the field of study that has actually been surveyed in the chapter. If the study was on "The Doctrine of God in Reformed Protestantism 1570-1640," do not conclude anything about the doctrine of God from the early Reformation. Do not conclude anything about the doctrine of God for later Protestantism or about Lutheranism. Do not conclude anything about the whole system of theology from arguments about the doctrine of God, except insofar as that doctrine obviously relates. Or if one is studying church polity in Geneva at the time of Calvin, do not draw conclusions for Presbyterian polity in general. The conclusions should fit exactly the bounds of the topic examined; the research itself thus sets the boundaries for the conclusion. The generalizations made in the conclusion are the generalizations that apply directly to what was attempted. Otherwise you are liable to be wrong — very wrong, possibly even absurd. It greatly devalues research if beginning scholars do not deal expertly with their conclusions, and

2. G. Kitson Clark, *Guide for Research Students Working on Historical Subjects,* 2nd ed. (Cambridge: Cambridge University Press, 1968), p. 19.

readers will be quick to notice this failure of discipline. Seldom, if ever, will modesty be criticized.

Conclusions may state implications for further research, but great caution should be exercised in this regard as well. It is best to deal with the possible implications for further research in an identifiable subsection, or simply hold these materials for future projects, since the motive for stating the possibility of further implications is often indistinguishable from the motive that leads to sweeping generalizations. This advice is directed primarily to young and beginning scholars. As one matures, judgment matures, and when a person's general command of a field becomes highly competent, then more may be claimed. This is one of a number of things that change over time. For example, beginning students often tend toward monocausal explanations of historical events. As their judgment matures, they begin to see the complexities of historical causation, and this leads them to become more tentative. Time spent in an area of research thus leads to maturity, which in turn produces more modesty and tentativeness than is often true of beginners. Similarly, one's command of the bibliography in a field will grow with time, one's preliminary survey of scholarship will broaden, and one's sense of fundamental issues will be enriched.

Conclusions, in short, should be "analytical" or "analytically descriptive." The student moves beyond the evidence to make an attempt at saying what the evidence means in a particular context. One can look at an individual writer or a group of writers on a topic, and then say what the structure and the various sources reveal about the breadth, the limitation, and the implications of their thought — where it came from, what it was doing, where it was going. But one should never say that this is the only way to describe the area, nor imply that the field is now exhausted, in a kind of prescriptive definition of what must be noted about the phenomenon. Rather, one moves off the description analytically, in terms of what can indeed be said about the shape of the phenomenon. The conclusion does remain somewhat open-ended, although one should have achieved a level of analysis that has not been attained before. The goal is to move off the material, throw new light on the evidence by means of a different set of antecedents and new material, and then say what this means for the phenomenon in brief, rather than make a strictly prescriptive statement about what must have happened.

Footnoting

The purpose of footnoting is to enable a reader to trace accurately, if not always in every detail, the steps of a scholar's research and to find the evidence upon which the argument is based. Most research students will be familiar with this principle. It is less likely that beginning students will have given any thought to the structure of footnotes. In writing essays, articles, and chapters there is a fairly predictable structure of footnotes that is related to the way we set up the initial paragraphs. An article will be very heavily documented in the first few pages because we are dealing with an entire field of literature. It is not uncommon for the first footnotes to take up more space than the text of the first two paragraphs. In surveying the field, one is dealing mainly with secondary sources. Once the current state of research is laid out and the thesis stated, the discussion moves on to primary sources. Generally speaking, in the ordering of materials, one moves from secondary sources into primary sources. As one begins to deal with primary documents, the chapter may once again require heavy documentation because of the initial citation of these sources, or perhaps the need to mention technical matters of method. Having examined the primary sources, the argument commonly turns to the substantive results of research, and typically, one will be documenting less and less along the way, because more attention is given to analysis. By the time the conclusion is reached, the documentation will dwindle to the vanishing point, and one is then able to state the conclusions on the basis of the material examined. In most well-written articles and chapters, one can discern this basic, predictable structure of footnoting and documentation. At the beginning of their research, students would do well to examine carefully the structure of a scholarly article, or a chapter in a well-received book, and consciously emulate these models.

It may happen that, following the introductory paragraphs, and after surveying the scholarship with an extensive apparatus of secondary documentation at the beginning, one discovers, toward the middle of the chapter, that one needs to present another large body of secondary documentation. In this case, the student or reader should ask whether his essay is in fact two distinct pieces, each with a separate apparatus. If it is one piece, has it been badly organized? Why does a new line of scholarship suddenly appear? Why did I not discuss these matters in my introductory paragraph and fold these references into the initial survey of scholarship? If the answer is that two basic issues are addressed in sequence in the essay and the form of the essay is clearly reflected by the division of the bibliography, or if there is some other logic that explains the anomaly, then the problem is solved. Such structural oddities, however, are often an indication that the student has inadvertently omitted something from the introductory discussion and inserted it at a later point, or that a second, unrelated topic that really does not belong in the chapter may have been added. Questions such as these should be asked throughout the process of constructing an essay.

The standard work on research by Barzun and Graff may justly be criticized on the question of what goes into a footnote. Barzun and Graff disagree with the maxim that if one wishes to elaborate a point in a footnote, it is either worth saying in the text (and not in the footnote) or it is not worth saying at all.[3] They cite several examples of where it is useful to elaborate a theme in a footnote, but the very nature of the exception, and the kind of exception that has to be shown (typically a commentary on or analysis of a point or a presentation of further information deemed unsuitable to the level of detail in the text), demonstrates the validity of the rule. In most cases it is inadvisable to develop long excurses in footnotes; if they are really important, they belong in the argument in the text of the paper. Less experienced scholars in particular tend to analyze primary sources in the text of their essays and to dialogue with secondary sources in the footnotes. This approach leads to long footnotes about the patterns and approaches of scholarship — and to a corresponding lack of dialogue with scholarly opinion in the context of the analysis of sources. Observations about the tendencies of scholarship, however, if they are really substantive, frequently belong in the text of an essay as part of the basic analysis of sources, with the footnote indicating where the secondary reference may be found. Kitson Clark was right to suggest that a long, argumentative footnote is often a symptom of mismanagement, and that part of the argument has been displaced from where it naturally belongs.[4]

Even so, footnotes should reflect the flow of the argument and normally not add new pieces to the essay's line of reasoning. It is just as important to engage other scholars in the argument as it is to present primary sources and analyze them: the line of reasoning in a scholarly

---

3. Barzun and Graff, *The Modern Researcher,* p. 297.
4. Kitson Clark, p. 34.

essay, thus, extends the line of the history of scholarship. Foreign-language quotations are an exception to the rule and do belong in footnotes, especially when a new translation of an original source appears in the text. Lengthy, untranslated passages may be a sign of erudition, but they also tend to disturb the line of argumentation, particularly since the translation itself is part of the interpretive process of the essay. Citation of the original text in the note offers readers the opportunity to check both the translation and the argument of the essay. A similar exception is properly made when a sentence or two is required to explain a necessary technical point, or to defend the choice of one edition over another acceptable edition of a primary source: these issues belong in a footnote.

This advice cuts against the characteristic temptation of the beginner. Graduate students wish to show that they are comprehensive, and while this is a good basic instinct, the discipline of excision needs to be exercised. One of the hardest things for a young writer to do is to blot out what needs to be blotted out, and to reduce what needs to be reduced. If it is not important enough for the text, students are well advised to transcend their instinct to preserve their work in a footnote. The fact that the student is acquiring information that is new to him or her, but that is by no means new to specialists in the field, means that invariably a large body of notes and possibly even long, well-crafted sections of a chapter will have to be left out of the final draft. Certain elements of background material can, of course, be utilized, but the distinction between what is new to the student and what is new to the field must constantly be kept in mind.

The question of whether or not to footnote material that is used for general or background information is not easily answered. Commonly, we footnote discrete bits of information, but if the task is focused on one particular source in detail, then the footnote can come at the end of the paragraph, because the whole paragraph identifies a unit of information. If, however, the paragraph is a compilation from an analysis of a whole series of different documents, then each discrete bit should be footnoted. Matters of general information, or matters of common knowledge, will often be covered in an introductory paragraph where the field and what has already been written about it are identified. If background material is extended over several pages, it is probably best to footnote it by saying, "The general content of this and the following three paragraphs are drawn from — " and then cite several of the best,

most recent secondary sources on the topic. This form is to be preferred
to citing those sources over and over again with a string of ibids.

As a general rule, all sentences that include quotations from
sources, either primary or secondary, ought to be footnoted. This practice prevents a confusion of sources or a question about the identity of
sources from arising. When a document is being paraphrased, a useful
practice is to add a footnote when the paraphrase passes from one page
of the document to the next, but to offer at least one footnote per
paragraph. A paragraph without footnotes is, to borrow a rabbinic
maxim about the vowel points of the Hebrew Bible, like a horse without
a bridle.

When citing primary sources, original printings or standard editions and translations must be referenced, with priority being given to
the original printing or standard edition. Thus, an initial reference to
Calvin's *Institutes* should first cite either the Latin text in the *Corpus
Reformatorum* or in the *Opera Selecta,* and then indicate which of the
standard translations, if any, has been followed or may be used by the
reader. If the translation has been followed, the author should indicate
this and indicate, as well, if he or she has made emendations of the
translation based on study of the original. Subsequent references may
simply cite the *Institutes* by book, chapter, and subsection. In the case
of citations from Calvin's commentaries, in which there is no standard
system of citation apart from the pagination of various editions, the
first reference should indicate the edition cited (again, probably, the
Corpus Reformatorum), the translation used, and the text of Scripture,
as a kindness to the reader. Subsequent references should include, first,
citation of the relevant volume and column in the *Corpus Reformatorum*
and, if the translation has been followed or emended, a reference to the
volume and page of the translation, as a courtesy to the reader. Scholarly
essays typically should not cite only the translation: this is acceptable
only if the point being made does not depend on a close exegesis of the
text and, in addition, if the essay is not a closely argued commentary
on the particular source in question.

Footnotes ought also to be constructed with careful consideration
of the method and logic of the work being cited. The practice of citing
Calvin's *Institutes* by book, chapter, and section, for example, is not
unique to Calvin but is the standard practice for the citation of classic
texts organized into such patterns and available in many editions and
translations. It would hardly make sense to have a footnote that read,

"*The Bible* (Chicago, IL: University of Chicago Press, 1935), p. 510" when the purpose of the reference is to direct the reader to Psalm 23:3 in the so-called "American Translation" of Smith and Goodspeed. Book, chapter, and verse must be used in citations of Scripture in view of the vast number of texts and translations. The principle also applies, however, to such works as Calvin's *Institutes,* Augustine's *City of God,* Irenaeus's *Against Heresies,* and so forth — although, in the case of the latter two works, each reference ought also, as a matter of courtesy, to include a citation of the volume and page or column of the edition or translation being used.

BIBLIOGRAPHIES

An enormous bibliography at the end of a chapter that bears little relationship to the footnotes is unacceptable. On the other hand, a direct correlation between the footnotes and the bibliography makes a separate bibliography for each chapter of a book or for a scholarly article entirely gratuitous. The first footnote reference should be a full bibliographical reference; after that, the item will be referred to in a shortened form. The sole purpose of a bibliography in a dissertation is to provide readers with ready access to the sources used in the work without having to go through all the footnotes. Or it gives the reader the possibility of finding a full reference on the basis of a partial reference in a footnote, without going through the whole book to find the first reference. It is even justifiable to have a "Select Bibliography," on the assumption that some of the items cited are cited only once and may play only an ancillary role in the thesis; such works need not be included in the bibliography. Furthermore, it is a common practice today to provide a bibliography of manuscript sources alone, without a bibliography of secondary sources.

If a full bibliography is required, it should be organized systematically under the two broad categories of primary and secondary sources. Under primary sources, one should list manuscripts and printed primary sources separately. Under secondary sources it is common to break a bibliography down further into categories of books, dissertations, and articles. Sometimes these three categories are run together alphabetically and sometimes they are not, but in either case, it is a good idea to work in this order and to think along these lines.

Some dissertations may have bibliographical essays rather than bibliographies, but it is not common to utilize annotated bibliographies. Generally, the sort of annotation found in the latter should occur in the first paragraphs of each chapter, or in the introductory chapter. This type of analysis is part of the work of producing the monograph or dissertation and belongs in the text itself.

Research with Computers

The increasingly lower prices of high-quality personal computers have made a wide range of word-processing, text storage, and text manipulation programs readily available to graduate students. We have already discussed the significant advantage to research that is made possible through the use of telecommunications that access local or nationwide databases. Among the options available, moreover, are notebook or laptop and portable computers, optical character scanners, databases that assist in taking notes and in the formation of bibliographies, and statistical and word-processing packages. The new technology is thus ideal for research as well as for the actual production of a dissertation, article, or book. Each of these areas has its own technical vocabulary, and some of them require highly specialized training and expertise. While in such short compass we will provide only the briefest of introductions to hardware options, leading technologies, and software packages, the references we include should be useful for further reading and exploration (App. V–VI).[5] Since all students will utilize a computer in the final production of their dissertation, we conclude with a separate, more detailed guide to word processing.

When one first sets out to purchase computer equipment, it is highly desirable to seek out the advice of a colleague or friend who has had some experience in the field. The technology in hardware is changing so rapidly that today's advice may be utterly passé tomorrow. Nevertheless, a few general guidelines may be offered. In order to utilize the best available software to its fullest extent, students who purchase computers ought to think in terms of high-end PCs with the fastest available microprocessor and very large capacity hard drives. This advice

5. For a much fuller discussion, see Janice Reiff, *Structuring the Past: The Use of Computers in History* (Washington: American Historical Association, 1991).

is based on the irreversible trend toward greater dependence on programs that utilize graphics. On the positive side, graphics simplify the use of various software programs, but this advantage comes at a cost; they require greater processor speed and they demand far greater disk space than mere text.

Students will also undoubtedly wish to weigh the advantages of a laptop, as over against a desktop computer. We expect that it will be the rare student who will enjoy the luxury of purchasing two machines, and today's laptop computers, as well as the heavier portable varieties that require an external electrical supply, offer many of the advantages, and few of the disadvantages, of the larger desktop machines. Large capacity hard disks as well as very fast telephone modems are now packed into the tiny confines of a notebook size case. The use of laptop computers for taking research notes, not to mention lecture notes, is now a common practice, even in tradition-bound environments like the main reading room of the British Library, which first approved the use of laptop machines as recently as 1991. The particular type of application should, of course, determine the exact configuration of hardware. Statistical procedures that just a few years ago required the power of a mainframe computer can now be performed on a top-end, desktop personal computer and most laptops as well.[6]

When recording research notes with a computer, the same general principles apply as in the practice of taking traditional, hard-copy notes; a single unit of thought is separated as a distinct "file" or "record" from the preceding and the following materials. This rule can be best applied with the assistance of a text-oriented database manager that is designed for research, such as "Notebook II Plus."[7] Units of data can be readily separated and identified and later organized by topic and subsection. In our experience, it has not been possible to avoid the use of hard-copy notes altogether, but we concede that a new generation of students may be able to develop the skills that will enable them to carry out the entire process

6. The Statistical Package for the Social Sciences for the PC was first made available in 1984, and it has since become far more usable by the addition of tutorials packaged with the software. See Konrad H. Jarausch, "SPSS/PC: A Quantitative Historian's Dream or Nightmare?" *Perspectives* 23, no. 2 (February 1985): 25-26.

7. David Y. Allen, "A Look at Notebook II," *Perspectives* 29, no. 5 (May-June 1991): 10-12. Of course, word processors alone can be used to manage text, but text-oriented databases, such as Notebook II, provide easier separation and manipulation of small, individual files.

of research and writing without paper and pencil, especially in some areas of research, such as the editing of texts. Notebook II and other comparable programs, such as Pro-Cite, offer the additional advantage of entering bibliographic data into a database format that can then be rearranged and re-sorted in a great variety of ways. Both programs allow the downloading of individual bibliographical references from national databases such as RLIN, and the importing of these references directly into a bibliography that can then be automatically reformatted for different university style sheets, or transformed through the use of keywords into footnote references that are readily inserted into word-processed documents.[8] The labor of retyping references for both footnotes and bibliographies is thereby greatly reduced, if not completely eliminated.

The preferred method of text entry is currently undergoing significant change. The rapid improvement in both the hardware and the software of optical character scanners seems, on the surface, to offer significant promise for note taking through the use of hand-held or full-page scanners. Hand-held scanners are presently sufficiently sophisticated to read eighteenth-century printed texts and, like modems, they are readily attached to laptop computers. Plans are currently being made, for example, to create a large database of eighteenth-century sermons by means of scanning them and hence greatly reducing the time required for data entry. The possibilities that this technology offers for research in a variety of fields are highly propitious, but the use of hand-held scanners is also fraught with no little danger for the beginning research student. If bibliographical references can be downloaded by modems and never pass through the keyboard of a computer, masses of quoted material can now be entered into a student's word processor without passing through her mind. The new technology thereby threatens to produce a fatal short circuit in the normal process of sifting and analysis, and because of this, it is a serious question whether or not the use of scanners will actually enhance people's work or save them time in the long run. Since the beginning research student is already tempted to quote sources excessively, the use of a scanner may result in a deadly glut of unassimilated, and finally unusable information. The one obvious exception to this concern would be in the case of scanning an

8. Pro-Cite uses add-on programs called Biblio-Links for downloading from specific databases, and these are expensive; the new program for Notebook II, called *LinkNB*, appears to be less fully automated, but is also less expensive.

entire class of full documents such as sermons, which would then be searched by the computer with a predefined set of carefully formulated questions.

Most of the important databases that research students are likely to use, such as the Thesaurus Linguae Graecae or the *Eighteenth-Century Short Title Catalog,* are packaged with retrieval software that is written specifically for these databases. Some projects, however, may require the searching of texts and the use of statistical analyses in stand-alone applications, and there are a number of excellent software programs that will greatly facilitate such projects. If a project entails the close analysis of words and phrases in several thousand pages of primary printed texts, then a text-based management system will be required.[9] Word processors, such as WordPerfect, have rudimentary forms of these programs, and words and phrases can be easily searched for and isolated. Students, however, should be aware that there are much faster and more efficient programs written specifically for this kind of task. "Soundex" (useful when searching for variant spellings of the same name) has a more expensive counterpart, "Sonar Professional," which supports virtually all forms of possible searches (Boolean, proximity, wildcard, synonym, and phonetic) and can search over 10,000 pages a second.[10]

For the organization and the manipulation of quantitative data, the PC version of the Statistical Package for the Social Sciences (SPSS) is an essential tool. This program will require some study to use effectively, but it does not necessitate the expertise of a statistician. If students master the pertinent sections of a basic textbook, like Hubert M. Blalock, Jr.'s *Social Statistics,* they will soon be able to utilize the most important statistical procedures packaged with SPSS. Moreover, one of the greatest advantages of this highly sophisticated program is the assistance it offers in organizing and displaying quantitative data.[11]

---

9. A helpful, brief discussion is found in Richard Jensen, "Offline 35," *Religious Studies News* 6, no. 5 (November 1991): 16-17.

10. Sonar is produced by Virginia Systems; its main drawback is cost. A cheaper and roughly comparable program is "Instant Recall" version 2.0 by Chronologic Corporation.

11. Changes are so rapid in the field of computer applications to quantitative data that advice concerning the best resources is bound to be dated. Beyond Janice Reiff's recent study, *Structuring the Past,* the older works by Roderick Floud, *An Introduction to Quantitative Methods for Historians* (London: Methuen & Co., 1973), and Susan Hockey, *A Guide to Computer Applications in the Humanities* (Baltimore: The Johns Hopkins University Press, 1980), set forth the central issues very lucidly.

Word Processing the Dissertation

It was not very long ago that the greatest agony suffered by doctoral students in moving toward the completion of the dissertation was the production of a fine, type-written product. Either the student accepted the burden of typing the dissertation himself, learned the difficult technique of placing footnotes at the bottom of the page, and mastered all of the other niceties of formatting, including retyping whole pages or even subsections to accommodate corrections — or the student contracted with a typist for the work, and even then remained responsible to see that the job was done properly. The personal computer has radically altered this situation and made possible the production of finely formatted and printed dissertations by students themselves. Indeed, the proper use of the word processor integrates the work of research and writing with the production of the final printed form of the dissertation. Several issues need to be dealt with in this regard (App. VII).

Students should acquaint themselves as quickly as possible with acceptable formats for footnotes, standard abbreviations, chapter headings and subheadings, tables of contents, and so forth. Much of the specific information needed on these matters is provided by such standard works as *The Chicago Manual of Style* and Turabian's *Manual for Writers of Term-Papers and Dissertations,* which is based on the Chicago Manual. Hudson and Townsend's *A Christian Writer's Manual of Style* is also useful for writers of specifically religious or theological dissertations.

Students should also be aware of the varying quality of printers. A dissertation requires either letter-quality dot-matrix printing (typically a 24-pin printer) or laser printing. It is also crucial that the printer be able to handle all of the commands necessary to the printing of the final product: for example, not all printers can print diacritical marks (accents, umlauts, etc.) in italicized words.

The best word-processing software available today will provide students with such capabilities as (1) the creation of different fonts (italics, underline, bold, larger and smaller size type, superscripted footnote numbers, etc.), (2) automatic placement of footnotes at the bottom of a page, (3) automatic renumbering of footnotes, (4) generation of large (i.e., book- or dissertation-length), continuously paginated master documents from a series of shorter files, (5) the ability to code headings and subheadings for the purpose of generating a table of contents, (6) the ability to code headings, pages, and notes in order to create patterns of internal cross-referencing automatically targeted to page, section, and footnote numbers, (7) the ability to introduce running heads for chapters and to suppress the header on initial or title pages, and so forth.

These features of advanced word processing programs can and should be used as an integral part of the process of research and writing: the word processor is a highly sophisticated tool, not a glorified typewriter. The same care ought to be taken in the use of a computer in research as noted above in the discussions of taking and collating notes, footnoting, and compiling a bibliography, and the basic principles indicated above ought to be adapted to the use of computer software. Thus, just as a researcher ought never to put more than a paragraph on a sheet or card, she ought similarly to limit the size of discrete bits of information entered into computerized research. One way to do this is simply to place a "hard page" code between paragraphs or, if excessive pagination is to be avoided, a common and easily searchable sign of a break in the material, like three asterisks at the left margin. The multiplication of files is to be avoided. (Typically separate files ought to be made for blocks of material drawn out of a single major source or for chapters or major chapter subsections in the eventual dissertation.)

Again, each discrete unit of research ought to be properly footnoted. When using a computer, it is wise to compile a master bibliography into which all new references are placed and to footnote each unit of research with a short title reference. Some software programs, like Nota Bene, allow coding of the master bibliography to permit retrieval of the information in various formats. It is also recommended strongly that "ibid." never be used in word processing: granting that footnotes are frequently not shown on the screen and that the editing process will include the block movement of paragraphs and sentences, it is all too easy to lose the identity of an "ibid." All references after the primary reference ought to be a short form, including the author's last name and a short form of a title, perhaps the first keyword. This form of footnoting can be expedited in WordPerfect through the creation of macros for short title references — the reference is then standardized and easily retrievable with a few keystrokes. (Researchers should also be aware of the ease with which word processing programs can translate bibliographic materials gathered from various library and periodical databases for incorporation into a research bibliography. Many libraries and virtually all periodical databases permit materials to be downloaded onto disk as well as printed out. Major bibliographical work can therefore be done simply by editing text from an extant database. See the discussion of online network databases and their use in the Appendix.)

Many software programs also offer table of contents generation. This feature can be useful, not only for the final draft of a dissertation or monograph, but also as part of the research and writing process: the table of contents is, after all, the outline of your research. As the research proceeds and the topic changes — headings omitted, moved, and added — the contents can be generated for the sake of producing a new outline of the research. In fact, the word processor permits a genuine reciprocity to occur between the outline and the growing text of a dissertation.

The selection of a particular word processing program for use in the writing of a dissertation should be made on the basis of a clear knowledge of the program's capabilities. It is not our purpose or intention here to recommend any particular software package. We would strongly advise against any package, however, incapable of performing *any one* of the above noted functions; Microsoft Word, WordPerfect, and Nota Bene admirably satisfy all of these criteria. It is useful to know, however, that Microsoft Word and the latest versions of WordPerfect are more graphically oriented than Nota Bene, and the graphical environment offers certain advantages in terms of ease of use and page layout. Nota Bene is the only major word processor that has not adopted some form of visual or graphic characteristics. But because it has focused all of its attention on the manipulation of text, Nota Bene is very efficient with editing shortcuts, and the seamless integration between the text editor and the text database is probably superior to any other word processor. In addition to reading through the manual of a given software package before purchase, a preliminary exercise well worth the effort is to run a "character map test" of the software on a potential printer to see if the advertised capability of the software is in fact compatible with the printer. In addition, students should be aware that major software programs are available to students at considerable discounts.

Software programs such as WordPerfect, Microsoft Word, and Nota Bene do provide good manuals for users. These manuals should be consulted regularly and used as a first line of attack, but they are often very terse and they offer virtually no concrete examples of word-processing techniques. They also give virtually no advice concerning choices between the various setup and programming options that they offer. The manual ought, therefore, to be supplemented by a solid guide-book such as those published by Que and Sybex noted in the Appendix. These supplementary manuals are far more detailed and often far easier to understand than the manuals packaged with the software, and they are full of useful examples.

Manuals such as these will provide examples of how to code bib-liographical references so that the text of the reference indents auto-matically below the first line of the reference — and does so in such a way that editing or changing the font size of the reference does not create any spacing or coding problems. If the first line of the reference is simply typed and then either indented or tabbed in for the second, the text will be unstable and any editing will destroy the neat formatting. These manuals also offer clear and useful advice for such WordPerfect features as "Macros" — which will be a great service in the use, for example, of short titles in footnotes.

The continuous use of a good software program like WordPerfect will become a self-improving exercise, since the techniques that are required to improve the manuscript are readily mastered. The various niceties of WordPerfect or Microsoft Word can be learned easily and then used consistently without any great problem of forgetting the basic command-structure. Students should keep pressing on the limits of their knowledge of techniques in all of the areas discussed in this chapter, since they are all so logical that learning is incremental and becomes almost second-nature.

6. *Preparing Lectures and Writing Monographs and Articles*

M ost graduate schools offer no guidance whatsoever in sound lecture preparation and teaching methods, and, as a result, a young teacher's first students may pay a heavy tariff for the privilege of studying under a well-qualified expert. In some cases, graduate programs seem to produce scholars who appear to know little outside the narrow confines of their concentration; alternatively, they occasionally result in people who are positively ill-equipped to teach undergraduates or Master's level seminarians. The challenge of preparing interesting lectures will often be compounded by the pressure to complete the dissertation, or to turn it into a monograph and then find a publisher. In addition, the experience of several years in a graduate program may yield the materials for an article or other pressing research project, and the new teacher will soon find that there is now less time to pursue such projects than there was before. This chapter will provide some basic guidance for outlining lectures, turning the dissertation into a book, dealing with publishers, preparing articles for publication, and coping with the unremitting pressures that will inevitably be encountered in one's first teaching position.

COURSE OUTLINE AND LECTURE PREPARATION

Most new graduates find that much of their energy in the first few years of teaching is directed toward the production of a series of lectures.[1] Beginning teachers commonly offer two major courses of lectures per quarter, at a minimum; and some smaller colleges and seminaries may demand as many as four or five series of lectures in a quarter. Without careful planning and some sense of method for the preparation of course outlines and lectures, the first years of teaching can be a devastating experience. The primary maxim of lecture preparation in teaching is, "Great industry in your first preparation is the foundation for leisure later on"; this principle, if possible, should be remembered in the midst of the inevitable early disorientation and panic one experiences in his or her first teaching assignment. Less facetiously stated, this is a variation on the theme expounded in the discussion on research methods: "Do it right the first time so that you will have something to build on."

In the first place, it is probably unwise and certainly repetitive (not to say boring) to lecture through the same material and to use the same approach as found in the assigned textbook. The most significant and constructive classroom lectures are those that supplement the assigned texts by focusing students' attention on the critical issues that emerge from their studies. A purely narrative approach that surveys long periods in history and effectively reproduces the textbooks is invariably deadening in effect. We prefer a topical approach that selects a pertinent and important aspect of history and emphasizes the details of that aspect or event in order to present a coherent view of the issues involved.[2] This topical approach does, however, result in a partial coverage of the period or subject under study, and it must be coordinated with a solid textbook and, preferably, with a well-selected reserve book list in the library.

The old-fashioned notion that teaching history primarily involves conveying information is perhaps the single greatest cause for the widespread lack of interest in the topic. A certain amount of factual data is undoubtedly conveyed in the approach we are advocating, but in the teaching of history, and in particular church history, far more is at stake than the dissemination of even the most edifying information. Any significant course of historical studies properly seeks to assist intellectual

---

1. Several helpful guides on this topic have appeared, including G. R. Elton, "Teaching," *The Practice of History* (New York: Thomas Y. Crowell, 1967), pp. 142-78; G. Kitson Clark and E. Bidder Clark, *The Art of Lecturing* (Cambridge: Heffer, 1970).

2. We have adopted an approach comparable to that of G. R. Elton, *The Practice of History*, pp. 165-66, though developed independently.

formation primarily in two areas: sharpening the students' analytical abilities and broadening their imaginative faculties.[3] In the specific disciplines of church history and Christian theology, these two intellectual qualities will naturally be accompanied by the cultivation of other, additional dispositions; analytic ability needs to be augmented by a positive estimation of the Christian tradition, and imagination by discernment. But even faith and discernment are gifts that can be supplemented by clear reasoning, comparison, and sound deduction. In other words, historical analysis, while insisting upon a critical and hence somewhat skeptical use of evidence, will not seek to produce skeptics, and nurturing the imaginative ability to grasp the larger whole of religious and churchly reality will not result in the reduction of all religious phenomena to the same bland, indiscriminate level of meaning. Ideally, teaching history will enable students to discriminate between the important and the unimportant, what should be retained in the tradition and what modified or discarded.

This approach to lecturing accomplishes several things; it enables students to observe a historian at work, collecting information, evaluating and ordering it, and interpreting it in discussion with other scholars. A teacher's candid display of excitement about some recent discovery or about a convincing new thesis in a book or article is one of the most important contributions that he or she can make to the educational process. Such personal involvement in lecturing invariably introduces an element of risk; a teacher's own favorite research projects should never be foisted onto a discussion of other issues, nor should they be allowed to dominate the discussion. Since a focus on issues invariably involves the evaluation of others' scholarship, it is also probably well to advise new teachers in particular to emphasize positive examples of scholarship rather than to dwell on the negative. Highlighting issues draws attention to the value of scholarly debate, it shows the way in which knowledge is advanced, and at its best it can reveal the way in which a community of scholarship functions. Conversely, when teachers are required to explain complex ideas and events to their students, their own powers of explication are enhanced, and hence teaching indirectly, but nevertheless truly, complements one's own program of research.[4]

---

3. Elton, *The Practice of History,* pp. 149, 161. Elton provocatively links the teaching of familiar historical topics to the development of analytical rigor, and the teaching of the unfamiliar to the mental quality of imagination and vision (p. 158).

4. Elton, *The Practice of History,* p. 143 on this complementarity.

In the actual preparation of a first set of lectures it is helpful to utilize standard textbooks, anthologies, and critical editions of collections of documents, in that order. One should begin by becoming fully conversant with several textbooks in the field, in addition to the one that is to be assigned to the class. This advice, while basic, offers several advantages that may not be obvious to the beginner. In the first place, it enables one to develop a general overview of the subject, a sense of subtopics and divisions of the subject, and a grasp of the ways in which the materials can best be presented. A survey of the best manuals in a given field is highly valuable if it generates fundamental methodological questions about the discipline: What are the principles of organization in this text? What is sound and useful about the organization? What is less than acceptable about it? What is useful in the author's basic outline? How does the outline have to be modified in the light of more recent scholarship, in the light of one's own attitudes about the material, or in the light of what other major scholars have done with the same material by way of organizing it? Once these questions have been asked, via the basic manuals, an outline can be generated for the course and a substantive series of lecture topics can be identified.

For example, a course-outline for the history of Christian doctrine ought to rest, in part, on an initial examination of such works as Seeberg's *History of Doctrines,* Harnack's *History of Dogma,* and various more specialized examinations of various periods in the history of the church, like Otto Ritschl's *Dogmengeschichte des Protestantismus.* A course-outline on American church history should rest, in part, on an examination of the standard surveys by Ahlstrom, Hudson, and Gaustad. An outline of the general history of the Christian church ought to evidence some contact with the standard works by Walker and Latourette. The lectures themselves should proceed from the outline to the sources — often after careful notice of the sources cited (and, sometimes, omitted) by the standard texts. We have noted in a previous chapter the value of bibliographic essays in the preparation of a first set of lectures. It will usually be impossible to examine all the recent scholarly articles that have appeared on the topic of the lecture, but if one has at least a general sense of the current state of research on a given topic, the authority of one's presentation will be enhanced accordingly. Some elements of the current state of research should be introduced into the lecture to illustrate to the students the ongoing nature of scholarly discourse.

Once the basic series of topics and the general outline of the individual lectures have been determined, however, do not use secondary literature in the form of textbooks as the foundation for discussion, but turn to standard anthologies and, if possible, collections of documents. For example, Bettenson's *The Early Christian Fathers: A Selection from the Writings of the Fathers from St. Clement of Rome to St. Athanasius* and *The Later Christian Fathers: A Selection from the Writings of the Fathers from St. Cyril of Jerusalem to St. Leo the Great* can be used as a basis for an initial presentation of patristic theology; or for the history of Christianity in the United States, one might turn to the superb anthology edited by Handy, Smith, and Loetscher, *American Christianity* (2 vols.), or to the more recent two-volume collection edited by Edwin Gaustad. Collections of texts and documents like these are available in almost every field. Used properly, they offer a point of entry into the original sources and thereby increase the authority and accuracy of one's presentation, even in subject areas beyond one's research specialization. In addition, their use establishes a sound basis on which subsequent lecture preparations can build. If more time is available for preparation, then the actual documents can be consulted either in their original manuscripts or printings, or in standard collections like the *Ante-Nicene Fathers* or the *Patrologia*. While it is certainly desirable to seek out and utilize the best critical editions of the original sources, to insist on such a practice would probably bring us to an unattainable counsel of perfection. In either case, however, if there is no time to transcribe quotations, it is not a bad idea to bring the source into the classroom and cite it directly (albeit judiciously and not at excessive length).

Careful forethought and a conscientious use of outlines should culminate in a commitment to a syllabus of lecture topics before the production of the lectures, even in the face of a heavy schedule and lectures in several different courses. Oftentimes newly appointed teachers must prepare lectures the night before they are to be presented. If an entire ten- or fourteen-week course has been outlined and the basic resources gathered (or at least identified) ahead of time, the topics will be clear at the point of preparation. This kind of commitment to a course syllabus is helpful both psychologically and emotionally: the pressure of preparation is usually assuaged by a clear definition of the task and a printed promise stated ahead of time in the syllabus.

Finally, as in the case of research notes, lecture notes ought to be taken very carefully, with accurate citation of primary and secondary sources, and with a view toward modification, expansion, and augmentation in the future. In the long run, a poorly prepared initial set of lectures will either linger on, unmodified, as the sum and substance of a particular class, resulting in extreme boredom on the part of both teacher and students, or it will have to be discarded. A well-prepared basic set of lectures can be expanded, new topics can be developed and added, and thereby the learning process can be extended to the professor as well as to the students. In time, the examination of the best critical editions of primary sources may become more than a pious wish, and the course of lectures may actually improve rather than degenerate.

In addition to supplementing lectures and expanding them into ancillary areas, lecture topics themselves should actually be changed from time to time, thereby providing an additional antidote to boredom with the subject, an experience that is almost bound to be translated directly to the students. The topic of vitality, interest, and freshness of approach leads us away from the subject of the lectures themselves to the equally demanding matter of style and presentation, though the two may never be entirely separated.

LECTURING AND TEACHING

When we turn to matters of style and the actual presentation of lectures, we recognize that there will be considerable variations between schools and teaching situations, and that many such matters are optional and properly suited to the taste and preference of the individual. For example, the intangible but essential quality of a teacher's commitment to the subject matter, his or her ability to display a high level of energy and to convey a sense of the worth of the endeavor, will have a great deal to do with the success or the failure of the teacher. While there is no substitute for this quality of passion, there is also no formula that will produce it and no set of exercises that will supply its absence. Similarly, a halting, dull form of lecture delivery will not easily be remedied by reading a few paragraphs in a book. Several issues that bear upon style, however, are universal, and some general guidelines concerning good form can be laid down.[5]

---

5. We will not digress here on the rudiments of public speaking. Kitson Clark, *The Art of Lecturing*, pp. 17-23, provides some very basic advice concerning one's posture, the use of the voice, gestures, blackboards, microphones, etc.

Lecture notes must be mastered before the lecture is given. If notes are read, the teacher must, at all costs, avoid the appearance of reading them, or being slavishly dependent on them. Eye contact with students is essential, even when they are dutifully taking down notes. If lectures are not fully memorized, it helps one avoid losing contact with the class to break the sections of a topic up with subheadings in one's notes that are grasped at a glance, with supporting points in the form of brief phrases. If lectures are written out word for word, in longhand, sentences should generally be shorter than one finds in written prose.[6] Attaining a balance between useful generalization and concrete example is an art, but it is an art that, if attended to, can be developed to a high and rhetorically powerful degree. A line of argument that is sustained too long without reference to a specific illustration will result in the loss of students' attention; conversely, a long series of stories or an undisciplined use of humor will lead students to conclude that the teacher is more interested in entertainment than in the course of study itself. Both extremes will produce understandable frustration in the student.

If outlines are useful in the preparation of lectures, they are also useful in the delivery of lectures. The psychological effect of a carefully prepared outline may be as important as the pedagogical effect, for it immediately communicates to the students that serious preparation has gone into the course. We have found that students on the whole appear to value outlines that serve as a basis for lectures, in part because they provide a sense of beginning, definition, and closure for the period spent in the classroom. Lecture outlines given to the class at the outset, or presented during the lecture via an overhead projector, will relieve part of the tedium of attentive listening, and they will be conducive to students taking meaningful notes. If this technique is adopted, the lecture should follow the outline (since there is nothing more frustrating in a student's classroom experience than finding no relation between the outline and the lecture), but it need not be followed slavishly. Digressions, especially those involving brief forays into technical topics that inform the general theme under discussion, or aspects of one's own research interests, are entirely acceptable, and, indeed, desirable.

We will not provide here an extended discussion of teaching aids and new techniques; other, more specialized sources will need to be

---

6. Kitson Clark, *The Art of Lecturing*, p. 25, has further detailed recommendations.

consulted on these topics.[7] However, we should note that the use of presentation graphics, developed to a fine art in the business community and now available in such software programs as "Power Point," does offer the interested teacher a highly versatile and powerful set of tools for teaching, and there can be little doubt about the value of utilizing charts and maps in the teaching of history. Such well-used sources as Charles S. Anderson's *Augsburg Historical Atlas* and Edwin S. Gaustad's *Historical Atlas of Religion in America* can profitably be assigned as supplementary texts. Two pieces of advice concerning audio and visual aids apply to almost all circumstances. First, the use of the device must be carefully planned so that it is smoothly integrated with the overall goals of the lecture. If a mechanical device is utilized, such as an over-head projector or a slide projector, it must be tested and the graphic display actually previewed ahead of time; there is no alternative method for assuring against disaster. Secondly, aids should always have the quality of transparency; the intended enhancement of a point must not be (though it commonly is) either a digression from the main point or a distraction. From a successful British source we find the following understated but pungent advice that well summarizes the essential points concerning teaching aids: "Fear your own preferences. Be ruthless in discarding. Strain always for simplicity, and plan your lectures as you would a campaign."[8]

Perhaps the single most important aspect of successful teaching is the quality of conviction noted at the outset of this section. Conviction as an essential quality of teaching does not entail dogmatically defending a particular line of argument; rather, it involves conveying a sense of the importance of the topic under discussion. This is not to suggest that a teacher should turn the lecture into a sermon; nor, conversely, do we mean to suggest that teachers should never own or advocate a position. But ownership of a position does not always need to be explicit; if it is always explicit, teaching may degenerate into propaganda. On the other hand, if a person's teaching lacks passion, it will produce boredom and indifference. If conviction concerning the importance of the topic must be evident, so, too, must the larger meaning of the topic and how it

---

7. *The History Teacher* is a quarterly journal that devotes the first of three sections to the "craft of teaching." For a good brief overview, see Janice L. Reiff, *Structuring the Past: The Use of Computers in History,* chapter 5, pp. 55-66.

8. Kitson Clark, *The Art of Lecturing,* p. 41.

contributes to the educational goal of the curriculum, and this must be made explicit more than once. In the teaching of history, what a lecturer demonstrates about clear thinking, the art of historical inquiry, and the evaluation of sources will often be as important as the topic at hand. Engaging the minds and the emotions of our students with fresh and interesting ideas is part of our task. If students are not inspired by history, if their imaginations are not stirred and their minds set running in new directions, and if their perceptual horizons are not extended, then we may rightly question whether history has been taught. This means, in our view, that the way in which the teacher handles the subject compares in importance with the subject itself, and thus, just as the content of a course of lectures should be subject to periodic review, a teacher's style should be regularly subjected to rigorous self-scrutiny.

PREPARING THE DISSERTATION FOR PUBLICATION

The revision of lectures should be an ongoing task, but the temptation to pour all of one's energy into improving course work must be resisted at some point. It is not a good idea to become so preoccupied with the polishing of lectures that one neglects the other tasks of writing that will, if done conscientiously, offer more substance to lectures than focusing solely on the teaching process. It is crucial for the beginning teacher to grasp that engaging in additional research and preparing the dissertation for publication and writing articles contributes in an indirect but powerful way to excellence in classroom performance. In our experience, teachers who concentrate solely on improving their lectures soon find that they lack depth of insight and power of analysis. The intimate connection between disciplined writing and articulate speech is commonly acknowledged, but there is an additional, intangible quality of authority in teaching that can only be cultivated by primary research. The teacher that separates these disciplines will soon discover an insurmountable barrier of mediocrity and sameness that can only be overcome by returning to first-level research and writing.

We recognize that teachers in small colleges and seminaries may be almost overwhelmed with their early course preparation. Considerable effort will be required to find time to pursue research and writing, but since the expenditure of such energy is a good investment, not only in the research itself, but indirectly in their classes and students, movement toward the preparation of the dissertation for publication should begin as soon as the dissertation is complete. This task is complicated by the fact that the aggressive copying program of University Microfilms International has made it increasingly difficult to publish even first-rate dissertations without significant revision based on further research. The preparation of the dissertation for publication today, therefore, involves far more than simply redrafting the prose and simplifying the argument. With few exceptions, publishers will require that revised dissertations demonstrate that substantial research has been undertaken beyond the original dissertation.

Armed with this knowledge, the wise mentor (or, for that matter, the student with foresight) will already have determined the way in which two or more chapters may be improved and reshaped. Ideally, this kind of planning should be done while the dissertation is perhaps only two-thirds complete. It may be that the chronological extent of the original work can be extended, or an entirely new genre of literature, properly excluded from the dissertation, may now be investigated. A new or revised chapter might adopt a different technique of investigation, and occasionally it may be possible to defend substantial revision simply on the basis of further research in similar sources. The basic method of revision advocated here is not unlike the method by which the topic was originally narrowed, though the process is now, as it were, done in reverse. The question is now one of how the work may be justifiably expanded, within reason, to qualify as a significantly revised piece of original research. One of the chief difficulties in this process is that substantial reworking must forfeit nothing of the originality of the project, while at the same time the bulk of the project cannot be greatly extended. Publishers will generally resist a typescript of more than 350 to 400 pages for a first book.

The publication of a dissertation may take several forms, but the current availability of unpublished dissertations through University Microfilms usually forces the discussion into two basic lines of argument. Some will advocate that the dissertation should be kept together as a single piece of research and published as a monograph. This advice is common in the humanities. Others, typically in those social sciences that are more quantitatively oriented, or in the physical sciences, will argue that a dissertation may be divided into several parts and published as a series of articles. One attraction of this second option is that it may require less reworking of the dissertation to turn at least some of the chapters into articles. But there is one major drawback to the second approach that must be carefully understood and weighed. Most academic institutions (and here we have in mind specifically administrators and committees of advancement and tenure in the humanities) will not weigh five scholarly articles with the same scale that they weigh a book. Although the amount of energy, insight, and sheer sweat that goes into an article, especially articles involving quantification, may actually exceed the effort put into a small monograph, the monograph tends to carry more weight than the article. It is for this reason that we think it wise, unless compelled by extraordinary circumstances, that research that has once taken the form of dissertation should be retained as a monograph.

Several useful books and pamphlets have appeared on the topic of how to develop a thesis into a book and how to approach publishers with a book-length manuscript.[9] The best single guide for all of the details of academic book publishing is *The Chicago Manual of Style*, itself a model of what a scholarly book should be. The latest edition of the style sheet of the *Modern Language Association* is also highly valuable. In all of this literature, and in our experience, several useful admonitions bear repeating. Aspiring authors should give careful attention to matters of prose style and the mechanics of bibliographic citation and footnote apparatus. At this preliminary stage of preparation, it is acceptable to adopt the footnote style of a major publisher, such as the University of Chicago. But no opportunity should be given to an editor to reject the typescript out of hand because the arguments are phrased poorly or ineptly. The scholar who dispatches a typescript to a publisher with grammatical, stylistic, or mechanical errors deserves to have it rejected.

A second key to finding a publisher is to examine the kinds of titles that publishers are printing. The book lists of university presses are actually more restricted than most people realize, and if a press has

9. Several useful pamphlets by the Modern Language Association have appeared, including, Oscar Cargill, William Charvat, and Donald D. Walsh, *The Publication of Academic Writing* (New York: Modern Language Association, 1967); and R. B. McKerrow and Henry M. Silver, *On the Publication of Research* (New York: Modern Language Association, 1964). See also Howard S. Becker, *Writing for Social Scientists: How to Start and Finish Your Thesis, Book, or Article* (Chicago: University of Chicago, 1986), Norman Fiering, *A Guide to Book Publication for Historians* (Washington: American Historical Association, 1979), and Beth Luey, *Handbook for Academic Authors*, revised (Cambridge: Cambridge University Press, 1990).

previously published no titles in the field of church history, it is unlikely that it will begin with a revised dissertation. Book catalogs and advertisements of books in major journals like the *American Historical Review* are the most convenient means of learning about the publishing parameters of various presses. In addition to university presses, beginning scholars may well want to look at the publishers who have adopted scholarly monograph series with limited press runs of several hundred copies of books, such as University Presses of America and Peter Lang Publishers.

Having determined the names of a half dozen or so publishers who are actively publishing in the area of one's specialization, the next step is to send a letter of inquiry to these publishers, along with the book's title page, table of contents, and one or two chapters, rather than the entire work. The cover letter should indicate that the typescript has been extensively revised from its earlier existence as a dissertation, and an attempt should be made to indicate to the editor the potential audience of the work. It is entirely legitimate, at this preliminary stage of inquiry, to send these materials to more than one publisher at a time. If the publisher indicates a serious interest in the manuscript, the editor will then declare whether house rules allow the simultaneous submission of entire typescripts to more than one publisher. (Simultaneous submissions are never allowed in the case of articles submitted to scholarly journals.) If a publisher disallows simultaneous submissions, then one is ethically bound either to narrow the choice to the one publisher, or proceed with several others that may allow more than one submission. Since it is not uncommon in the process of evaluation for typescripts to be tied up for six months or more, the attraction of simultaneous submissions is obvious. On the other hand, it is usually the less well-established and hence less prestigious presses that allow the practice. If a publisher wishes to see the entire typescript, it may be wise to obtain the style sheet of the publisher or publishers that will be pursued, and then meticulously adopt the style and the recommendations of that publisher in detail.

Finally, even the most gifted and promising young scholar commonly faces the disappointment of having a typescript rejected, sometimes repeatedly. Most typescripts are refereed by two specialists in a field, but editors may unknowingly rely on referees who are constitutionally ill-equipped to appreciate the line of argument that the book espouses; the quirkiness of some evaluations, to our minds, remains

absolutely baffling. The only redress that one has in this world of uncertainty is to take the rejections in stride and turn immediately to other
publishers. Carefully done, well-written scholarship that does make a
contribution to a field of study will eventually be rewarded with publication, assuming that the author can manifest sufficient persistence
and courage.

Ongoing Research: Articles and Book-Length Projects

In this chapter, we have been advocating the idea that there is a vital,
creative, and sustaining connection between a teacher's ongoing research projects and the best classroom experience where students become excited about learning. On the one hand, lectures should contain
not only information about the old issues and debates, but new interpretations and, in some cases, new information that brings fresh insight
to bear on the perennial issues. This can only be accomplished by serious
scholars who are working in the primary sources. On the other hand,
interaction with students impresses upon us our own limited conceptual
frameworks and thrusts us back into the sources with new and different
questions. In a word, the most effective teachers are often the most
careful scholars, and the scholar's quality of work in the guild is formed
in part by the experience of teaching.

No matter what one's own level of commitment to publishing,
students of history who aspire to be good teachers should aim to research and write something, since the two enterprises properly nurture
each other. One will occasionally meet scholars that only write books
and never debate issues at the more discrete level of the journals; conversely, a few scholars never venture into the realm of writing books in
the form of unified, book-length essays, but instead write a series of
disparate, disconnected articles, and yet somehow find a publisher to
publish them as if they were in fact a book. Ideally, however, the two
enterprises belong together, and something can be said for the way that
articles and book-length projects are mutually supportive.

One key to the writing of articles is to think of them as smaller,
ancillary projects that stimulate and feed a larger, long-term project,
and these long-term projects, in turn, should fit into an even broader
pattern of a person's lifework. Occasionally, one will stumble across a
perfectly self-contained topic that sparks one's interest and has little

bearing on anything else, and still it may deserve the time and energy required to turn it into an article. For the most part, however, articles should be viewed as smaller parts of the larger whole of one's research and writing program. It is at this point that long-term planning can be useful: done well, it can save one from engaging in a series of disparate, and finally unrelated and useless projects. No hard-and-fast rules can be laid down, and an individual's style and his or her own particular way of arranging work will undoubtedly vary dramatically from person to person.

In conclusion, what we can state with confidence is that the best teaching and the best research are interdependent, and generations of past scholars have defined useful categories of discrete literary forms, such as the article and the monograph, that still provide the best avenue for displaying the results of research and actually extending the scope of human learning. The scholarly guild properly demands a certain depth of investment in research for one's writing to attain a hearing, and these conventions are not likely to change in our lifetime. Much of the opposition that is expressed to the integration of scholarship and teaching arises from those who have never worked effectively in both fields or, worse, have failed in one or the other.[10] Those who suppose that graduate-level or seminary teaching can proceed without ongoing first-level research would sell the enterprise too cheaply, and the same applies to undergraduate teaching as well.

Given the reality and the utility of these structures, young scholars would do well to think carefully about the interdependence of research and teaching. It would be wise for them to consider that a dissertation left unpublished and an article set aside half finished are probably sound indicators that a course of lectures will not be revised, and that they are likely to grow increasingly dull and cold. Similarly, the historian who publishes only with the denominational journal and refuses to risk public statements in the wider world of scholarship must wonder whether there is not a discernible sectarian slant in his or her teaching. In some cases, of course, this kind of focus may be a matter of one's

---

10. Recent statements include Robert W. Ferris, *Renewal in Theological Education: Strategies for Change* (Wheaton: The Billy Graham Center, 1990); and Bryan Barnett, "Teaching and Research are Inescapably Incompatible," *The Chronicle of Higher Education* (June 3, 1992). Much of the recent literature on spiritual formation in theological education seems to work with similar assumptions.

calling, but in other cases it may signal a loss of nerve or a failure of vision. In reality, the advantages of adopting the conventions and standards of the guild and attempting to work broadly within a variety of fora and scholarly genre far outweigh the risks. For the historian of the church and Christian doctrine, this seems to us the only possible way to make a viable and lasting contribution to the field.

Bibliography:
Selected Aids to the Study of Church History and Historical Theology

I. Church History: Reference and Research Tools

A. Dissertations and Theses

Bilboul, Roger R., ed. *Retrospective Index to Theses of Great Britain and Ireland, 1716-1950*. Associate Editor, Francis L. Kent. 5 vols. Santa Barbara: American Bibliographical Center, ABC-Clio, 1975-1977. Supplements the Aslib *Index to Theses* by offering comprehensive coverage for the period before 1950.

The BRITS Index: An Index to the British Theses Collections, 1971-1987, Held at the British Document Supply Centre and London University. 3 vols. Godstone, Surrey, England: British Theses Service, 1989. Includes dissertations completed in the universities of the United Kingdom during the years indicated; these dissertations were not included in the UMI database.

Dissertation Abstracts International. Ann Arbor: University Microfilms International. This work collects, catalogs, and publishes virtually all North American doctoral dissertations. It is published monthly and is one of the most important tools for students of church history. UMI also has a computerized database that contains dissertations dating back to 1861, and it may be searched through DIALOG, Ovid Online, or EPIC, a service of OCLC (see the Appendix). Many research libraries also provide searching capabilities through CD-ROM. Dissertations from the United Kingdom from 1988 forward are included; for the period before 1988, see *The BRITS Index*.

Doctoral Dissertations in Church History, in the journal *Church History*, are

167

indexed and abstracted yearly from vol. 23 (1954, going back as far as 1949) and through vol. 42 (1973). Very thorough listings through the 1950s and 1960s, trailing off in the 1970s.

Doctoral Dissertations in History. Washington, DC: American Historical Association, Institutional Services Program, 1976-; semiannual. Unlike DAI, this source covers work in progress.

Gilbert, V. F., and D. S. Tatla, comps. *Women's Studies: A Bibliography of Dissertations, 1870-1982.* New York: Blackwell, 1985. Categorizes over 12,000 unpublished dissertations from American and British Universities.

Historical Research for University Degrees in the United Kingdom: Theses Completed. List no. 15- . London: University of London, Institute of Historical Research, 1954- ; annual.

Historical Research for University Degrees in the United Kingdom. 14 vols. Bulletin of the Institute of Historical Research, supplements 1-14. London: Longmans, Green and Company, 1933-1953.

Index to Theses Accepted for Higher Degrees by the Universities of Great Britain and Ireland. London: Aslib, 1953- , covering the period 1950 to the present. The British index does not contain abstracts, nor is there a computerized database.

Jacobs, Phyllis M., comp. *History Theses, 1901-70: Historical Research for Higher Degrees in the Universities of the United Kingdom.* London: University of London, Institute of Historical Research, 1976. This is the British counterpart to Kuehl.

Kuehl, Warren F. *Dissertations in History: An Index to Dissertations Completed in History Departments of United States and Canadian Universities.* Lexington: University Press of Kentucky. Vol. 1, 1873-1960 (1965); vol. 2, 1961-70 (1972).

Kuehl, Warren F. *Dissertations in History, 1970-June 1980: An Index to Dissertations Completed in History Departments of United States and Canadian Universities.* Santa Barbara: ABC-Clio Information Services, 1985.

La Noue, George R. *A Bibliography of Doctoral Dissertations Undertaken in American and Canadian Universities, 1940-1962, on Religion and Politics.* New York: Published for the Dept. of Religious Liberty by the Office of Publication and Distribution, National Council of Churches, 1963.

Master's Abstracts. Ann Arbor: University Microfilms International. Published Quarterly.

Montgomery, Michael S., comp. *American Puritan Studies: An Annotated Bibliography of Dissertations, 1882-1981.* Westport, CT: Greenwood Press, 1984.

Reynolds, Michael M. *Guide to Theses and Dissertations: An International Bibliography of Bibliographies.* Revised and enlarged. Phoenix: Oryx Press, 1985. This reference must be consulted for national guides to dissertations for non-English-speaking countries.

Young, Arthur P., and E. Jens Holley, with Annette Blum. *Religion and the*

American Experience, 1620-1900: A Bibliography of Doctoral Dissertations. Westport, CT: Greenwood Press, 1992.

B. Periodical Directories and Abstracts

Alkire, Leland G., Jr. *Periodical Title Abbreviations.* 2 vols. 9th ed. Detroit, Washington, DC, London: Gale Research, 1994. Vol. I is by abbreviation, vol. II by title: the work is international in scope and quite exhaustive.

Arts and Humanities Citation Index. Philadelphia: Institute for Scientific Information, 1976- . This international, comprehensive index covers all of the humanities, including religion, and it examines more than 200 journals in history. It is second in importance to *America: History and Life* and *Historical Abstracts,* and like the latter it can be searched online to 1980 through DIALOG, as well as through Ovid Online (see the Appendix).

Boehm Eric H., and Lalit Adolphus. *Historical Periodicals: An Annotated World List of Historical and Related Serial Publications.* Santa Barbara: ABC-Clio, 1961.

Boehm, Eric H., Barbara H. Pope, and Marie S. Ensign, eds. *Historical Periodicals Directory.* Santa Barbara: ABC-Clio, 1981-86. 5 vols. Vol. 1 covers the U.S. and Canada, and vols. 2 and 3, Europe. The directory examines some 8,200 periodicals, four times as many entries in the field of history as *Ulrich's International Periodical Directory* and *Irregular Serials and Annuals.* It supersedes the earlier work by Boehm and Adolphus.

British Humanities Index. London: Library Association Publishing, 1962- .

The Catholic Periodical and Literature Index. 1930 to date. Haverford, PA: Catholic Library Association. Bimonthly. This index was entitled the *Catholic Periodical Index* until 1968.

Elenchus of Biblica, formerly *Elenchus Bibliographicus Biblicus,* is part of the *Ephemerides* project.

Ephemerides Theologicae Lovanienses. University of Louvain. 1924 to date.

Historical Abstracts: Bibliography of the World's Periodical Literature. E. H. Boehm, ed. Santa Barbara: ABC-Clio, 1955- . In two parts: Part A, *Modern History Abstracts 1450-1914,* and Part B, *Twentieth Century Abstracts 1914-Present.* Published four times a years, this is the leading index for history for the period after 1450 (excluding the U.S. and Canada, for which see under American History, Periodical Guides). The index abstracts and annotates articles from 2,100 journals published in some 80 countries utilizing 40 languages. A retrospective index published in 1988 is available and the entire database may be searched on DIALOG (see Appendix).

Irregular Serials & Annuals: An International Directory. 10th edition. New York and London: R. R. Bowker, 1985. Absorbed by Ulrich in 1988.

Pauck, Wilhelm, "Church Historical Societies and Their Journals." *Church History* 21 (1952): 73-75.

Periodical Abstracts Ondisc. Ann Arbor, MI: University Microfims International, 1988- . This index now provides abstracts for the articles in 450 current periodicals with sophisticated searching software. However, its retrospective power is very limited; for 1988 it covers only ten journals.

The Philosopher's Index: A Retrospective Index to U.S. Publication from 1940. 3 vols. Bowling Green, OH: Philosophy Documentation Center, Bowling Green State University, 1978. A thesaurus was published for the Index in 1979, and there is a separate index to non-English-language publications from 1940 (1980).

The Philosopher's Index: An International Index to Philosophical Periodicals. 1967 to date. Published quarterly, the Index abstracts articles in some 150 journals and can be searched online through DIALOG.

Recently Published Articles was published three times a year by the American Historical Association. Each issue is approximately 150 pages and provides a comprehensive, up-to-date listing of articles by country and time period. 1976-91.

Regazzi, John J., and Theodore C. Hines. *A Guide to Indexed Periodicals in Religion.* Metuchen: Scarecrow Press, 1975.

Religion Index One: Periodicals; A Subject Index to Periodical Literature, Including an Author Index with Abstracts, and a Book Review Index. Vol. 1- . Chicago: American Theological Library Association, 1949- . One of the most important publications of the American Theological Library Association, *Religion Index One* is published semiannually with biennial cumulation. The databases for Religion Index One and Two are available for online computer search and via CD-ROM. The database is updated monthly.

Religion Index Two: Multi-Author Works. Vol. 1- . Chicago: American Theological Library Association, 1976- . An annual publication.

Ulrich's International Periodicals Directory. 28th ed. New York: R. R. Bowker, 1989. History, vol. 2, pp. 1853-1956. 3 vols. with quarterly updates.

C. Scholarly Journals

Archiv für Reformationsgeschichte. Has a yearly volume of abstracts of Reformation studies. Began publishing in 1903.

Archives d'histoire doctrinale de littéraire du moyen âge. Paris, 1926ff.

Bulletin de la Société de l'histoire du protestantisme français. 1866 to date.

Catholic Historical Review. 1915 to date.

Church History. 1889 to date. Three cumulative indexes, 1889-1980.

Franciscan Studies. 1924 to date.

Journal of the Canadian Church Historical Society. 1950 to date. Semiannual.

Journal of Church and State. 1959 to date. Triannual. Includes "Recent Doctoral Dissertations on Church and State."
Journal of Early Christian Studies. 1933 to date.
Journal of Ecclesiastical History. 1950 to date.
Journal of Medieval Latin. 1991 to date. A new journal by the North American Association of Medieval Latin.
Journal of Medieval and Renaissance Studies. 1971 to date.
Journal of Presbyterian History. 1901 to date.
Journal of Religious History. Sydney, 1960 to date. Semiannual.
Renaissance Quarterly. Supersedes *Renaissance News.* 1948 to date.
Revue d'Histoire Ecclésiastique. Louvain, 1900 to date.
The Second Century: A Journal of Early Christian Studies. 1981 to 1989.
Sixteenth Century Journal. 1972 to date. *Speculum.* 1926 to date. Each issue has a "Bibliography of American Periodical Literature." A journal of mediaeval studies.
Theologische Literaturzeitung. Leipzig, 1876 to date. Includes subject categories of church history and systematic theology.
Vigiliae Christianae: A Review of Early Christian Life and Language. 1947 to date.
Zeitschrift für Kirchengeschichte. 1876 to date.

D. Handbooks, Bibliographical Guides, and General Surveys

Adams, Charles Kendall. *A Manual of Historical Literature, Comprising Brief Descriptions of the Most Important Histories in English, French, and German . . .* 3rd ed., revised and enlarged. New York: Harper & Brothers, 1889.
Baker, Derek, ed. *The Materials, Sources and Methods of Ecclesiastical History.* Studies in Church History, 11. New York: Harper & Row, 1975. A promising title, but in reality a series of highly specialized studies.
Ballou, Patricia K. *Women: A Bibliography of Bibliographies.* 2nd ed. Boston: G. K. Hall, 1986.
Berkowitz, David S. *Bibliographies for Historical Researchers.* Waltham, Mass., 1969.
Bibliografía Teológica Comentada. Vol. 1- . Buenos Aires: Instituto Superior Evangélico de Estudios Teológicos, 1973- . An annual publication of approximately 5,000 books and articles on Latin American theology.
Bibliographia internationalis spiritualitatis. Vol. 1- . Rome: Pontifico Instituto di Spiritualità, 1966- . Published annually. The major resource for articles on spirituality, organized topically, with an author index.
Bindoff, S. T., and James T. Boulton. *Research in Progress in English and Historical Studies in the Universities of the British Isles.* New York: St. Martin's, 1971.

Blockx, Karel. *Bibliographical Introduction to Church History.* Louvain: Acco, 1982. This list is not annotated and it lacks a title index.

Case, Shirley Jackson, et al., eds. *A Bibliographical Guide to the History of Christianity.* Chicago: University of Chicago Press, 1931. Rev. ed. New York: Smith, 1951.

Chadwick, Henry, and Owen Chadwick, gen. eds. *Oxford History of the Christian Church.* New York: Oxford University Press, 1977- . A projected 20-vol. series.

Chadwick, Owen. *The History of the Church: A Select Bibliography.* 3rd ed. London: Historical Association, 1973.

Christensen, Torben, Jokols H. Grønback, Erik Nørv, and Jørgen Stenback. *Kirkehistorisk Bibliograf.* Copenhagen: G. E. C. Gad, 1979.

Collinson, Robert L. *Bibliographies, Subject and National.* 3rd ed., rev. London: Lockwood, 1968.

Coulter, Edith M., and Melanie L. Hoseh. *Historical Bibliographies: A Systematic and Annotated Guide.* 1935. Reprint. New York: Russell & Russell, 1965. A useful guide to older materials.

Darling, James. *Cyclopedia Bibliographica: A Library Manual of Theological and General Literature.* 3 vols. London: Darling, 1834. Vols. 1-2 offer an alphabetical listing by author. Darling frequently gives the titles of individual works in volumes of collected works. Vol. 3 proceeds by subject. Remains a significant resource for sixteenth-, seventeenth-, and eighteenth-century theological studies.

The Eighteenth Century: A Current Bibliography. New York: AMS Press, 1978- . International, interdisciplinary, and comprehensive review of books and articles, but no longer "current"; the volume for 1985 was published in 1990. Published as part of the *Philological Quarterly* in an interdisciplinary format since 1970, it came under the auspices of The American Society of Eighteenth-Century Studies in 1978. The section on philosophy, science, and religion runs to seventy pages a year.

Fischer, Clare B. *Breaking Through: A Bibliography of Women and Religion.* Berkeley: Graduate Theological Union Library, 1980.

Fritze, Ronald H., Brian E. Coutts, and Louis A. Vyhnanek. *Reference Sources in History: An Introductory Guide.* Santa Barbara: ABC-Clio, 1990. The best, most recent, comprehensive guide.

Gorman, G. E., and Lyn Gorman. *Theological and Religious Reference Materials: General Resources and Biblical Studies.* Bibliographies and Indexes in Religious Studies, 1. Westport, CT: Greenwood Press, 1984.

Gorman, G. E., and Lyn Gorman. *Theological and Religious Reference Materials: Systematic Theology and Church History.* Bibliographies and Indexes in Religious Studies, 2. Westport CT: Greenwood Press, 1985. This is the best recent guide for the literature of church history and historical theology, but the second volume in the series must be used in conjunction with the first, since there is much material on church history in the first volume. These two volumes provide detailed annotations for most reference works in church history, but the organization is poor. Standard denominational bibliographies are dispersed throughout the volumes, but can be located through the indices.

Historische Bibliographie. 1986 to date. Arbeitsgemeinschaft Ausseruniversitarer Historischer Forschungseinrichtungen in der Bundesrepublik Deutschland. An annual supplement to Historische Zeitschrift.

Howe, George F., et al. *Guide to Historical Literature.* The American Historical Association. New York: Macmillan, 1967. A major topical bibliography to serials, series, bibliographical tools, books, articles, etc., in all fields of historical investigation, annotated. Covers intellectual and religious history but needs to be supplemented in the specific areas of philosophy and theology.

Jedin, Hubert, and John Dolan, eds. *History of the Church.* New York: The Seabury Press, 1979. 10 vols. A standard reference by Catholic scholars. Each volume has a bibliography of 50 to 100 pages.

Kepple, Robert J., and John R. Muether. *Reference Works for Theological Research.* 3rd ed. Lanham: University Press of America, 1992. Church history is covered briefly on pp. 129-65 with every item annotated.

Le Leannec, Bernard. *Church and State: International Bibliography, 1973-1977, Indexed by Computer/Église et État: Bibliographie Internationale, 1973-1977, Établié par Ordinateur.* RIC Supplément, no. 35-38. Strasbourg: CERDIC Publications, 1978.

Loeb, Catherine R., Susan E. Searing, Esther F. Stineman, with assistance of Meredith J. Ross. *Women's Studies: A Recommended Core Bibliography, 1980-1985.* Littleton, CO: Libraries Unlimited, 1987.

McCabe, James. *A Critical Guide to Catholic Reference Books.* Research Studies in Library Science, 2. Littleton, CO: Libraries Unlimited, 1971.

Menendez, Albert J. *Church-State Relations: An Annotated Bibliography.* Garland Reference Library of Social Science, 24. New York: Garland Publishing Company, 1976.

Nouvelle Histoire de l'Eglise. Paris: Editions du Seuil, 1963- . Thus far, five volumes have been published, bringing the study through Vatican II. Bibliographies: v. 1, 535-71; v. 2, 564-81; v. 3, 539-80; v. 4, 505-49; v. 5, 757-870.

Peirce, David Roland. *A Select Bibliography of History.* 3rd ed. Cambridge, MA: Harvard University Press, 1966.

Poulton, Helen J. *The Historian's Handbook: A Descriptive Guide to Reference Works.* Norman, OK: University of Oklahoma Press, 1972. A standard work for years, it is now superseded by Ronald Fritze, et al., *Reference Sources in History.*

Ritchie, Maureen. *Women's Studies: A Checklist of Bibliographies.* London: Mansell, 1980.

Rothbart, Margarete J., and Ulrich Helfenstein. *Bibliographie internationale des travaux historiques publiés dans les volumes de "mélanges."/International bibliography of historical articles in Festschriften and miscellanies.* Paris: A. Colin, 1955- . (Vol. 1 covers 1880-1939; vol. 2 covers 1940-50 plus addenda to vol. 1.)

Thils, Gustave. *Theologica e Miscellaneis.* Louvain: E. Warny, 1960. Reprint, 1968. Index of articles appearing in selected miscellanies and festschriften, 1918-58.

Untersuchungen zur Kirchengeschichte. Witten, 1965- .

E. Dictionaries and Encyclopedias

The use of dictionaries and encyclopedias in scholarly work can be a source of trouble and dismay to the uninitiated. An initial, necessary distinction must be made between the encyclopedias and topical dictionaries written for the general public and those written by scholars for students in scholarly fields and for other scholars. The former, including such famous and prestigious works as the *Britannica, Americana, Colliers Encyclopaedia,* and the *World Almanac,* ought to be avoided as conceived on a level below that of graduate scholarship. The latter, some of which follow, are of considerable value and worthy of citation in scholarly studies. Basic language dictionaries like *Webster* and *Cassell* are not cited, but are also excluded from the above caveat.

1. Linguistic Tools: Dictionaries and Paleographical Aids

Blaise, Albert. *Lexicon Latinitatis Medii Aevi: praesertim ad res ecclesiasticas investigandas pertinens* (Dictionnaire latin-français des auteurs du Moyen-Age). Turnhout: Brepols, 1975.

————. *Manuel du latin chrétien.* Reprint. Turnhout: Brepols, 1986.

Cappelli, Adriano. *Lexicon Abbreviaturarum: Dizionario di Abbreviature Latine ed Italiane usate nelle Carte e Codici specialmente del Medio-evo.* 6th ed. Milan: Hoepli, 1961. Reprint, 1985.

Abréviations latines médiévales: supplement au "Dizionario di Abbreviature Latine," ed. *Italiane de Adriano Cappelli.* 2nd ed. Louvain and Paris: Publications Universitaires / Nauwelaerts, 1966.

Chassant, A. *Dictionnaire des abréviations latines et françaises du moyen âge.* Paris, 1849. 5th ed., 1884.

————. *Paléographie des chartes et des manuscrits du XIe an XVIIe siècle.* 8th ed. Paris, 1885.

Dictionnaire de l'ancienne langue française et de tous dialectes du IXe au XVe. siècle. Par Frédéric Godefroy. 10 vols. Paris: F. Vieweg, 1881-1902. Reprint. Vaduz: Kraus Reprints, 1965.

Dictionnaire Latin-Français des Auteurs Chrétiens. Edited by Albert Blaise and Henri Chirat. Strasbourg: Le Latin Chrétien, 1954. A theological dictionary in essence defining the vocabulary of Latin Christianity; useful for the Middle Ages.

Du Cange, Charles. *Glossarium Mediae et Infimae Latinitatis.* 10 vols. Reprint. Graz: Akademische Druck, 1954.

Grandsaignes d'Hauterive, Robert. *Dictionnaire d'ancien français, moyen âge et renaissance.* Paris: Larousse, 1947.

Hector, Leonard C. *The Handwriting of English Documents.* 2nd ed. London: Edward Arnold, 1966. An essential guide for English medieval documents.

Huguet, Edmond. *Dictionnaire de la langue française du seizième siècle.* 7 vols. Paris: Champion, 1925-67.

Lampe, G. W. H., ed. *A Patristic Greek Lexicon.* Oxford: Clarendon Press, 1961-68.

A Lexicon of St. Thomas Aquinas Based on the Summa Theologica and Selected Passages of His Other Works. Edited by Roy Deferrari, et al. 5 vols. Washington, DC: Catholic University of America Press, 1948-53. Important not only for an understanding of Aquinas, but also for comprehension of medieval philosophical and theological vocabulary.

Lindsay, W. M. *Notae Latinae: An Account of Abbreviation in Latin MSS. of the Early Miniscule Period (c. 700-850).* Cambridge, 1915.

Martin, Charles T., comp. *The Record Interpreter: A Collection of Abbreviations, Latin Words and Names used in English Historical Manuscripts and Records.* 2nd ed. London: Stevens and Sons, 1910. Reprint. Hildesheim: Georg Olms Verlag, 1969.

Marucchi, O. *Christian Epigraphy.* Translated by J. Armine Willis. Cambridge: Cambridge University Press, 1912.

Medieval Latin Word-List from British and Irish Sources. Prepared by James Huston Baxter and Charles Johnson. London: Oxford University Press, 1934.

Newton, K. C. *Medieval Local Records: A Reading Aid.* Helps for Students of History, 83. London: Historical Association, 1971.

Niermeyer, Jan F. *Mediae Latinitatis Lexicon Minus: A Medieval Latin-French/English Dictionary.* Leiden: E. J. Brill, 1976.

———. *Mediae Latinitatis Lexicon Minus: Abbreviationes et Index Fontium.* Leiden: E. J. Brill, 1976.

The Oxford English Dictionary. 2nd ed. Prepared by J. A. Simpson and E. S. C. Weiner. 20 vols. Oxford: Clarendon Press, 1989.

Souter, Alexander. *A Glossary of Later Latin to 600 A.D.* Oxford: Clarendon Press, 1949.

Thompson, E. M. *An Introduction to Greek and Latin Paleography.* Oxford, 1912.

Thoyts, E. E. *How to Decipher and Study Old Documents: Being a Guide to the Reading of Ancient Manuscripts.* 3rd ed. London, 1909.

2. Biographical Dictionaries and Encyclopedias

Allgemeine deutsche Biographie. 55 vols. Leipzig, 1875-1912.

Biographie nationale, publiée par l'académie royale de Belgique. Brussels, 1866- .

Biographie universelle. 2nd ed. 45 vols. Paris, 1845-65.

Biographisch Lexicon voor de Geschiedenis van het Nederlandse Protestantisme. 2 vols. Kampen: J. H. Kok, 1983.

Biographisch woordenboek der Nederlanden. 27 vols. Haarlem: Brederode, 1852-78.

Biographisches Lexikon des Kaisertums Öesterreich. Edited by C. von Wurzbach. 60 vols. Vienna, 1856-91.

Dictionary of American Biography. Edited by Allen Johnson. 20 vols. New York: Scribners, 1928-36. Eight Supplements, through 1970.

Dictionary of National Biography. Edited by Leslie Stephen and Sidney Lee. London: University Press, H. Milford, ed., 1986. Vols. 1-22 are pre-1900 covering A-Z and supplement. Vols. 23-30 cover 1901-1971/80.

Dictionary of Scientific Biography. Edited by Charles Coulston Gillespie. New York: 1970- .

Dictionnaire de biographie française. Edited by J. Balteau, A. Rastoul, and M. Prévost. Paris: Letouzy et Ané, 1929- . 17 vols. as of 1989.

Dictionnaire historique et biographique de la Suisse. Neûchatel: Attinger, 1920-34.

Dizionario biografico degli italiani. 32 vols. Rome: Instituto della Enciclopedia Itialiana, 1960- .

Jocher, Christian Gottlieb. *Allgemeines Gelehrten Lexikon.* 11 vols. Leipzig, 1750-1897. A major source for sixteenth- and seventeenth-century biographies not found in more recent dictionaries.

Laffont, Robert, and Valentino Bompiani. *Dictionnaire biographique des auteurs de tous les temps et de tous les pays.* 2 vols. Paris: S.E.D.E., 1957-58.

New Century Cyclopedia of Names. 3 vols. New York: Appleton-Century-Crofts, 1954.

Nieuw nederlandsch biografisch woordenboek. 10 vols. Leiden: Sijthoff, 1911-37.

Who Was Who. London: A. & C. Black, 1920- .

3. Dictionaries of Anonyms and Pseudonyms

Atkinson, Frank. *Dictionary of literary pseudonyms: a selection of popular modern writers in English.* 4th enl. ed. London: Bingley; Chicago: American Library Association, 1987.

Barbier, Antoine-Alexandre, Olivier Alexandre Barbier, Paul Billard, René Billard, and J.-M. Querard. *Dictionnaire des ouvrages anonymes. Supercheries littéraires devoileés.* 3rd ed., rev. et augm. 4 vols. in 8 parts. Paris: P. Daffis, 1872-79.

Coston, Henry. *Dictionnaire des pseudonymes.* Paris, 1961.

Cushing, William. *Anonyms: a dictionary of revealed authorship.* 1889; repr. Waltham, MA: Mark Press, 1963.

Cushing, William. *Initials and pseudonyms: a dictionary of literary disguises.* 2 vols. 1885-88; repr. Waltham, MA, Mark Press, 1963.

Franklin, Alfred. *Dictionnaire des noms, surnoms et pseudonymes latins de l'histoire littéraire du moyen âge [1100 a 1530].* Paris: Firmin-Didot et cie, 1875.

Halkett, Samuel, John Laing, et al. *Dictionary of Anonymous and Pseudonymous English Literature.* Edinburgh, 1926- . 9 vols. 3rd ed., rev. and enlarged. Edited by John Horden. Harlow: Longman, 1980.

Holzmann, Michael, and Hanns Bohatta. *Deutsches Anonymen-Lexikon, 1501-1850.* 7 vols. 1902-28; repr. Hildesheim: G. Olms, 1961.

Holzmann, Michael, and Hanns Bohatta. *Deutsches Pseudonymen-Lexikon.* 1906; repr. Hildesheim: G. Olms, 1961.

Kempenaer, A. de, and Jan Izaak van Doorninck. *Vermomde Nederlandsche en Vlaamsche schrijvers.* Leiden: A. W. Sijthoff, 1928. A dictionary of Dutch and Flemish anonyms and pseudonyms.

Melzi, Gaetano. *Dizionario di opere anonime e pseudonime di scrittori italiani, o come che sia aventi relazione all'Italia.* 3 vols. New York: B. Franklin, 1960.

Passano, Giovanni Battista, Gaetano Melzi, and Emmanuele Rocco. *Dizionario di opere anonime e pseudonime, in supplemento a quello di Gaetano Melzi.* New York: B. Franklin, 1960.

Querard, J.-M. *Les supercheries littéraires devoileés. Galerie des auteurs apocryphes, supposés, déguises, plagiaires et des editeurs infideles de la littérature française pendant les quatre derniers siècles: ensemble les industriels littéraires et les lettres qui sont anoblis à notre époque.* 5 vols. Paris: Lediteur: 1847-53.

Stonehill, Charles Archibald, Andrew Block, Andrew and H. Winthrop Stonehill. *Anonyma and pseudonyma.* 4 vols. London, 1926-27.

Weller, Emil Ottokar. *Die falschen und fingierten Druckorte: Repertorium der seit Erfindung der Buchdruckerkunst unter falscher Firma erschienenen deutschen, lateinischen und franzosischen Schriften.* 2 vols. 1864; repr. Hildesheim: G. Olms, 1960. A unique and significant effort to identify falsely given places of publication.

Weller, Emil Ottokar. *Lexicon pseudonymorum. Worterbuch der Pseudonymen aller Zeiten und Volker; oder, Verzeichnis jener Autoren, die sich falscher Namen bedienten.* Hildesheim: G. Olms, 1963.

4. Theological and Church-Historical Dictionaries and Encyclopedias

An asterisk [*] precedes those items which represent the results of advanced research and which stand as suitable documentation of points made in scholarly research. Items without an asterisk are useful general tools suitable for citation in introductory or survey footnotes. Note that all dictionaries here included may be cited at any time as sources of basic definitions.

*Altenstaig, Johann. *Vocabularius theologiae.* Hagenau: Heinrich Gran, 1517. Necessary for understanding the terms of late medieval and early Reformation theology.

————. *Lexicon theologicum.* Koln, 1619. Reprint. Hildesheim: Olms, 1973.

Brauer, Jerald C., ed. *The Westminster Dictionary of Church History.* Philadelphia: The Westminster Press, 1971. The emphasis is upon the modern church and the American church in particular. Sketchy bibliographies.

Concise Theological Dictionary. By Karl Rahner and Herbert Vorgrimler. Edited by Cornelius Ernst. Translated by Richard Strachan. 2nd ed. London: Burns and Dortes, 1983.

Cyclopaedia of Biblical, Theological, and Ecclesiastical Literature. Edited by J. McClintock and J. Strong. 10 vols., plus supplement (2 vols.). New York: Harper & Bros., 1867-87. Outdated, but a solid work in its day; excellent for data on the eighteenth and nineteenth centuries.

Dictionary of Christian Biography, Literature, Sects, and Doctrines. Edited by W. Smith and H. Wace. 4 vols. Boston: Little, Brown, 1877-87. Deals with the first eight centuries only.

A Dictionary of Christian Theology. Edited by A. Richardson. Philadelphia: Westminster, 1969.

Dictionary of Philosophy. Edited by Dagobert D. Runes. A new edition, revised and enlarged. New York: Philosophical Library, 1983.

Dictionary of Theology. By Karl Rahner and Herbert Vorgrimler. Translated by Richard Strachan. 2nd ed. New York: Crossroad, 1981.

Dictionnaire apologétique de la foi catholique contenant les preuves de la verité de la religion et les résponses aux objections tirées des sciences humaines. Edited by A. D'Ales. 4th ed. 4 vols., plus index vol. Paris: G. Beauschesne, 1928-35.

* *Dictionnaire de spiritualité, ascétique et mystique, doctrine et histoire.* Edited by Marcel Viller, et al. Paris: G. Beauchesne, 1932- .

* *Dictionnaire de théologie catholique, contenant l'exposé des doctrines et de la théologie catholique.* Edited by A. Vacant, E. Mangenot, and E. Amann. 15 vols. Paris: Librairie Letouzey et Ané, 1923-50 (hereafter cited as DTC).

Dizionario di erudizione storico-ecclesiastica da S. Pietro sino ai nostri giorni. 103 vols. Compiled by Gaetano Moroni Romano. Venice, 1840-61; index, 6 vols. Venice: Tipografia Emiliana, 1878-79.

Douglas, J. D., ed. *The New International Dictionary of the Christian Church.* Rev. ed. Grand Rapids: Zondervan, 1978. Good articles on the Evangelicals; weak bibliography.

Dupin, Louis Ellies. *Bibliothèque des auteurs écclesiastiques du dix-huitième.* 50 vols. Paris, 1698-1704. Reprint. Farnborough, UK: Greg International, 1970.

* *Encyclopaedia of Religion and Ethics.* Edited by James Hastings. 12 vols. New York: Scribners, 1908-34. Reprint. Scribners, 1961.

*The Encyclopedia of Philosophy. Edited by P. Edwards. 8 vols. New York: Macmillan, 1972.

The Encyclopedia of Religion. Edited by Mircea Eliade. 16 vols. New York: Macmillan, 1987.

Encyclopedia of Theology: The Concise Sacramentum Mundi. Edited by Karl Rahner. New York: Seabury, 1975.

Encyclopédie des sciences religieuses. Publiée sous la direction de F. Lichtenberger. 13 vols. Paris: Sandoz et Fischbacher, 1877-82.

Evangelical Dictionary of Theology. Edited by Walter A. Elwell. Grand Rapids: Baker, 1984.

Haag, Eugene, and Emile Haag. *La France Protestante.* 10 vols. Paris: J. Cherbuliez, 1846-59.

————. 2nd ed. 6 vols. (A-Gasparin only.) Paris, 1877-88. To be cited as definitive only for authors not listed in recent, critical works.

Hurter, H., ed. *Nomenclator literarius theologiae catholicae.* 3 vols. Vol. I edited by F. Pangerl, 4th ed. Vienna, 1926. Vols. I-III, 3rd ed. Oenipointe: Libraria Academica Wagneriana, 1903-13. To be cited as definitive only for thinkers not located in DTC.

*Lexikon für Theologie und Kirche. Edited by J. Hofer and K. Rahner. 10 vols., index, and supplement (3 vols.) on the Second Vatican Council. Freiburg: Herder, 1957-67.

Muller, Richard A. *Dictionary of Latin and Greek Theological Terms Drawn Principally from Protestant Scholastic Theology.* Grand Rapids: Baker Book House, 1985.

*The New Catholic Encyclopedia. Edited by William J. McDonald, et al. 15 vols. New York: McGraw-Hill, 1967. This is a massive scholarly effort, undertaken by many editors and writers — virtually the definitive work on Roman Catholicism in English.

*The New Schaff-Herzog Encyclopedia of Religious Knowledge. Edited by Samuel Macauley Jackson, et al. 12 vols. New York: Funk & Wagnalls, 1908-14.

The Oxford Dictionary of the Christian Church. Edited by F. L. Cross and A. E. Livingston. 2nd ed. London and New York: Oxford University Press, 1974.

*Realencyclopaedie für protestantische Theologie und Kirche. Edited by A. Hauck. 24 vols. 3rd ed. Leipzig: J. C. Hinrich, 1896-1913.

*Reallexikon für Antike und Christentum: Sachwörterbuch zur Auseinandersetzung des Christentums mit der antiken Welt. Edited by Franz Joseph Dolger and Hans Lietzmann. 11 vols. to date. Stuttgart: A. Hiersmann Verlags — G.M.B.H., 1950- . With Supplement, 1985.

*Die Religion in Geschichte und Gegenwart: Handwörterbuch für Theologie und Religionswissenschaft. 3rd ed. Edited by H. von Campenhausen, et al. 7 vols. Tübingen: Mohr, 1957-65.

*Sacramentum Mundi: An Encyclopedia of Theology. Edited by K. Rahner, et al. 6 vols. New York: Herder & Herder, 1968-70.

Theologische Realenzyklopaedie. Edited by Gerhard Krause and Gerhard Mueller. New York and Berlin: Walter de Gruyter, 1977. A work of massive scholarship, destined to be definitive.

Twentieth Century Encyclopedia of Religious Knowledge. Edited by Lefferts A. Loetscher. 2 vols. Grand Rapids: Baker, 1955. An extension of the New Schaff-Herzog.

Wetzer, Heinrich J., and Benedict Welte. *Kirchenlexikon oder Encyklopaedie der Katholischen Theologie.* 12 vols. Freiburg im Breisgau, 1847-60. 2nd ed. by Joseph Cardinal Hergenroether and Franz Kaulen. 13 vols. Freiburg im Breisgau: Herder, 1882-1903.

The Westminster Dictionary of Christian Theology. Edited by Alan Richardson and John S. Bowden. Philadelphia: Westminster, 1983.

F. Historical Atlases and Guides to Historical Geography

Bischoff, H. T., and J. H. Moeller. *Vergleichendes Wörterbuch der alten, mittleeren, und neuen Geographie.* Gotha, 1892.

Deschamps, Pierre. *Dictionnaire de geographie ancienne et moderne à l'usage du librairie et de l'amateur de livres.* Berlin: J. Altman, 1922. Reprint. Paris: Maisonneuve & La Rose, 1964.

Dictionnaire d'histoire et de géographie ecclésiastique. Edited by A. Baudrillart, et al. Paris: Letouzey, 1912- .

Freeman, Edward A. *Atlas to the Historical Geography of Europe.* 3rd ed. London: J. B. Bury, 1903. To be used in conjunction with the preceding study.

Freeman, Edward A. *The Historical Geography of Europe.* 2 vols. London, 1881. 3rd ed. by J. B. Bury. London, 1903.

Graesse, Johann Georg Theodor (1814-85). *Orbis latinus;* oder, Verzeichniss der lateinischen benennungen der bekanntesten städte, meere, seen, berge und flüsse in allen theilen der erde, nebst einem deutsch-lateinischen register derselben. Dresden: G. Schonfeld, 1861.

Hammond Historical Atlas: A Collection of Maps Illustrating Geographically the most Significant Periods and Events in the Development of Western Civilization. Maplewood, NJ: Hammond Incorporated, 1960. Good detail on boundaries, cities, and geographical features.

Hartmann, Karl. *Atlas-Tafel-Werk zu Bibel und Kirchengeschichte: Karten, Tabellen, Erläuterungen.* 5 vols. Stuttgart: Quell Verlag, 1979- . Superb! Unexcelled in the field for church-historical materials. (There are better Bible-atlases.)

Heussi, Karl, and Hermann Mulert. *Atlas zur Kirchengeschichte: 66 Karten auf 12 Blättern.* 3 vols. Tübingen: J. C. B. Mohr, 1937.

Himly, Auguste. *Histoire de la formation territoriale des états de l'Europe centrale.* 2 vols. 2nd ed. Paris: Hachette, 1894.

Jedin, Hubert, Kenneth Scott Latourette, and Jochen Martin, eds. *Atlas zur*

Kirchengeschichte; Die Christlichen Kirchen in Geschichte und Gegenwart. Freiburg im Breisgau: Herder, 1970.

Kinder, Hermann, and Werner Hilgemann. *The Anchor Atlas of World History.* Translated by Ernest A. Menze, with maps designed by Harald and Ruth Bukor. 2 vols. New York: Doubleday, 1974-78. Notable for its running text in which the history, primarily of the Western world, is presented in tandem with the maps. Strong in the areas of economic and political history, with considerable depth on twentieth-century warfare.

Littell, Franklin H. *The Macmillan Atlas History of Christianity.* Cartography by E. Hausman. Prepared by Carta, Jerusalem. New York: Macmillan, 1976.

McClure, E. *Historical Church Atlas.* London, 1897.

McEvedy, Colin. *The Penguin Atlas of Ancient History.* Baltimore: Penguin Books, 1967.

————. *The Penguin Atlas of Medieval History.* Baltimore: Penguin Books, 1961. Both volumes are excellent for economic history and movement of populations, but weak on geographical features, detail of boundaries, cities, etc.

Meer, Frederik van der, and Christine Mohrmann. *Atlas of the Early Christian World.* Translated and edited by Mary F. Hedlund and Harold H. Rowley. London: Thomas Nelson and Sons, 1958.

Muir, Ramsey. *Muir's Historical Atlas: Ancient, Medieval and Modern.* 10th ed. Edited by Reginald F. Treharne and Harold Fullard. New York: Barnes and Noble, 1964.

Moore, R. I., ed. *Historical Atlas of the World.* Chicago and New York: Rand McNally, 1989. Excellent, clear political maps, but hampered by the broad scope and brevity of the volume.

Oesterley, H. *Historisch-geographisches Wörterbuch des deutschen Mittelalters.* 2 vols. Gotha: J. Perthes, 1883.

Poole, R. L. *Historical Atlas of Modern Europe from the Decline of the Roman Empire.* Oxford: Clarendon Press, 1902.

Shepherd, William R. *Historical Atlas.* 9th ed. New York: Barnes and Noble, 1969.

Spruner, K. von, and T. Menke. *Handatlas für die Geschichte des Mittelalters und der neuren Zeit.* 3rd ed. Gotha, 1880.

Thompson, James M. *An Historical Geography of Europe (800-1789).* London: H. Milford, 1929.

Webster's Geographical Dictionary: A Dictionary of Names of Places with Geographical and Historical Information and Pronunciations. With maps and illustrations. Springfield, MA: G. & C. Merriam, 1988. This volume includes cross-references from non-English place names to the English forms and contains a useful series of historical maps of Europe together with maps of continents and subcontinents.

G. Guides to Archives[1]

Baier, Helmut. *Aus kirchlicher Archiv- und Verwaltungspraxis: Dokumentation der Gemeinsamen Tagung für Kirchenjuristen und Kirchenarchivare, Celle 1989.* [Veroffentlichungen der Arbeitsgemeinschaft der Archive und Bibliotheken in der Evangelischen Kirche Bd. 16] Neustadt an der Aisch: Degener, 1990.

Bar, Max. *Ubersicht über die bestande des K. Staatsarchivs zu Hannover.* Leipzig: S. Hirzel, 1900. [One of numerous volumes devoted to the archives of individual German principalities: search "Germany, Archives."]

Brogan, Martha L. *Research guide to libraries and archives in the Low Countries.* New York: Greenwood Press, ca. 1991.

Brucker, Jean Charles. *Les archives de la ville de Strasbourg anterieures a 1790.* Strassburg: J. H. E. Heitz, 1873.

Burkhardt, Carl August Hugo. *Hand- und Adressbuch der deutschen Archive: im Gebiete des Deutschen Reiches, Luxemburgs, Oesterreich-Ungarns, der russischen Ostseeprovinzen und der deutschen Schweiz.* 2 vols. Leipzig: Grunow, 1887. [Has the obvious disadvantage of having been written before the two World Wars! Still worth consulting.]

Enschede, A. J. *Inventaris van het archief der stad Haarlem.* 3 vols. Haarlem: A. C. Kruseman, 1866.

[France] Archives departementales du Bas-Rhin. *Inventaire analytique du fonds de la Chambre imperiale de Wetzlar: XVe-XVIIe siècles.* Strasbourg: Archives du Bas-Rhin, 1978.

Gardy, Frédéric. *Catalogue de la partie des archives Tronchin acquise par la Sociéte du Musée historique de la Réformation.* Geneva: A. Jullien, 1966.

German Historical Institute. *Guide to inventories and finding aids of German archives at the German Historical Institute, Washington, D.C.* Edited by Axel Frohn, with the assistance of Anne Hope. Washington, DC: The Institute, 1989.

[Germany, East] *Ubersicht über die Bestande des Deutschen Zentralarchivs Potsdam.* Ed. Helmut Lotzke and Hans Stephan Brather. Berlin: Rutten & Loening, 1957.

Kahlenberg, Friedrich P. *Deutsche Archive in West und Ost: zur Entwicklung d. staatl. Archivwesens seit 1945.* Düsseldorf: Droste, 1972.

Klein, Michael. *Die Handschriften der Staatsarchive in Baden-Wurttemberg.* Wiesbaden: O. Harrassowitz, 1987.

Largiader, Anton. *Die Papsturkunden des Staatsarchivs Zurich von Innozenz III.*

---

1. This section of the bibliography offers a very abbreviated sampling of available guides and inventories to major archives. For Modern British and American Guides, see below under III.F. and IV.G. Researchers should prepare themselves to run searches of library databases using the name of a country followed by the qualifier "archives and," for example, in the case of Germany to find well over a hundred items in a major database.

bis Martin V.; ein Beitrag zum Censimentum Helveticum. Zurich [Staatsarchiv des Kantons Zurich]: Schulthess, 1963.

Martin, Paul Edmond. *Catalogue de la collection des manuscrits historiques* [Archives d'Etat de Genève]. Genève: A. Jullien, 1936.

[Netherlands] Ministerie van Onderwijs, Kunsten en Wetenschappen. *De rijksarchieven in Nederland; overzicht van de inhoud van de Rijksarchiefbewaarplaatsen.* 's Gravenhage, 1953.

Niedersachsisches Staatsarchiv. *Findbuch zum Bestand Reichskammergericht (1515-1806).* Edited by Hans-Heinrich Ebeling. [Inventar der Akten des Reichskammergerichts, Bd. 11] 2 vols. Osnabruck: Kommissionsverlag H. Th. Wenner, 1986. [Note that these volumes are only part of a much larger series.]

Okkema, J. C. *Inventaris van de synodale archieven van de Gereformeerde Kerken in Nederland.* Kampen: Kok, 1975.

Welsch, Erwin K. *Libraries and archives in Germany.* Pittsburgh: Council for European Studies, 1975.

Zeeden, Ernst Walter. *Repertorium der Kirchenvisitationsakten aus dem 16. und 17. Jahrhundert in Archiven der Bundesrepublik Deutschland.* Stuttgart: Klett-Cotta, 1982- .

II. Church History: By Period[2]

A. Early Church

1. Guides, Manuals, and Encyclopedias

Altaner, Berthold. *Patrologie: Leben, Schriften, und Lehre der Kirchenväter.* 8th ed. Freiburg: Herder, 1978. The English translation of the 5th German ed. of 1960 is available as *Patrology.* New York: Herder and Herder, 1961.

Bengtson, Hermann. *Introduction to Ancient History.* Translated from the 6th ed. by R. I. Frank and Frank D. Gilliard. Berkeley: University of California Press, 1970.

Cayré, Fulbert. *Manual of Patrology and History of Theology.* Paris: Society of St. John the Evangelist, Desclée and Co., 1936-40. 3 vols. Bibliography: vol. 1, pp. xxxi-xxxvii. Unlike most patrologies, Cayré extends through the Middle Ages.

Chréstou, Panagiotis C. *Greek Patrology II: The Literature of the Period of Persecutions.* History of Christian Literature, 2. Thessaloniki: Patriarchical Institute for Patristic Studies, 1978.

---

2. We have refrained, for reasons of length and for fear of overemphasizing the obvious, from the inclusion of critical editions of the works of individual authors. We have, however, cited large-scale collections of works by many authors.

Encyclopedia of Early Christianity. Edited by Everett Ferguson. New York: Garland, 1990.

Encyclopedia of the Early Church. Edited by Angelo Di Berardino. Translated by Adrian Walford with bibliographical amendments by W. H. C. Frend. 2 vols. New York: Oxford University Press, 1992.

Hazlett, Ian, ed. *Early Christianity: Origins and Evolution to A.D. 600* — In Honour of W. H. C. Frend. Nashville: Abingdon, 1991. Far more than a typical *festschrift,* this book surveys current scholarship and provides guidance for further research on a wide range of topics.

The Oxford Classical Dictionary. Edited by N. G. L. Hammond and H. H. Scullard. Second ed. Oxford: Clarendon Press, 1970.

Quasten, Johannes. *Patrology.* 4 vols. Utrecht: Spectrum; Westminster, MD.: Christian Classics, 1950-86. With the fourth volume, Quasten becomes the most complete English-language patrology — an excellent bibliographical resource, to be supplemented by more recent efforts.

Paulys Real-Encyclopädie der classischen Altertumswissenschaft. New edition, ed. Georg Wissowa. 33 vols. in 49, with supplements. Stuttgart: Drückenmüller, 1894- . Frequently identified as "Pauly-Wissowa," this resource remains resource *sine qua non* in classical studies.

Reallexikon für Antike und Christentum; Sachwörterbuch zur Auseinandersetzung des Christentums mit der antiken Welt. Edited by Theodor Klauser. Stuttgart: Hiersemann, 1950- .

Tixeront, Joseph. *A Handbook of Patrology.* Translation based upon the 4th French edition. St. Louis: Herder, 1951.

Young, Frances. *From Nicea to Chalcedon: A Guide to the Literature and Its Background.* Philadelphia: Fortress, 1983.

2. Bibliographies

Bibliographia Patristica: Internationale Patristische Bibliographie. Berlin: Walter de Gruyter for the Patristische Komision der Academien der Wissenschaften in der Bundesrepublik Deutschland, vol. 1- , 1959- . This annual publication covers books, articles, and dissertations.

Halton, Thomas P., and Robert D. Sider. *A Decade of Patristic Scholarship, 1970-1979.* [*The Classical World,* col. 76, #2, 6 (1982/83)] Pittsburgh: Duquesne University Press, 1982-83. Doubly useful because its pattern of organization follows Quasten.

Metzger, Bruce Manning. *Index of Articles on the New Testament and the Early Church Published in Festschriften.* Philadelphia: Society of Biblical Literature Monograph Series, 1951.

Robinson, Thomas A., with Brent D. Shaw. *The Early Church: An Annotated Bibliography of Literature in English.* ATLA Bibliography Series, 33. Metuchen, NJ: Scarecrow Press, 1993.

Rounds, Dorothy. *Articles on Antiquity in Festschriften, An Index: The Ancient*

Near East, the Old Testament, Greece, Rome, Roman Law, Byzantium. Cambridge, MA: Harvard University Press, 1962.

Stewardson, Jerry L. *A Bibliography of Bibliographies on Patristics.* Evanston, IL: Garrett Theological Seminary Library, 1967.

3. Editions of Texts and Concordances

Benoit, André, et al. *Biblia Patristica: Index des citations et allusions Bibliques dans la littérature patristique.* 3 vols. *Supplément, Philon d'Alexandrie.* Paris: Éditions du Centre national de la recherche scientifique, 1975-87.

Cetedoc Library of Christian Latin Texts. Turnhout: Brepols. A CD-ROM project designed to encorporate the entire *Corpus Christianorum, Series Latina.*

Clavis Patrum Graecorum. Edited by Mauritius Geerard. 5 vols. Turnhout: Brepols, 1983-89. A bibliographical supplement to *Corpus Christianorum,* alphabetized by author, that lists editions and basic studies.

Corpus Christianorum: Series Graeca. Turnhout: Typographi Brepols, 1977- . The *Corpus Christianorum,* in its *Series Graeca* and *Series Latina,* is gradually superseding Migne as the best critical text of the fathers, following the conspectus of Dekkers.

Corpus Christianorum: Series Latina. Turnhout: Typographi Brepols, 1953- .

Corpus Christianorum: Thesaurus Patrum Latinorum. Turnhout: Typographi Brepols, 1992- . A computer-compiled microfiche thesaurus of the entire *Corpus,* supplemented by separate volumes devoted to Augustine, Bernard of Clairvaux, John Cassian, Gregory the Great, Jerome, and Peter Lombard's *Sentences.*

Corpus scriptorum ecclesiasticorum latinorum. Edited by the Academy of Vienna. Vienna, 1866ff. A major effort, intended to supersede Migne's *Patrologia graeca* with a modern, critical text.

The Fathers of the Church: A New Translation. Edited by R. J. Deferrari, et al. Washington, DC: CUA Press, 1947ff. 70 vols. to date.

Dekkers, Dom E. *Clavis Patrum Latinorum.* Steenbrugis: in Abbatia Sancta Petri, 1961. Published first in 1951, this remains an important guide to the manuscripts and edited texts of the fathers.

Glorieux, Palémon. *Pour Revaloriser Migne: Tables Rectificatives.* Cahier Supplémentaire aux Mélanges de Science Religieuse, 9. Lille: Facultés Catholiques, 1952. This volume should be used in conjunction with Hamman's supplement (listed under Migne) for corrections and additions to Migne.

Goodspeed, Edgar. *Index Apologeticus sive Clavis Iustini Martyris Operum Aliorumque Apologetarum Pristinorum.* Leipzig: J. C. Hinrichs Buchhandlung, 1912.

———. *Index Patristicus sive Clavis Patrum Apostolicorum Operum.* 1907. Reprinted with corrections. Naperville, IL: R. Allenson, 1960.

Die griechischen christlichen Schriftsteller der ersten drei Jahrhunderte. Edited by the Academy of Berlin. Berlin, 1897ff. This series, despite its title, reaches beyond the third century and is designed as a complement to the *Corpus scriptorum ecclesiasticorum latinorum.*

Kraft, Heinrich. *Clavis Patrum Apostolicorum.* Munich: Kösel Verlag, 1963. Supersedes Goodspeed on the Apostolic Fathers.

Lenfant, David. *Concordantiae Avgvstinianae, sive Collectio omnivm sententiarvm quae sparsim reperivntvr in omnibus S. Augustini operibus. Ad instar concordantiarvm Sacrae scriptvrae.* 2 vols. Bruxelles: Culture et Civilisation, 1965.

Migne, J. P., ed. *Patrologia Graeca Cursus Completus.* 161 vols. Paris: Vives, 1857-66. Still the exhaustive source, but superseded where more modern critical editions exist. A Latin translation accompanies the Greek text.

Patrologiae Cursus Completus accurante I.-P. Migne index locupletissimus. Edited by Theodorus Hopfner. 2 vols. Paris: Gouthier, 1928-36. A significant work, granting the absence of indices from the original *Patrologia Graeca.*

Migne, J. P., ed. *Patrologia Latina Cursus Completus.* 221 vols. Paris: Vives, 1844-55. Not the most critical text, but still the most exhaustive source, well indexed. Now available on CD-ROM.

Patrologiae Cursus Completus. Series Latina: Supplementum. Edited by Gauthier Adalbert Hamman. 4 vols. Paris: Garnier, 1958-1971. A revision of Migne organized by volume that summarizes more recent scholarship on authorship and texts.

Sources Chrétiennes: Textes, Traductions, Introductions et Notes. Paris: Editions du Cerf, 1941- . Extending to more than 160 volumes, this series of Greek and Latin texts of the fathers has French translations.

Thesaurus Linguae Graecae. Irvine: University of California. A vast resource on CD-ROM: see annotation in appendix.

B. Medieval and Renaissance

1. Surveys

The Cambridge Medieval History. 2nd ed. 9 vols. Cambridge: Cambridge University Press, 1966- .

Dictionary of the Middle Ages. 13 vols. Joseph R. Strayer, ed. New York: Scribner, 1982-89.

The New Cambridge Modern History. 14 vols. Cambridge: Cambridge University Press, 1957-79.

2. Guides, Indices, and Concordances

Boyce, Gray Cowan, comp. and ed. *Literature of Medieval History, 1930-1975: A Supplement to Louis John Paetow's "Guide to the Study of Medieval History."* 5 vols. Millwood, NY: Kraus International Publications, 1981.

Boyle, Leonard E. *A Survey of the Vatican Archives and Its Medieval Holdings.* Subsidia Mediaevalia, 1. Toronto: Pontifical Institute of Medieval Studies, 1972.

Chenu, M.-D. *Toward Understanding St. Thomas.* Trans. Albert M. Landry and Dominic Hughes. Chicago: Regnery, 1964. An excellent introduction, in the style of a patrology — with discussion of St. Thomas's milieu and works, with extensive bibliographies of texts, editions, collections, and periodicals.

Deferrari, Roy J., and M. Inviolata Barry. *A Complete Index of the "Summa Theologica" of St. Thomas Aquinas.* Baltimore: n.p., 1956. Note also Deferrari's Lexicon, above, under dictionaries.

Evans, Gillian, ed. *A Concordance to the Works of St. Anselm.* 4 vols. Millwood, NY: Kraus, 1982.

Fawtier, Robert, ed. *Les sources de l'histoire de France, des origines à la fin du XVᵉ siècle.* Vol. 1- . Paris: Editions Picard, 1971- . Will be definitive when finished; see Molinier, below.

Guide to the Sources of Medieval History. R. C. Van Caenegem, with F. L. Ganshof. Amsterdam: North-Holland Publishing Company, 1978.

Halphen, Louis, and Jean Berthold Mahn. *Initiation aux études d'historie du Moyen Age.* Paris: Presses Universitaires de France, 1940.

Index Thomisticus: Sancti Thomae Aquinatis Operum Omnium Indices et Concordantiae. . . . Vol. 1- . Stuttgart: Fromann-Holzboog, 1974- . The standard resource — will be definitive when complete in ca. 30 volumes; coordinated with the Leonine edition of St. Thomas's works.

Molinier, Auguste. *Les Sources de l'historie de France: des origines aux guerres d'Italie (1494).* 6 vols. Paris: Picard, 1900-1904. Together with the multi-volumed works of Bourgeois and Hauser (above, under Reformation) a dated but for its time exhaustive guide to French historical sources. Will be superseded by Fawtier.

North Carolina. University Library. Humanities Division. *Medieval and Renaissance Studies: A Location Guide to Selected Reference Works and Source Collections in the Libraries of the University of North Carolina at Chapel Hill and Duke University.* Chapel Hill, 1967.

Paetow, Louis J. *A Guide to the Study of Medieval History.* New York: F. S. Crofts, 1931.

Potthast, August. *Bibliotheca historica medii aevi. Wegweiser durch die geschichtswerke des europaischen mittelalters bis 1500.* 2 vols. Graz: Akademische druch-u. Verlagsanstalt, 1954. Also note the *Repertorium fontium historiae Medii Aevi.* Rome: Istituto storico italiano per il Medio Evo, 1962, based on Potthast.

Powell, James M., ed. *Medieval Studies: An Introduction.* 2nd ed. Syracuse: Syracuse University Press, 1992.

3. Periodical Guides

International Guide to Medieval Studies; A Quarterly Index to Periodical Litera-
ture. Darien, CT: American Bibliographic Service, 1961- . Alphabetical
author listing.
International Medieval Bibliography. Minneapolis, and Leeds, England, by the
University of Leeds, 1967- . Published semiannually, this superb reference work includes articles, collections of essays, and essays in *festschrif-*
ten, but not books.

4. Bibliographies

Altschul, Michael. *Anglo-Norman England, 1066-1154.* Conference on British
Studies Bibliographical Handbooks. Cambridge: Cambridge University
Press, 1969.
Bak, Janos H., Heinz Quirin, and Paul Hollingsworth. *Medieval Narrative*
Sources: A Chronological Guide: With a List of Major Letter Collections.
New York: Garland, 1987.
Berkhout, Carl T., and Jeffrey B. Russell. *Mediaeval Heresies: A Bibliography,*
1960-1979. Toronto: Pontifical Institute of Medieval Studies, 1981.
Bibliographie Internationale de l'Humanisme et de la Renaissance. Geneve,
1965- .
Bibliothèque d'Humanisme et Renaissance. 1941 to date.
Bulletin de théologie ancienne et médiévale. Louvain, 1929- .
Chevalier, Ulysse. *Répertoire des Sources Historiques du Moyen Age; I, Bio-*
bibliographie. New ed. 2 vols. Paris: A. Picard, 1905-7.
Chevalier, Ulysse. *Répertoire des Sources Historiques du Moyen Age; II, Topo-*
bibliographie. Paris: A. Picard, 1884-99.
Cosenza, M. *Biographical and Bibliographical Dictionary of the Italian*
Humanists and of the World of Classical Scholarship in Italy, 1300-1800. 6
vols. Boston: Hall, 1962-67.
Cottineau, L. *Repertoire Topo-bibliographique des Abbayes et Prieures.* Macon:
Protat Brothers, 1935-70.
Dahlman, Friedrich Christoph, and George Waitz. *Quellenkunde der Deutschen*
Geschichte. Berlin: Walter de Gruyter, 1959-61. 10 vols. First published,
1830.
Fabricius, Johann A. *Bibliotheca Latina Mediae et Infimae Aetatis.* Edited by
J. D. Mansi. 6 vols. Florence, 1858-59.
Farrar, Clarissa Palmer, and Austin Patterson Evans. *Bibliography of English*
Translations from Medieval Sources. Records of Civilization: Sources and
Studies, no. 39. New York: Columbia University Press, 1946. Gives full
bibliographical details on nearly 4,000 translations of medieval docu-
ments. Extremely valuable for teachers.
Ferguson, Mary Anne. *Bibliography of English Translations from Medieval*

Sources, 1943-1967. Records of Civilization: Sources and Studies, no. 88. New York: Columbia University Press, 1974. Brings Farrar and Evans up to date.

Ghellinck, Joseph de. *L'Essor de la Litterature Latine au XIIe Siècle.* 2 vols. 2nd ed. Brussels: Desclée, De Brower, 1955.

Glorieux, Palémon. *Répertoire des maîtres en théologie de Paris au XIIIe siècle.* 2 vols. Paris: Vrin, 1933-34. A significant survey of thirteenth-century theologians, listing works, editions, and locations of manuscripts.

Graves, Edgar B. *A Bibliography of English History to 1485: Based on "The Sources and Literature of English History from the Earliest Times to about 1485," by Charles Gross.* Oxford: Clarendon Press, 1975.

Guth, DeLloyd J. *Late Medieval England, 1377-1485.* Conference on British Studies Bibliographical Handbook. Cambridge: Cambridge University Press, 1976.

Kingsford, Charles L. *English Historical Literature in the Fifteenth Century.* Oxford, 1913.

Kohl, Benjamin G. *Renaissance Humanism: A Bibliography of Materials in English.* New York: Garland Publishers, 1985.

Kristeller, Paul O., and Cranz F. Eduard. *Catalogus Translationum et Commentatorium: Medieval and Renaissance Translations, Commentaries, Annotated Lists and Guides.* Washington, DC: Catholic University of America Press, 1960- .

La Serna Santander, Charles Antoine de. *Dictionnaire bibliographique choisi du quinzieme siècle, ou Description par ordre alphabetique des editions les plus rares et les plus recherchees du quinzieme siècle.* 3 vols. Bruxelles: J. Tarte, 1805-07.

Manitius, Max. *Geschichte der Lateinischen Literatur des Mittelalters.* 3 vols. Munich: Beck, 1911-33.

Margolin, Jean-Claude. *Douze Années, de Bibliographie Érasmienne (1950-61).* Paris: J. Vrin, 1963.

Medieval Studies: A Bibliographical Guide. Everett U. Crosby, C. Julian Bishko, and Robert L. Kellogg. New York: Garland, 1983.

Renaudet, Augustin. *Préréforme et Humanisme à Paris Pendant les Premières Guerres d'Italie, 1494-1517.* 2nd ed., rév. Paris: Librairie d'Argences, 1953. Bibliographie: xix-lxiv.

Répertoire International des Medievistes. Poitiers: Université de Poitiers, 1951/52- .

Rouse, Richard H., et al. *Serial Bibliographies for Medieval Studies.* Berkeley: University of California Press, 1969.

Stegmüller, Friedrich. *Repertorium Biblicum Medii Aevi.* 7 vols. Matriti: Institute Francisco Suarez, 1940-51.

Stegmüller, Friedrich. *Repertorium Commentariorum in Sententias Petri Lombardi.* 2 vols. Würzburg: F. Schöningh, 1947.

Wilkinson, Bertie. *The High Middle Ages in England, 1154-1377.* Conference

on British Studies Bibliographical Handbook. Cambridge: Cambridge
University Press, 1978.

Williams, Harry Franklin. *An Index of Medieval Studies Published in Festschrif-*
ten, 1865-1946, with Special Reference to Romanic Material. Berkeley:
University of California Press, 1951.

5. Editions and Series of Texts and Translations

[N.B. given the vast number of editions and series the following represents
only a sampling: the researcher should consult the specialized guides of Paetow
and Boyce, cited above, section 2.]

Beiträge zur Geschichte der Philosophie des Mittelalters. Münster, 1891ff. A significant series of texts and studies.

Cistercian Fathers Series. Kalamazoo, MI: Cistercian Publications.

The Classics of Western Spirituality: A Library of the Great Spiritual Masters.
Ramsay, NJ: Paulist Press, 1978ff. A series of translations, extending from
the patristic to the modern period, with fine introductions, quite significant for its presentation of many previously untranslated works of medieval spirituality.

Corpus Christianorum: Continuatio Medievalis. Turnhout: Typographi Brepols,
1953- .

The Fathers of the Church, Mediaeval Continuation. Edited by R. J. Deferrari,
et al. Washington, DC: CUA Press, 1989ff.

Migne, J.-P., ed. *Patrologia Latina Cursus Completus.* 221 vols. Paris: Vives,
1844-55. Includes medieval authors as far as A.D. 1216: still the most
exhaustive collection.

Monumenta Germaniae Historica (500-1500). Ed. G. H. Perta, T. Mommsen, et
al. Berlin, 1826ff. [N.B. the *Monumenta* appeared in two distinct series,
one bound in folio, the other in quarto.]

Regesta pontificum Romanorum. Ed. P. F. Kehr. 7 vols. Berlin, 1926-25.

Regesta pontificum Romanorum, inde ab anno post Christum natum 1198 as
annum 1304. Ed. A. Potthast. 2 vols. Berlin, 1874-75.

Rerum Brittanicarum medii aevi scriptores: or, Chronicles and memorials of Great
Britain and Ireland during the Middle Ages. 244 vols. London, 1858-96.

Rolls Series. See: *Rerum Brittanicarum medii aevi scriptores.*

Sacrorum conciliorum nova et amplissima collectio. Ed. J. D. Mansi, et al. 31 vols.
Florence, 1759-98; new edition, with continuation [vols. 32-53]. Paris,
1901ff.

Société de l'histoire de France. Publications. Paris, 1835ff. Original sources;
exceeds 250 vols.

Sources Chrétiennes: Textes, Traductions, Introductions et Notes. Paris: Editions
du Cerf, 1941-.

6. Studies in Series

American Philosophical Society. *Monograph Series.*
Cistercian Studies Series. Kalamazoo, MI: Cistercian Publications.
Classified Index to the Publications of the American Philosophical Society: A list of Papers, Monographs, Treatises and Books Published by the Society, 1769-1940, Classified According to Subject. Philadelphia, 1940.
London. Warburg Institute. *Mediaeval and Renaissance Studies.* 1944/45- .
Mediaeval Academy of America. *Publications.*
New York (State). State University at Binghamton. Center for Medieval and Early Renaissance Studies. *Monograph Series.*
Renaissance Society of America. *Studies in the Renaissance.* 1954-74; *absorbed by Renaissance Quarterly.*
Southeastern Institute of Medieval and Renaissance Studies. *Medieval and Renaissance Series.* Chapel Hill: University of North Carolina Press, 1966- .
Toronto. Pontifical Institute of Medieval Studies. *Medieval Studies.* 1939- .
Traditio: Studies in Ancient and Medieval History, Thought and Religion. 1943- .
University of California at Los Angeles. Center for Medieval and Renaissance Studies. *Monograph Series.*
University of Nebraska. *Studies in Medieval and Renaissance History.* 1964-73.

C. Reformation and Post-Reformation Europe

1. Bibliographies and General Surveys

Allison, Antony F., D. M. Rogers, and W. Lottes. *The Contemporary Printed Literature of the English Counter-Reformation between 1558 and 1640: An Annotated Catalogue.* Aldershot, UK: Scholar Press; Brookfield, VT: Gower, 1989- . One of several projected volumes currently available.
Archiv für Reformationsgeschichte, Beiheft: Literaturbericht/Archive for Reformation History. Supplement: Literature Review. St. Louis, MO: American Society for Reformation Research; Gütersloh: Gutersloher Verlagshaus Gerd Mohn, 1972- . Annual annotated index to articles, books, and dissertations.
Bainton, Roland H. *Bibliography of the Continental Reformation: Materials Available in English.* Chicago: The American Society of Church History, 1935. 2nd ed., rev., enlarged by Bainton and Eric W. Gritsch. Hamden, CT: Archon Books, 1972.
Baker, Derek, ed. *The Bibliography of the Reform, 1450-1648, Relating to the United Kingdom and Ireland for the Years 1955-1970.* Oxford: Blackwell, 1975.
Benzing, Josef. *Lutherbibliographie; Verzeichnis der Gedruckten Schriften Martin Luthers bis zu dessen Tod.* Baden-Baden: Heitz, 1966.

Boehmer, Eduard. *Bibliotheca Wiffeniana. Spanish Reformers of the Two Centuries from 1520. Their Lives and Writings, According to the Late Benjamin B. Wiffen's Plan and with the Use of His Materials.* 3 vols. 1874-1904. Reprint. New York: Burt Franklin, 1962.

Bourgeois, Émile, and Louis André. *Les Sources de l'histoire de France: XVIIe siècle (1610-1715).* 4 vols. Paris: Picard, 1913-24. With the other works in the series (Hauser and Molinier), a superb tool.

Bourilly, E., et al. *Calvin et la Réforme en France.* 2nd ed., rev. Aix-en-Provence: Librairie Dragen, 1974. "Bibliographie Calvinienne abrégée," 137-64.

Calvin Theological Journal. No. 2 of each year contains the annual "Calvin Bibliography."

Cameron, Euan. *The European Reformation.* Oxford: Clarendon Press, 1991. Contains a useful, up-to-date bibliography of bibliographies, collections, and histories.

Catalogue général des livres imprimés de la Bibliothèque Nationale. 231 vols. Paris: Imprimé Vie Nationale, 1897-1981.

―――. idem. *Supplément, 1960-1964.* Paris Bibliothèque Nationale, 1964-67.

Catalogue of Books Printed on the Continent of Europe, 1501-1600, in Cambridge Libraries. Compiled by Herbert M. Adams. 2 vols. Cambridge: Cambridge University Press, 1967.

Catalogus librorum impressorum Bibliothecae Bodelianae in Academia Oxoniensi. 4 vols. Oxford, 1843-51.

Chambers, Bettye T. *Bibliography of French Bibles: Fifteenth- and Sixteenth-Century French-Language Editions of the Scriptures.* Geneva: Droz, 1983.

Chrisman, Miriam Usher. *Bibliography of Strasbourg Imprints, 1489-1599.* New Haven: Yale University Press, 1982.

Commission internationale d'histoire écclésiastique comparée. *Bibliographie de la Réforme, 1450-1648; ouvrages parus de 1940 à 1955.* 8 vols. to date.

Dagens, Jean. *Bibliographie Chronologique de la Littérature de Spiritualité et de Ses Sources (1501-1610).* Paris: Desclée de Brouwer, 1952.

Dickens, A. G. *The English Reformation.* New York: Schocken Books, 1965. Bibliography: pp. 341-63.

Dickens, A. G., and John M. Tonkin, with Kenneth Powell. *The Reformation in Historical Thought.* Cambridge: Harvard University Press, 1985.

Dickerson, G. Fay, ed. *Luther and Lutheranism: A Bibliography Selected from ATLA Religion Database.* Chicago: ATLA Religion Indexes, 1982.

Donnelly, John Patrick, S.S., with Robert M. Kingdon. *A Bibliography of the Works of Peter Martyr Vermigli,* With a Register of Vermigli's Correspondence by Marrin W. Anderson. Sixteenth Century Essays and Studies XIII. Kirksville, MO: Sixteenth Century Journal Publishers, 1990.

Eder, Karl. *Die Geschichte der Kirche im Zeitalter des Konfessionellen Absolutimus (1555-1648).* Wien: Herder, 1949. Bibliography: pp. 371-436.

Erichson, Alfred. *Bibliographia Calviniana; Catalogus Chronologicus Operum Calvini.* 1900. Reprint. Nieuwkoop: B. De Graaf, 1965.

Eys, Willem J. van. *Bibliographie des Bibles et des Nouveaux Testaments en langue française des XVe et XVIe siècles.* 2 vols in 1. Nieuwkoop: De Graaf, 1963.

Geisendorf, Paul-F. *Bibliographic Raisonné de l'Histoire de Genève des Origines a 1798.* Memoires et documents de la Société d'histoire et d'archéologie de Genève XLIII. Geneva: Alex. Jullien, 1966.

Goeze, Johann Melchior. *Versuch einer Historie der gedruckten Niedersachsischen Biblen vom Jahr 1470 bis 1621.* Hildesheim: Olms, 1976.

Graesse, Jean Georg Theodor. *Trésor de livres rares et précieux ou, nouveau dictionnaire bibliographique.* 7 vols. Dresden, Geneva, London, Paris: B. Kuntz, 1859-69.

Hagen, Kenneth, and Franz Possett. *Annotated Bibliography of Luther Studies, 1977-1983.* Sixteenth Century Bibliography, 24. St. Louis: Center for Reformation Research, 1985.

Hammer, Wilhelm. *Die Melanchthonforschung im Wandel der Jahrhunderte.* 3 vols. Gütersloh: Gerd Mohn, 1967-81. Vol. 1: 1519-1799; vol. 2: 1800-1965; vol. 3: addenda and corrections, 1519-1970.

Hauser, Henri. *Les Sources de l'histoire de France: XVIe siècle (1494-1610).* 4 vols. Paris: Picard, 1906-15.

Herbert, Arthur Sumner, et al. *Historical Catalogue of Printed Editions of the English Bible: 1525-1961.* London: British & Foreign Bible Society; New York: American Bible Society, 1968.

Hillerbrand, Hans J. *A Bibliography of Anabaptism, 1520-1630.* St. Louis: Center for Reformation Research, 1975.

International Committee of Historical Sciences. *Bibliographie de la Réforme, 1450-1648; Ouvrages parus de 1940 á 1955.* 2nd ed. Leiden: E. J. Brill, 1958- .

Kempff, D. *A Bibliography of Calviniana, 1959-1974.* Leiden: E. J. Brill, 1975. A useful one-volume work covering a period after Niesel, but not as exhaustive as the yearly bibliographies in *Calvin Theological Journal.*

Kuczynski, Arnold. *Thesaurus libellorum historiam reformationis illustrantium. Verzeichniss einer Sammlung von nahezu 3000 Flugschriften Luthers und seiner Zeitgenossen.* Leipzig: T. O. Weogel, 1870.

Lutheran Research Since 1945. Lutheran World, XIII, 3 (1966). Entire issue.

Lutherjahrbuch: Organ der Internationalen Lutherforschung. Vol. 1- . Göttingen: Vandenhoeck und Ruprecht, 1919- ; annual. Titles of books, articles, and theses other than those in German or English are translated.

Lauchert, Friedrich. *Die Italienischen Literarischen Gegner Luthers.* Reprint. Nieuwkoop: DeGraaf, 1972.

Lortz, Joseph. *The Reformation in Germany.* London: Longman and Todd; New York: Herder and Herder, 1968. 2 vols. Bibliography: vol. 2, pp. 362-94.

McConica, James K. *English Humanists and Reformation Politics under Henry VIII and Edward VI.* Oxford: Clarendon Press, 1968. Bibliography: pp. 295-308. Index of 16th Century Books by English Humanists, pp. 308-19.

McKim, Donald K., ed. *Encyclopedia of the Reformed Faith.* Louisville: Westminster, John Knox, 1992.

Manning, Roger B. *Religion and Society in Elizabethan Sussex: A Study of the Enforcement of the Religious Settlement, 1558-1603.* Leicester, UK: Leicester University Press, 1969. Bibliography: 282-301.

Niesel, Wilhelm. *Calvin-Bibliographie, 1901-1959.* Munich: C. Kaiser, 1961.

Ozment, Stephen, ed. *Reformation Europe: A Guide to Research.* St. Louis: Center for Reformation Research, 1982.

Pegg, Michael A. *A Catalogue of German Reformation Pamphlets (1516-1546) in the Libraries of Great Britain and Ireland.* Baden-Baden: V. Koerner, 1973.

Peter, Rodolphe, and Jean-François Gilmont. *Bibliotheca Calviniana: Les oeuvres de Jean Calvin publiées an XVIᵉ siècle. I: Écrits théologiques, littéraires et juridiques, 1532-1554.* Travaux d'Humanisme et Renaissance, CCLV. Geneva: Droz, 1991.

Pipkin, H. Wayne. *A Zwingli Bibliography.* Pittsburgh: Pickwick Press, 1972.

Ragatz, Lowell, J. *A Bibliography for the Study of European History, 1815-1939.* Ann Arbor, MI: Edwards Brothers, 1942. Supplements, 1943- .

Roach, John, ed. *A Bibliography of Modern History.* London: Cambridge University Press, 1968. A bibliographical supplement to the *New Cambridge Modern History* representing the work of 170 scholars.

Ruchat, Abraham, and Louis Vulliemin. *Histoire de la reformation de la Suisse.* 7 vols. Lausaunne: Ducloux, 1835-38.

Scholars of Early Modern Studies. Kirksville, MO: Sixteenth Century Journal Publishers. Formerly *Historians of Early Modern Europe, SEMS* offers a worldwide listing by country of scholars, giving addresses, information on research, and select publications, plus a listing of doctoral candidates, dissertations, and advisors.

Schottenloher, Karl. *Bibliographie zur Deutschen Geschichte im Zeitalter der Glaubensspaltung, 1517-1558.* 2nd ed. 7 vols. Stuttgart: A. Hiersemann, 1956-66.

Skarsten, Trygve R. *The Scandinavian Reformation: A Bibliographical Guide.* Sixteenth Century Bibliography, 25. St. Louis: Center for Reformation Research, 1985.

Smeeton, Donald D. *English Religion, 1500-1540: A Bibliography.* Macon, GA: Mercer University Press, 1988.

Les Sources de l'histoire de France. See: Bourgeois; Molinier; and Hauser, this section.

Staehelin, Ernst. *Oekolampad-Bibliographie.* 2nd ed. Nieuwkoop: De Graaf, 1963.

Tedeschi, John A. *The Literature of the Italian Reformation: An Exhibition Catalogue.* Chicago: The Newberry Library, 1971.

Van der Walt, B. J. *Contemporary Research on the Sixteenth Century Reformation.* Potchefstroom, South Africa: Potchefstroomse University, 1979. A brief but useful survey of research centers, institutes, and societies worldwide.

Williams, George Huntston. *The Polish Brethren: Documentation of the History and Thought of Unitarianism in the Polish-Lithuanian Commonwealth and in the Diaspora 1601-1685.* 2 vols. Missoula, MT: Scholars Press, 1980.

Williams, George Huntston. *The Radical Reformation.* 3rd ed., rev. and expanded. Kirksville, MO: Sixteenth Century Journal Publishers, 1992.

Wolf, Gustav. *Quellenkunde der deutschen Reformationsgeschichte.* 3 vols. in 2. 1914-16. Reprint. Nieuwkoop: De Graaf, 1965. Old, but still significant analysis of literature on the later Middle Ages and Reformation.

2. Collections of Sources

Archiv für die schweizerische Reformations-Geschichte. 3 vols. Freiburg im Breisgau: Herder, 1869-75. Note that this and other similar local and national archives, *Aktensammlungen,* etc. are only representative samples: researchers should consult databases under such headings as "Reformation — Switzerland — Sources" or "Reformation — Germany — Sources."

The Center for Reformation Research Microform Holdings. 8 vols. St. Louis, 1977-79. See annotation in Appendix under IV. B.

Corpus Catholicorum. Werke catholischer Schriftsteller im Zeitalter der Glaubensspaltung. Münster: Aschendorff, 1919- . Includes works by many of the important sixteenth-century Catholic authors, such as Eck, Cochlaeus, and Cajetan.

Corpus Reformatorum. Edited by Karl G. Bretschneider, et al. 101 vols. Halle, Berlin, Leipzig, and Zurich, 1834-1962. Includes the complete works of Melanchthon (vols. 1-28), Calvin (vols. 29-87), and Zwingli (vols. 88-101).

Durr, Emil. *Aktensammlung zur Geschichte der Basler Reformation in den Jahren 1519 bis Anfang 1534. Im Auftrage der Historischen und antiquarischen Gesellschaft zu Basel.* 6 vols. Basel: Verlag der Historischen und antiquarischen Gesellschaft, 1921-50.

Early English Books I, 1475-1640 and *Early English Books II, 1641-1700* are microfilm collections selected from the short title catalogs of Pollard and Redgrave, and Wing, published by University Microfilms International. See annotations under III.C. below and the Appendix.

Early Printed Bibles: Printed Bibles and Bible Translations in the 15th and 16th Centuries and Philological Tools on Microfiche. Ed. Fritz Büsser. Leiden: IDC Microform Publishers. See annotation in the Appendix under Inter Documentation Company.

Egli, Emil. *Aktensammlung zur Geschichte der Zurcher Reformation in den Jahren 1519-1533.* Zurich, 1879; repr. Nieuwkoop: De Graaf, 1973.

Fatio, Olivier. *Registres de la Compagnie des pasteurs de Genève.* Genève: Droz, 1962- .

Franz, G., ed. *Quellen zur Geschichte des Baurenkrieges.* Munich, 1963.

Kidd, B. J. *Documents Illustrative of the Continental Reformation.* Oxford: Clarendon Press, 1911.

The Lutheran Reformation: Sources, 1500-1650 on Microfiche. Edited by W. S. Maltby. Leiden: IDC Microform Publishers. Approximately 1750 titles are projected for the series. See annotation in the Appendix under Inter Documentation Company.

D. Martin Luthers Werke. Kritische Gesamtausgabe. Weimar: H. Böhlau, 1883-1987.

Monumenta Reformationis Lutheranae ex tabulariis secretioribus S. Sedis, 1521-1525. Edited by Petrus Balan. Regensburg: Pustet, 1884.

Pahl, Irmgard. *Coena Domini, I: Die Abendmahlsliturgie der Reformationskirchen im 16./17. Jahrhundert.* Freiburg: Universitätsverlag, 1983.

Reformed Protestantism: Sources of the 16th and 17th Centuries on Microfiche. I.A. *Heinrich Bullinger and the Zurich Reformation;* I.B. *Geneva;* 2.A. *Strasbourg;* 2.B. *France;* 3. *The Netherlands and Germany.* Leiden: IDC Microform Publishers. See annotation in the Appendix under Inter Documentation Company.

Reu, Johann Michael. *Quellen zur Geschichte des kirchlichen Unterrichts in der evangelischen Kirche Deutschlands zwischen 1530 und 1600.* 4 vols. in 9. Gütersloh, 1904-1935; repr. Hildesheim, New York: G. Olms, 1976.

Scherer-Boccard, Theodor, et al. *Archiv für die schweizerische Reformations-Geschichte.* 3 vols. in 4. Amsterdam: John Benjamins, 1972.

Sehling, Emil. *Die evangelischen Kirchenordnungen des XVI. Jahrhunderts.* 8 vols. to date. Leipzig: O. R. Reisland/Tübingen: Mohr, 1902- .

Sixteenth Century Pamphlets in German and Latin. Edited by Hans-Joachim Köhler. Part 1: 1501-30; Part 2: 1531-1600. Leiden: IDC Microform Publishers, 1978- . A major series of pamphlets reflecting political, social, and religious conflict. At its completion, the series will contain nearly 10,000 pamphlets.

Strickler, Johannes. *Actensammlung zur schweizerischen Reformationsgeschichte in den Jahren 1521-1532: im Anschluss an die gleichzeitigen eidgenossischen Abschiede.* 5 vols. Zurich: Theologische Buchhandlung, 1989.

Urkundliche Quellen zur hessischen Reformationsgeschichte. 4 vols. Marburg: Elwert, 1951-57.

III. MODERN BRITISH SOURCES

A. Bibliographical Guides and Handbooks

Altholz, Josef L. *Victorian England, 1837-1901.* Conference on British Studies Bibliographical Handbooks. Cambridge: Cambridge University Press, 1970. All of the publications in this useful series include the most important books, articles, and editions of texts.

Annual Bibliography of British and Irish History. Brighton: Royal Historical

Society, 1975- . Covers books, articles, edited works, and reference materials, categorized by period and topic.

Annual Bibliography of English Language and Literature. 1920 to date. Cumulated through 1969.

Annual Bulletin of Historical Literature. London: Historical Association, 1910- . Unlike the *Annual Bibliography,* the *Bulletin* is not comprehensive with respect to Britain, but though selective, it is attentive to trends in historiography, particularly in Britain, and it covers other nations as well.

Brown, Lucy M., and Ian R. Christie. *Bibliography of British History, 1789-1851.* Oxford: Clarendon Press, 1977.

Davies, Godfrey. *Bibliography of British History, Stuart Period, 1603-1714.* Oxford: The Clarendon Press, 1928. 2nd ed., edited by Mary Frear Keeler, 1970. Issued under the Direction of the American Historical Association and the Royal Historical Society of Great Britain.

Grose, Clyde L. *A Select Bibliography of British History, 1660-1760.* Chicago: University of Chicago Press, 1939.

Hadidian, Dikran Y., comp. *Bibliography of British Theological Literature, 1850-1940.* Bibliographia tripotamopolitana, no. 12. Pittsburgh: Pittsburgh Theological Seminary, 1985.

Handbook of British Chronology. 3d ed. E. B. Fryde, et al. London: Royal Historical Society, 1986. The focus of this book is on officeholders, both secular and ecclesiastical.

Handbook of Dates for Students of English History. Edited by C. R. Cheney. London: Royal Historical Society, 1945.

Hanham, H. J. *Bibliography of British History, 1851-1914.* Oxford: Clarendon Press, 1976.

Lancaster, Joan C. *Bibliography of Historical Works Issued in the United Kingdom, 1946-1956.* London: University of London, Institute of Historical Research, 1957.

Levine, Mortimer. *Tudor England, 1485-1603.* Conference on British Studies Bibliographical Handbooks. Cambridge: Cambridge University Press, 1968. Surveys literature through 1966.

Macgregor, Malcolm Blair. *The Sources and Literature of Scottish Church History.* Glasgow: J. McCallum and Co., 1934.

Morgan, William Thomas. *A Bibliography of British History (1700-1715) with Special Reference to the Reign of Queen Anne.* Indiana University Studies, vols. XVIII-XIX, XXIII-XXVI; studies no. 94-95, 114-24. Bloomington, Ind., 1934-42.

Pargellis, Stanley M., and D. J. Medley. *Bibliography of British History: The Eighteenth Century, 1714-1789.* Oxford: The Clarendon Press, 1951.

Read, Conyers. *Bibliography of British History, Tudor Period, 1485-1603.* 2nd ed. Oxford: Clarendon Press, 1959.

Sachse, William L. *Restoration England, 1660-1689.* Conference on British Studies Bibliographical Handbook. Cambridge: Cambridge University Press, 1971.

Smith, Robert A. *Late Georgian and Regency England, 1760-1837.* Conference on British Studies Bibliographical Handbook. Cambridge: Cambridge University Press, 1984.

Writings on British History, 1901-1933. 5 vols. in 7. London: Royal Historical Society, 1968-70.

Writings on British History. London: Royal Historical Society, 1937- . Irregular. This series is comprehensive and international; with some lapses, it continues the thorough treatment of the series for 1901-33, but because of the bulk of material and its failure to remain current, it will be discontinued with the volume for 1974. For British history, students should turn to the *Annual Bibliography of British and Irish History.*

B. Periodicals and Newspapers: Guides and Indexes

Altholz, Josef L. *The Religious Press in Britain, 1760-1900.* Contributions to the Study of Religion, 22. New York: Greenwood Press, 1989.

Houghton, Walter E., ed. *The Wellesley Index to Victorian Periodicals, 1824-1900.* Toronto: University of Toronto Press, 1966-89.

Linton, David, and Ray Boston. *The Newspaper Press in Britain: An Annotated Bibliography.* London and New York: Mansell Publishing, 1987.

Nelson, Carolyn W., and Matthew Seccombe. *British Newspapers and Periodicals, 1641-1700: A Short-Title Catalogue of Serials Printed in England, Scotland, Ireland, and British America.* New York: Modern Language Association, 1988.

Palmer's Index to the Times Newspaper. Subsequently, *The Times Index.* 1790 to date.

Woodworth, David, comp. *Guide to Current British Journals.* London: British Library, 1970.

C. National Bibliography and Guides to Sources

Averley, G., et al. *Eighteenth-Century British Books: A Subject Catalogue Extracted from the British Museum General Catalogue of Printed Books.* 4 vols. Folkestone, UK: Dawson, 1979. Volume 1 deals with philosophy and religion.

British Library. *The Eighteenth Century Short Title Catalogue: The British Library Collections.* Editor, R. C. Alston; assistant editor, M. J. Crump. London: The British Library, 1983.

The British Library General Catalogue of Printed Books to 1975. London: Bingley; London: K. G. Saur, 1980-87. 360 vols. Many libraries will have the older edition, entitled *British Museum General Catalog of Printed Books to 1955,* that runs to 263 vols. Supplements and microfiche of the earlier edition bring the catalog up to 1986.

Dr. Williams's Library, London, Catalogue of Asccessions. 2 vols. London: Dr. Williams's Trust, 1955-61. Accessions 1900-50 and 1951-60. Updated annually by *Bulletin of Dr. Williams's Library.*

Early Nonconformity, 1566-1800: A Catalogue of Books in Dr. Williams's Library, London. 12 vols. Boston, MA: G. K. Hall, 1968.

The Eighteenth-Century Short Title Catalog. The North American branch of this ongoing project is now located at the University of California Riverside, under the direction of Henry L. Snyder. Computer searches can now be done through RLIN or through CD-ROM. As of mid-1990, all the North American imprints are on-line. Microfilm of many of the works in this catalog are available through Primary Source Media's *The Eighteenth Century* project (see Appendix).

Gillett, Charles Ripley, comp. and ed. *Catalogue of the McAlpin Collection of British History and Theology.* 5 vols. New York: Union Theological Seminary, 1927-30. Approximately 15,000 entries covering the period 1500-1700. The supplement, which adds about 3,000 titles, is entitled *Catalog of the McAlpin Collection of British History and Theology; Acquisitions, 1924-1978.* New York: G. K. Hall, 1979.

Kanner, Barbara. *Women in English Social History, 1800-1914: A Guide to Research.* 2 vols. New York: Garland Publishing Co., 1990.

Mead, Herman Ralph. *Incunabula in the Huntington Library.* San Marino: The Huntington Library, 1937. Books printed in the 15th century.

Nineteenth-Century Short Title Catalogue. Series I, 1801-15, 6 vols.; Series II, 1816-70, 7 vols. to date. Newcastle upon Tyne, UK: Avero Publications Ltd., 1984- . The period covered by the first series (1801-15) listed as many titles as the total for the eighteenth century. This project draws only upon catalogs of the British deposit libraries, and many novels (and other ephemera as well) were not retained by the copyright libraries. See Appendix for Chadwyck-Healey's project to microfilm specified subject areas of titles in the catalog.

Pollard, Alfred W., and Gilbert R. Redgrave. *A Short Title Catalogue of Books Printed in England, Scotland, and Ireland and of English Books Printed Abroad, 1475-1640.* London: The Bibliographical Society, 1926. 2 vols. 2nd ed., revised and enlarged by W. A. Jackson, F. S. Ferguson, and Katherine F. Pantzer. London: The Bibliographical Society, 1976, 1986. Almost all of the works listed in Pollard and Redgrave are available on microfilm in *Early English Books I, 1475-1640,* published by University Microfilms International (see Appendix).

Rider, Philip R. *A Chronological Index to the Revised Edition of the Pollard and Redgrave Short-Title Catalogue.* London: Bibliographical Survey, 1978.

Robinson, F. J. G., et al. *Eighteenth-Century British Books: An Author Union*

Catalog: Extracted from the British Museum General Catalog of Printed Books, the Catalogue of the Bodleian Library, and of the University Library, Cambridge. 5 vols. Folkestone, UK: Dawson, for the University of Newcastle upon Tyne, 1981.

Robinson, F. J. G., et al. *Eighteenth Century British Books: An Index to the Foreign and Provincial Imprints in the Author Union Catalog.* Newcastle upon Tyne: Avero Publications Ltd., 1982.

Smith, Hilda L., and Susan Cardinale. *Women and the Literature of the Seventeenth Century: An Annotated Bibliography based on Wing's Short Title Catalogue.* Bibliographies and Indexes in Women's Studies, 10. New York: Greenwood Press, 1990.

Wing, Donald. *Short-Title Catalogue of Books Printed in England, Scotland, Ireland, Wales and British America and of English Books Printed in Other Countries, 1641-1700.* 6 vols. New York: The Index Society, 1945. The second edition, revised and enlarged, appeared in 3 vols. New York: The Modern Language Association, 1972-88. Many of the works in Wing are available on microfilm through the collection entitled *Early English Books II, 1641-1700,* published by University Microfilms International (see Appendix).

D. Biographical Dictionaries

Allibone, Samuel Austin. *A Critical Dictionary of English Literature and British and American Authors.* Philadelphia: J. B. Lippincott, 1891. 3 vols. with 2 supplements.

Boase, Frederic. *Modern English Bibliography.* 6 vols. London: Netherton and Worth, 1892-1914.

Dictionary of National Biography. 24 vols. with supplements.

E. Atlases and Dictionaries

Currie, Robert, Alan Gilbert, and Lee Horsley. *Churches and Churchgoers: Patterns of Church Growth in the British Isles since 1700.* Oxford: Clarendon Press, 1977.

Gay, John D. *The Geography of Religion in England.* London: Gerald Duckworth, 1971.

Gilbert, Martin, with cartography by Arthur Banks. *British History Atlas.* London: Weidenfeld and Nicolson, 1968.

Huggett, Frank E. *A Dictionary of British History 1815-1973.* Oxford: Blackwell, 1974.

Steinberg S. H., and I. H. Evans. *Steinberg's Dictionary of British History.* 2nd ed. London: Edward Arnold, 1970.

F. Guides to Archives and Manuscripts

Catalogue of Additions to the Manuscripts in the British Museum. 1836 to date. Cumulated to 1945. London: The British Library.

Emmison, Frederick G. *How to Read Local Archives, 1500-1700.* Helps for Students of History, 82. London: Historical Association, 1967. Provides illustrations and typescripts of early modern handwriting, including vestry minutes and church wardens' accounts.

Field, Clive D. "Sources for the Study of Protestant Non-conformity in the John Rylands University Library of Manchester," *Bulletin of the John Rylands University Library of Manchester* 71 (1989): 103-39.

Foster, Janet, and Julia Sheppard. *British Archives: A Guide to Archive Resources in the United Kingdom.* 2nd ed. New York: Stockton Press, 1989. This indispensable guide includes major and minor depositories, including the county record office network.

Guide to British Historical Manuscripts in the Huntington Library. San Marino, CA: The Library, 1982. Almost every research library will publish its own guide to manuscript collections, and this is a good example.

Index of Manuscripts in the British Library. 11 vols. Teaneck, NJ: Chadwyck-Healey, 1984-85.

Kitson Clark, G., and G. R. Elton. *Guide to Research Facilities in History in the Universities of Great Britain and Ireland.* 2nd ed. Cambridge: Cambridge University Press, 1965. A listing, by university, of major collections, including manuscripts and material in microform.

Mullett, Michael. *Sources for the History of English Nonconformity, 1660-1830.* London: British Records Association, 1991. *Papers of British Churchmen, 1780-1940.* Guides to Sources for British History, 6. London: Her Majesty's Stationery Office, 1987.

Pitschmann, Louis. *A Scholar's Guide to Washington D.C., for Northwest European Studies.* Belgium, Denmark, Finland, Great Britain, Greenland, Iceland, Ireland, Luxembourg, the Netherlands, Norway, Sweden. Scholar's Guide to Washington, D.C., no. 10. Washington, DC: Woodrow Wilson International Center for Scholars; Smithsonian Institute Press, 1984.

Purvis, John S. *An Introduction to Ecclesiastical Records.* London: St. Anthony's Press, 1953. An introduction to Anglican ecclesiastical records and record offices, superseded on the local level by the latest edition of Tate.

Record Repositories in Great Britain. 6th ed. Her Majesty's Stationery Office, 1979. A good, brief guide that provides the addresses, and lists the services, of many of the archives in Great Britain. The names and addresses of organizations that will help students locate specific records are also listed. Every repository listed is in a position to provide simple photocopies of materials, upon payment.

Tate, William E. *The Parish Chest: A Study of the Records of Parochial Administration in England.* 3rd ed. Cambridge: Cambridge University Press, 1969.

G. Recent Historiography

Elton, G. R. *Modern Historians on British History 1485-1945: A Critical Bibliography 1945-1969.* London: Methuen, 1970.
Furber, Elizabeth Chapin, ed. *Changing Views on British History: Essays on Historical Writing since 1939.* Cambridge, MA: Harvard University Press, 1966.
Schlatter, Richard, ed. *Recent Views on British History: Essays on Historical Writing since 1966.* New Brunswick: Rutgers University Press, 1984.

IV. American Church History

A. Bibliographical Guides and Handbooks

Braden, Charles S. *These Also Believe.* New York: Macmillan, 1949, 1967. Appendix B: "A Brief Dictionary of Modern Cults and Minority Religious Groups in America."
Brunkow, Robert De V., ed. *Religion and Society in North America: An Annotated Bibliography.* Clio Bibliography Series, 12. Santa Barbara: ABC-Clio, 1983. Some 4,300 abstracts of journal articles, worldwide, for the period 1973-80.
Burr, Nelson R. *A Critical Bibliography of Religion in America.* 2 vols. Princeton: Princeton University Press, 1961.
Ellis, John Tracy, and Robert Trisco. *Guide to American Catholic History.* 2nd ed. Revised and enlarged. Santa Barbara: ABC-Clio, 1982.
Freidel, Frank, with assist. of Richard K. Showman, eds. *Harvard Guide to American History.* Rev. ed. 2 vols. Cambridge: The Belknap Press, 1974.
Gaustad, Edwin Scott. *American Religious History.* Washington: Service Center for Teachers of History, 1967.
Haber, Barbara. *Women in America: A Guide to Books, 1963-1975, With an Appendix on Books Published 1976-1979.* Urbana: University of Illinois Press, 1981.
Harrison, Cynthia Ellen, ed. *Women in American History: A Bibliography.* 2 vols. Santa Barbara: American Bibliographical Center-Clio Press, 1979-85.
Kelly, James. "Sermons and Addresses," *American Catalogue of Books, 1861-1866.* Pp. 278-82.
Mead, Frank S. *Handbook of Denominations in the United States.* 9th ed. Edited and revised by Samuel S. Hill. Nashville: Abingdon Press, 1990.
Mode, Peter G. *Source Book and Bibliographical Guide for American Church History.* Menasha, WI: The Collegiate Press, 1921.
Piepkorn, Arthur Carl. *Profiles in Belief: The Religious Bodies of the United States and Canada.* 4 vols. New York: Harper & Row, 1979.
Religious Books, 1876-1982. New York: R. R. Bowker, 1983. 4 vols. The most

comprehensive bibliography of late nineteenth- and twentieth-century books on religion in North America; approximately 130,000 titles organized by subject, with author and title indexes.

Sandeen, Ernest R., and Frederick Hale. *American Religion and Philosophy: A Guide to Information Sources.* Detroit: Yale Research Company, 1978. This book surveys the literature that has appeared since Burr's work was published in 1961.

Spiller, Robert Ernest, et al., eds. *Literary History of the United States.* 4th ed., rev. 3 vols. New York: Macmillan, 1974. Vol. 3 is a bibliography.

Yearbook of the American Churches. 1916 to date.

B. Periodical Guides and Indexes

Adkins, Nelson F., ed. *The Index to Early American Periodicals 1730-1860.* New York: Readex Microprint Corporation, 1962.

America: History and Life. 1964 to date. Supplement to vols. 1-10, 1964-73. Edited by Eric H. Boehm. Santa Barbara: American Bibliographical Center of ABC-Clio, 1980. With five issues annually, this is the leading index for the history of the U.S. and Canada. Each volume offers abstracts or citations of more than 7,000 articles from some 2,000 journals. The index also abstracts book reviews and dissertations. The complete file can be searched on DIALOG (see Appendix).

Cameron, Kenneth W. *Research Keys to the American Renaissance: Scarce Indexes to the Christian Examiner, North American Review and the New Jerusalem Magazine.* Hartford: Transcendental Books, 1967.

Cushing, Helen G., and Adah V. Morris, eds. *Nineteenth Century Readers' Guide to Periodical Literature, 1890-1899: With Supplementary Indexing 1902-1922.* New York: H. W. Wilson Co., 1944.

Gohdes, Clarence L. F. *The Periodicals of American Transcendentalism.* Durham: Duke University Press, 1931.

The Guide to Catholic Literature. Vol. I: 1888-1940. Haverford, PA: Catholic Library Association. Quadrennial.

Index to Religious Periodical Literature. 1949 to date.

Index to the Titles and Authors of Articles in the Journal of the Presbyterian Historical Society, 1901-1946.

Methodist Reviews Index 1818-1985: A Retrospective Index of Periodical Articles and Book Reviews. Compiler and Editor, Elmer J. O'Brien. Nashville: Board of Higher Education and Ministry, The United Methodist Church, 1989.

Mott, Frank Luther. *A History of American Magazines, 1741-1930.* 5 vols. Cambridge, 1939-68.

Poole's Index to Periodical Literature, 1802-1906. With a Cumulative Author Index, edited by C. E. Wall. Ann Arbor: Pierian Press, 1971. The major resource for nineteenth-century English and American periodicals, although it lists articles only by subject (i.e., not by author and title). The problem is remedied, however, by Wall, C. Edward (see below).

Readers' Guide to Periodical Literature: An Author and Subject Index. 1900 to date. Edited by Helen G. Cushing and Adah V. Morris. New York: H. W. Wilson, 1944.

Richardson, Ernest. *An Alphabetical Subject Index . . . to Periodical Articles on Religion, 1890-1899.* New York, 1907.

Roorbach, O. A. "List of Periodicals Published in the United States," *Bibliotheca Americana, 1820-1852.* New York: P. Smith, 1939. Pp. 644-52.

Social Sciences and Humanities Index. New York: H. W. Wilson, 1907-74. After 1974, this guide was divided into the *Humanities Index* and the *Social Sciences Index.* The *Humanities Index* includes citations of articles and book reviews on history, religion, philosophy, language, and literature. Both indices are now available online through Ovid Online.

Spence, Thomas H., Jr. "Southern Presbyterian Reviews," *The Union Seminary Quarterly Review* 61, 2 (February 1945): 93-109.

Stroupe, Henry Smith. *The Religious Periodical Press in the South Atlantic States.* Durham: Duke University Press, 1956.

Union List of Serials in Libraries of the United States and Canada. 3rd ed. 5 vols. New York: H. W. Wilson Co., 1965.

Wall, C. Edward. *Cumulative Author Index for Poole's Index to Periodical Literature, 1802-1906.* Ann Arbor: Piernan, 1971.

Writings on American History: A Subject Bibliography of Articles. 1902 to 1990 (excluding 1941-47). Index volume, 1902-40. This series, like *Recently Published Articles,* has been engulfed by the exponential increase in the number of publications, and it has yielded to computerized indices such as *America: History and Life.* The first series, concluding in 1961, listed books and articles; the second series, only articles. Separate cumulative sets were assembled for the years 1962-73, thereby covering an earlier gap between the old and new series, but in the period after 1976, there is much overlap on the topic of American history with *Recently Published Articles.*

C. Newspaper Guides

Gregory, Winifred. *American Newspapers, 1821-1936.* New York: H. W. Wilson, 1937.

New York Times Index. 1851 to date.

Schwarzlose, Richard. *Newspapers: A Reference Guide.* New York: Greenwood Press, 1987.

United States Newspaper Program: National Union List. 4th ed. Dublin, OH: OCLC, 1993. See the Appendix, Microform Guides and Sources.

D. General Reference and Research Tools

1. National Bibliography and Sources

A Checklist of American Imprints, 1820- . Metuchen, NJ: Scarecrow Press, 1972- .

Bristol, Roger P. *Supplement to Charles Evans' American Bibliography.* Charlottesville: The Bibliography Society of America, 1970. Index in separate volume. This adds over 10,000 items to Evans.

Evans, Charles. *American Bibliography: A Chronological Dictionary of all Books, Pamphlets and Periodical Publications Printed in the United States of America from the Genesis of printing in 1639 down to and including the year 1820.* 14 vols. Chicago: The Blakely Press, 1903-59. Evans lists over 39,000 titles.

Library of Congress Catalog: A Cumulative List of Works: Represented by Library of Congress Printed Cards. Books: Subjects. Washington: U.S. Library of Congress, 1950- . Quarterly, with annual and quinquennial cumulations.

National Union Catalogue of Pre-1956 Imprints. Chicago and London: Mansell, 1968- . An exhaustive listing, alphabetically by author, of all editions of every book printed before 1956 and held by libraries belonging to the National Union/Library of Congress system. Each listing indicates the libraries that have the book. Now exceeds 700 volumes.

Roorbach, Orville Joseph. *Bibliotheca Americana. Catalogue of American Publications, Including Reprints and Original Works, from 1820 to 1852.* 4 vols. Supplements to 1861. Reprint. Metuchen, NJ: Mini-Print Corporation, 1967.

Sabin, Joseph, with Wilberforce Eames and R. W. C. Vail. *Bibliotheca Americana: A Dictionary of Books Relating to America, from its Discovery to the Present Time.* 28 vols. New York: Joseph Sabin, 1868-92; New York: Bibliographical Society of America, 1928-35.

Shaw, Ralph R., and Richard H. Shoemaker. *American Bibliography: A Preliminary Checklist for 1801-1819.* New York: The Scarecrow Press, Inc., 1958-66. This series changed its title to *American Imprints* with the volume for 1820; it has been under the direction of various editors. There are author and title indices.

Shipton, Clifford K., ed. *Early American Imprints, 1639-1800.* Worcester: American Antiquarian Society. Readex Microprint Corporation, 1962. This edition of microcard reproductions of entire books and pamphlets (but not serials) includes about 30,000 of the items listed in Evans's bibliography and an additional 8,000 items listed in Shipton and Mooney's *National Index.* Most major research libraries have this series, some in the older microcard format, and others in a newer microfiche edition of 1981-82 that adds additional titles.

Shipton, Clifford K., James E. Mooney, and John B. Hench. *Early American Imprints, Second Series, 1801-1819.* New York: Readex Microprint Corporation, 1964- . This is the sequel to the Readex Microprint edition of early books and extends to approximately 50,000 items.

Shipton, Clifford K., and James E. Mooney, eds. *National Index of American Imprints through 1800: The Short-Title Evans.* 2 vols. Boston: American Antiquarian Society, 1969. This guide is arranged alphabetically to the microprint edition of *Early American Imprints, 1639-1800,* but it also updates Evans's bibliography for the period by adding 10,035 titles, most of which are from the labors of Roger Bristol.

Waters, Willard O. "American Imprints, 1648-1797 in the Huntington Library, Supplementing Evans's American Bibliography," *The Huntington Library Bulletin* 3 (1933): 1-95.

2. Denominations

(For a more comprehensive listing of denominational bibliographies, see G. E. Gorman and Lyn Gorman, above, under I.D.)

(Baptist) Starr, Edward C., comp. *A Baptist Bibliography Being a Register of Printed Material by and about Baptists.* 25 vols. Philadelphia: Published by the Judson Press for the Samuel Colgate Baptist Historical Collection, Colgate University, 1947-76.

(Brethren) Durnbaugh, Donald F. *Guide to Research in Brethren History.* Elgin, IL: Church of the Brethren Historical Committee, 1968.

(Catholic) Vollmar, Edward R. *The Catholic Church in America: An Historical Bibliography.* 2nd ed. New York: Scarecrow Press, 1963.

(Congregational) Dexter, Henry Martyn. *The Congregationalism of the Last Three Hundred Years, as Seen in Its Literature.* For the period 1546-1879. New York: Harper and Brothers, 1880.

(Mennonite) Springer, Nelson P., and A. J. Klassen, comps. *Mennonite Bibliography, 1631-1961.* 2 vols. Scottsdale, PA: Herald Press, 1977.

(Methodist) Baker, George C., Jr. *An Introduction to the History of Early New England Methodism, 1789-1839.* Bibliography: pp. 85-138. Durham: Duke University Press, 1941.

(Methodist) Little, Brooks B., ed. *Methodist Union Catalog of History, Biography, Disciplines and Hymnals.* Lake Junaluska, NC: Association of Methodist Historical Society, 1967.

(Methodist) Rowe, Kenneth E., ed. *Methodist Union Catalog: Pre-1976 Imprints.* 6 vols. Metuchen: Scarecrow Press, 1975- . The project will be completed in 20 vols.

(Mormon) Kirkpatrick, L. H. *Holdings of the University of Utah, on Utah and the Church of Jesus Christ of Latter-Day Saints.* Salt Lake City, 1954.

(Presbyterian) Parker, Harold M., Jr. *Bibliography of Published Articles on American Presbyterianism, 1901-1980.* Westport, CT: Greenwood Press, 1985.

(Presbyterian) Prince, Harold B., ed., comp. *A Presbyterian Bibliography: The*

Published Writings of Ministers Who Served in the Presbyterian Church in the United States . . . 1861-1961. ATLA Bibliography series. Metuchen: Scarecrow Press, 1983.

(Presbyterian) Trinterud, Leonard J., comp. *A Bibliography of American Presbyterianism during the Colonial Period.* Philadelphia: Presbyterian Historical Society, 1968.

3. Specialized

(African American Studies) *Dictionary Catalog of the Schomburg Collection of Negro Literature and History.* Boston: G. K. Hall, 1962- . 9 vols. with 5 supplements printed to date.

(African American Studies) Jones, Charles E. *Black Holiness: A Guide to the Study of Black Participation in Wesleyan Perfectionist and Glossolalic Pentecostal Movements.* ATLA Bibliography Series. Metuchen: Scarecrow Press, 1987.

(African American Studies) Krash, Ronald, and Gail Juris, comps. *Black America: Research Bibliography.* St. Louis: Pius XII Memorial Library Publications, 1970.

(African American Studies) Leffall, Dolores C., comp. *The Black Church: An Annotated Bibliography.* Washington: Minority Research Center, 1973.

(African American Studies) Smith, Dwight La Vern, ed. *Afro-American History: A Bibliography.* Clio Bibliography series, 2. Santa Barbara: ABC-Clio, 1974.

(Evangelical) Blumhofer, Edith L., and Joel A. Carpenter. *Twentieth-Century Evangelicalism: A Guide to the Sources.* New York: Garland, 1990.

(Evangelical) Jones, Charles E., comp. and ed. *A Guide to the Study of the Holiness Movement.* ATLA Bibliography series, 1. Metuchen, NJ: Scarecrow Press, 1974.

(Evangelical) Magnuson, Norris A., and William G. Travis. *American Evangelism: An Annotated Bibliography.* West Cornwall, CT: Locust Hill Press, 1990.

(Evangelical) Peterson, Paul D., ed. *Evangelicalism and Fundamentalism: A Bibliography Selected from the ATLA Religion Database.* 1st rev. ed. Chicago: ATLA Religion Indexes, 1983.

(Italian American) Tomasi, Silvano, and Edward C. Stibili. *Italian Americans and Religion: An Annotated Bibliography.* New York: Center for Migration Studies, 1978.

(Pentecostal) Jones, Charles E. *A Guide to the Study of the Pentecostal Movement.* 2 vols. ATLA Bibliography Series. Metuchen: Scarecrow Press, 1983.

(Pentecostal) Mills, Watson E. *Charismatic Religion in Modern Research: A Bibliography.* Macon, GA: Mercer University Press, 1985.

(Science and Religion) Eisen, Sidney, and Bernard V. Lightman. *Victorian Science and Religion: A Bibliography with Emphasis on Evolution, Belief,*

and Unbelief, Comprised of Works Published from C. 1900-1975. Hamden,
CT: Archon, 1984.
(Women's History) Bass, Dorothy C., and Sandra Hughes Boyd. *Women in
American Religious History: An Annotated Bibliography and Guide to
Sources.* Boston: G. K. Hall, 1986.

4. Bibliographies of Bibliographies

Beers, Henry Putney. *Bibliographies in American History: Guide to Materials for
Research.* Rev. ed. New York: H. W. Wilson Company, 1942.
Bibliographic Index. A cumulative bibliography of bibliographies, 1937 to date.

E. Biographical Dictionaries and Directories

(African American) DuPree, Sherry Sherrod. *Biographical Dictionary of Afri-
can-American, Holiness-Pentecostals, 1880-1990.* Washington, DC: Mid-
dle Atlantic Press, 1989.
Biography Index. 1946 to date. A Cumulative Index to Biographical Material in
Books and Magazines. Vol. 1, January 1946/July 1949. Triennial. New
York: H. W. Wilson Co.
(Catholic) Delaney, John J., and James Edward Tobin. *Dictionary of Catholic
Biography.* Garden City, NY: Doubleday, 1961.
Dictionary of American Biography. 20 vols. with indexes and supplements.
Dictionary of American Religious Biography. Henry W. Bowden, with Edwin S.
Gaustad. Westport, CT: Greenwood Press, 1977.
(Methodist) *Who's Who in the Methodist Church.* Nashville: Abingdon Press,
1966.
National Cyclopaedia of American Biography. Compiled by H. A. Harvey and
Raymond D. McGill. 62 vols. and vols. labeled A-N63. New York: James T.
White and Co., 1892-1984. Use in conjunction with the *Index: National
Cyclopedia of American Biography* (1984).
The New York Times Obituaries Index, 1858-1968. New York: New York Times,
1970. Index II, 1969-78. 1980.
(Presbyterian) Witherspoon, E. D., Jr., ed. *Ministerial Directory of the Presby-
terian Church, U.S., 1861-1967.* Doraville, GA: Foote and Davies, 1967.
(Protestant) Sprague, William B. *Annals of the American Pulpit.* 9 vols. New
York: Carter, 1859-69. Reprint. New York: Arno Press, 1969. Includes
Congregational, Presbyterian, Episcopalian, Baptist, Methodist, Unitar-
ian, Lutheran, and Reformed.
(Specialized) Fothergill, Gerald. *A List of Emigrant Ministers to America, 1690-
1811.* London: E. Stock, 1904.
(Specialized–African American clergy) Williams, Ethel L. *Biographical
Directory of Negro Ministers.* 3rd ed. Boston: G. K. Hall, 1975.

F. Encyclopedias and Atlases

(Adventist) *Seventh-Day Adventist Encyclopedia*. Washington, DC: Review and Herald Publishing Association, 1966.

(African Methodist Episcopal) *Encyclopaedia of African Methodism*. Compiled by Richard Robert Wright, Jr. 2nd ed. Philadelphia: n.p., 1947.

(Baptist) *Encyclopedia of Southern Baptists*. 4 vols. Nashville: Broadman Press, 1958-82. Index to vols. 1-4. Nashville: Broadman Press, 1972.

(Brethren) *The Brethren Encyclopedia*. Philadelphia: Brethren Encyclopedia, Inc., 1983.

(Lutheran) Bodensieck, Julius, ed. *The Encyclopedia of the Lutheran Church*. 3 vols. Minneapolis: Augsburg Publishing House, 1975.

(Lutheran-Missouri Synod) Lucker, Erwin L., ed. *Lutheran Cyclopedia*. Rev. ed. St. Louis: Concordia Publishing House, 1975.

(Mennonite) *The Mennonite Encyclopedia: A Comprehensive Reference Work on the Anabaptist-Mennonite Movement*. 5 vols. Hillsboro, KS: Mennonite Brethren Publishing House, 1955-90. Index of Titles, 1960.

(Methodist) *The Encyclopedia of World Methodism*. Edited by Nolan B. Harmon. 2 vols. Nashville: United Methodist Publishing House, 1974.

(Methodist) Simpson, Matthew. *Cyclopaedia of Methodism*. 5th rev. ed. Philadelphia: L. H. Everts, 1882.

(Presbyterian) Nevin, Alfred, ed. *Encyclopaedia of the Presbyterian Church in the United States of America*. Philadelphia: Presbyterian Encyclopedia Publishing Co., 1884.

(Reformed) Vandeburge, Peter N., et al., eds. *Historical Directory of the Reformed Church in America, 1628-1978*. 2nd ed. Grand Rapids: Eerdmans, 1978.

Carroll, Jackson W., Douglas W. Johnson, and Martin Marty. *Religion in America: 1950 to the Present*. New York: Harper and Row, 1979. This brings Gaustad's atlas up to date.

Gaustad, Edwin Scott. *Historical Atlas of Religion in America*. Rev. ed. New York: Harper and Row, 1976.

Hill, Samuel S. *Encyclopedia of Religion in the South*. Macon, GA: Mercer University Press, 1984.

Lippy, Charles H., and Peter W. Williams. *Encyclopedia of the American Religious Experience*. 3 vols. New York: Charles Scribner's Sons, 1988.

G. Archives and Manuscripts

Allison, William Henry. *Inventory of Unpublished Material for American Religious History in Protestant Church Archives and Other Repositories*. Washington: Carnegie Institution of Washington, 1910. Though dated, this is still a valuable guide for locating major collections and identifying pertinent material in local archives.

Catlett, Stephen J., ed. *A New Guide to the Collections in the Library of the American Philosophical Society.* Philadelphia: American Philosophical Society, 1987.

Crick, Bernard R., and Miriam Alman. *A guide to manuscripts relating to America in Great Britain and Ireland.* Published for the British Association for American Studies by the Oxford University Press, 1961.

Cuthbert, Norma B. *American Manuscript Collections in the Huntington Library for the History of the Seventeenth and Eighteenth Centuries.* San Marino: The Huntington Library, 1941.

Griffin, Grace Gardner. *A Guide to Manuscripts Relating to American History in British Depositories.* Washington: Library of Congress, 1946.

Hamer, Philip M., ed. *A Guide to Archives and Manuscripts in the United States.* New Haven: Yale University Press, 1961.

Hinding, Andrea, and Suzanna Moody, eds. *Women's History Sources: A Guide to Archives and Manuscript Collections in the United States.* 2 vols. New York: R. R. Bowker, 1979.

Johnson, Clifton H. *American Missionary Association Archives as a Source for the Study of American History.* New York: American Missionary Association.

Lind, William E. "Methodist Archives in the United States," *The American Archivist* 24, 4 (October 1961): 435-40.

Manross, William W. *The Fulham Papers in the Lambeth Palace Library: American Colonial Section.* Oxford: Clarendon Press, 1965.

H. Henry Meeter Center for Calvin Studies. Calvin Theological Seminary, Grand Rapids, MI.

National Union Catalog of Manuscript Collections. Washington, DC: Library of Congress, 1962- . Published annually with summary cumulations for each five-year period. *NUCMC* is indexed by name, place, subject, and genre of material. Students should also consult the recently published *Index to Personal Names in the National Union Catalog of Manuscript Collections, 1959-1984.* 3 vols. Alexandria, VA: Chadwyck-Healey, 1988.

Rede, Wyllys. "The Maryland Diocesan Library — A Mine of Historical Material," *Historical Magazine of the Protestant Episcopal Church* I, 2 (June 1932): 102-10.

Sweet, William Warren. "Church Archives in the United States," *Church History* 8 (1939): 43-53.

[United States] National Historical Publications and Records Commission. *Directory of archives and manuscript repositories in the United States.* 2nd ed. Phoenix: Oryx Press, 1988.

H. Recent Historiography

Annals. Vol. 256 (March 1948). *Organized Religion in the United States;* vol. 387 (January 1970). *The Sixties: Radical Change in American Religion;* vol. 332 (November 1960). *Religion in American Life.*

Bass, Herbert J., ed. With Introduction. *The State of American History.* Chicago: Quadrangle Books, 1970. See especially Sydney Ahlstrom, "The Moral and Theological Revolution of the Sixties and Its Implications for American Religious Historiography."

Bowden, Henry W. *Church History in the Age of Science: Historiographical Patterns in the United States, 1876-1918.* Chapel Hill: University of North Carolina Press, 1971.

Bowden, Henry W. *Church History in an Age of Uncertainty: Historiographical Patterns in the United States, 1906-1990.* Carbondale and Edwardsville: Southern Illinois University Press, 1991.

Brauer, Jerald C., R. Pierce Beaver, et al., eds. *Reinterpretation in American History.* Vol. V: *Essays in Divinity.* Chicago: University of Chicago Press, 1968.

Cadden, John Paul. *The Historiography of the American Catholic Church, 1785-1943.* Washington, 1944. Reprint. New York: Arno Press, 1978.

Daedalus. Winter 1967. *Religion in America.*

V. Historiography and Historical Method

Aron, Raymond. *Introduction to the Philosophy of History: An Essay on the Limits of Historical Objectivity.* Translated by George Irwin. Boston: Beacon, 1961.

Barnes, Harry Elmer. *A History of Historical Writing.* 2nd ed. New York: Dover, 1937. Reprint, 1967.

Barzun, Jacques, and Henry F. Graff. *The Modern Researcher.* 4th ed. New York and San Diego: Harcourt, Brace, Jovanovich, 1977.

Bebbington, David. *Patterns in History: A Christian Perspective on Historical Thought,* 1979. Reprint, with new preface and afterword. Grand Rapids: Baker Book House, 1990.

Berlin, Sir Isaiah. *Vico and Herder: Two Studies in the History of Ideas.* London: Hogarth, 1976.

Birkos, Alexander S., and Lewis A. Tambs. *Historiography, Method, and History Teaching: A Bibliography of Books and Articles in English.* Hamden, CT: Linnet Books, 1975.

Bloch, Marc. *The Historian's Craft.* New York: Vintage, 1953. The classic "nuts and bolts" approach to the archaeological data of history by a great historian.

Breisach, Ernst. *Historiography: Ancient, Medieval and Modern.* Chicago: University of Chicago Press, 1983.

Brown, Colin. *History and Faith: A Personal Exploration.* Grand Rapids: Zondervan, 1987.

Butterfield, Herbert. *The Whig Interpretation of History.* New York: Norton, 1965.

Butterfield, Herbert. *Man on His Past: The Study of the History of Historical Scholarship.* Cambridge: Cambridge University Press, 1955.

Carr, Edward H. *What is History?* New York: Vintage Books, 1961. In juxtaposition with Bloch and Elton, a view of history as primarily interpretation.

Collingwood, R. G. *The Idea of History.* New York and London: Oxford University Press, 1956. A historical approach, by an idealist philosopher of history; a classic essay.

Danto, Arthur C. *Analytical Philosophy of History.* Cambridge: Cambridge University Press, 1968.

Dilthey, Wilhelm. *Pattern and Meaning in History: Thoughts on History and Society.* Edited and with an introduction by H. P. Rickman. New York: Harper & Row, 1962. A significant selection of materials from an eminent philosopher of history who was also a superb practicing historian.

Elton, G. R. *The Practice of History.* New York: Crowell, 1967. History as bruta facta: an answer to E. H. Carr.

Fitzsimons, Matthew A., et al. *The Development of Historiography.* Harrisburg, PA: Stackpole, 1954.

Fling, F. M. *The Writing of History: An Introduction to Historical Method.* New Haven: Yale University Press, 1920.

Flint, Robert. *History of the Philosophy of History.* Edinburgh and London: William Blackwood, 1893.

Gallie, W. B. *Philosophy and the Historical Understanding.* 2nd ed. New York: Schocken, 1968.

Garraghan, Gilbert J. *A Guide to Historical Method.* Edited by J. Delanglez. New York: Fordham University Press, 1946.

Gooch, George P. *History & Historians in the Nineteenth Century.* Boston: Beacon, 1959.

Gottschalk, Louis. *Understanding History: A Primer of Historical Method.* 2nd ed. New York: Knopf, 1969. Not as eminent or up to date as Barzun and Graff, but nonetheless worth examining for an occasional alternative approach.

Gustavson, Carl G. *A Preface to History.* New York: McGraw-Hill, 1955. Excellent introduction to historical thinking at the level of general history.

Harvey, Van A. *The Historian and the Believer: The Morality of Historical Knowledge and Christian Belief.* New York: Macmillan, 1969.

Hughes, H. Stuart. *History as Art and as Science: Twin Vistas on the Past.* New York: Harper & Row, 1964.

Johnson, A. *The Historian and Historical Evidence.* New York, 1926.

Langlois, Charles V., and Charles Seignobos. *Introduction to the Study of History.* Translated by G. G. Berry. London, 1898. Reprint. New York: Barnes & Noble, 1966. The classic objectivistic manual.

McIntire, C. T., and Ronald A. Wells, eds. *History and Historical Understanding.* Grand Rapids: Eerdmans, 1984.

Mandelbaum, Maurice. *The Problem of Historical Knowledge: An Answer to Relativism.* New York: Liveright, 1938.

Maritain, Jacques. *On the Philosophy of History.* Edited by Joseph Evans. New York: Scribner, 1957.

Marwick, Arthur. *The Nature of History.* New York: Knopf, 1970.

Meinicke, Friedrich. *Historism: The Rise of a New Historical Outlook.* Translated by J. E. Anderson; foreword by Isaiah Berlin; introduction by Carl Hinrichs. New York: Herder and Herder, 1972.

Meyerhoff, Hans. *The Philosophy of History in Our Time: An Anthology.* Garden City: Doubleday, 1959.

Nevins, Allan. *The Gateway to History.* Boston: Heath, 1938.

Popper, Karl. *The Poverty of Historicism.* 1957. Reprint. New York: Harper & Row, 1964.

Renier, G. J. *History: Its Purpose and Method.* New York: Harper & Row, 1950.

Richardson, R. C. *The Study of History: A Bibliographical Guide.* Manchester: Manchester University Press, 1988.

Scott, E. *History and Historical Problems.* Oxford, 1925.

Spengler, Oswald. *The Decline of the West: I. Form and Actuality; II. Perspectives of World-History.* Translated by Charles Atkinsom. New York: Knopf, 1926-28. A one-volume abridgment by Helmut Werner and Arthur Helps was published by The Modern Library in 1962.

Stephens, Lester D. *Historiography: A Bibliography.* Metuchen, NJ: Scarecrow Press, 1975.

Stern, Fritz, ed. *The Varieties of History: from Voltaire to the Present.* Cleveland: World, 1956.

Tholfsen, Trygve R. *Historical Thinking: An Introduction.* New York: Harper & Row, 1967.

Thompson, J. Westfall, with B. J. Holm. *A History of Historical Writing.* 2 vols. New York: Macmillan, 1942.

Toynbee, Arnold J. *A Study of History.* 12 vols. New York: Oxford University Press, 1934-64. Meta-history at its best (or worst, depending on one's point of view; i.e., is this kind of eminence a "bad eminence"?).

Walsh, W. H. *Philosophy of History: An Introduction.* New York: Harper & Row, 1960.

White, Morton. *Foundations of Historical Knowledge.* New York: Harper & Row, 1965.

VI. General Reference Works for the Profession

American Library Directory. 2 vols. 45th ed. New York and London: R. R. Bowker, 1992-93. A listing of all U.S. libraries, alphabetized by state and city, that provides the address of the library, names of current librarians, lists of major collections, and statistics on holdings.

Annual Register of Grant Support. Chicago: Marquis Professional Publications. Updated every several years.

De George, Richard T. *The Philosopher's Guide to Sources, Research Tools, Professional Life and Related Fields.* Lawrence, KS: Regents Press, 1980.

Directory of Historical Societies and Agencies in the United States and Canada. Nashville: American Association for State and Local History, 1956- . Triennial.

Directory of Publishing Opportunities in Journals and Periodicals. 5th ed. Chicago: Marquis Professional Publications, 1981.

Fellowships and Grants of Interest to Historians. Washington: American Historical Association, Institutional Services Program, 1977- .

Fiering, Norman. *A Guide to Book Publication for Historians.* Washington: American Historical Association, 1979.

Harrold, Ann, ed. *Libraries in the United Kingdom and the Republic of Ireland.* Chicago: American Library Association, 1989.

Luey, Beth. *Handbook for Academic Authors.* New York: Cambridge University Press, 1987.

Steiner, Dale R. *Historical Journals: A Handbook for Writers and Reviewers.* Santa Barbara: ABC-Clio, 1981. Covers 350 U.S. and Canadian Journals in history.

Appendix:
Computer Applications in Research and Writing and New Sources in Microform

I. Online Network Databases

Dialog. Knight-Ridder Information Inc., 2440 El Camino Real, Mountain View, CA 94040. 800-334-2564; 415-254-7000. Referred to as the world's largest online retrieval service, DIALOG is the online source for *The Philosopher's Index,* and the ABC-Clio databases, including *America: History and Life* and *Historical Abstracts. Dissertation Abstracts International* may also be searched on DIALOG.

Online Computer Library Center (OCLC). Online Computer Library Center Inc., 6565 Frantz Road, Dublin, OH 43017-0702. 800-848-5800; 614-764-6000. OCLC offers its own massive database of hundreds of linked libraries, nationwide and foreign, as well as guidance for manuscript and newspaper collections. OCLC is currently converting the records of the *National Register of Microform Masters* to its online database and the project on U.S. newspapers will provide comprehensive access to the location of newspapers. (See below under Microform Guides and Sources.) OCLC has an ongoing project of cataloging some 17,000 eighteenth-century books and pamphlets on philosophy and religion at Emory University. For specialists in seventeenth- and eighteenth-century church history, it will be useful to know that OCLC now includes the shelf list of the Clark Library of UCLA. EPIC is OCLC's reference tool that provides access to a variety of databases for librarians and scholars through Compuserve. "FirstSearch," a subset of EPIC, is available online through Internet.

Ovid Online (formerly Bibliographic Retrieval Services). Ovid Technologies, 5650 South Green St., Murray, MT 84123. 800-950-2371; 801-281-3884;

United Kingdom, 011-4481-748-3777. Ovid Online provides access to *Dissertation Abstracts International,* updated monthly, in addition to the H. W. Wilson Bibliographic and Humanities Indices and *Current Contents.*

Research Libraries Information Network (RLIN). The RLIN Information Center, The Research Libraries Group, Inc., 1200 Villa Street, Mountain View, CA 94041-1100. 800-537-7546. RLIN provides online access to the Eighteenth-Century Short Title Catalog and many records of archival collections. The database of books now numbers more than 30,000,000 and there are currently 200,000 records pertaining to archival materials.

II. ONLINE PUBLIC ACCESS CATALOGS

Several basic items of information must be known before dialing the number of an online library. All of the following online systems accept the modem setting of 8 data bits, 1 stop bit, and non-even parity, unless otherwise noted. The user should know the baud rate of the modem; some systems have different telephone numbers for different baud rates, although, increasingly, library systems will adjust automatically to the baud rate of any modem. Upon a successful connection, many online library systems require the user to press "enter" once or twice before any instructions are given: this enables the host computer to sense the speed of the modem. Most systems require that one type in the "terminal emulation type," and for most PCs, this will be VT100. Most libraries provide directions for logging off; if specific instructions are lacking, the modem may simply be disconnected. The libraries listed here all allow public access, and they illustrate the ease with which one can locate a research library within all broad geographic regions of the country.

Boston University: (TOMUS) 617-353-9601. Upon connecting, at the "BUnet:" prompt, type "telnet library," and then follow the instructions. The computer will ask for terminal type and give several options. A help screen with a variety of options for searches follows. Voice assistance is available at 617-353-3704.

Harvard University: (HOLLIS) 617-496-8500. Set modem software for 7 data bits, 1 stop bit, and even parity. Upon connecting, press "return" and the prompt "enter terminal type" will appear. After entering terminal type, type "HOLLIS." A directory screen will then lead one into the various library options.

Princeton Theological Seminary: 609-921-2360. Set the modem to 7-1-E. At connect, press "enter" two or three times and then respond to the prompt for terminal type. Commands are case sensitive. From the menu, type B and return, and then follow menu.

University of California, Irvine: (MELVYL) 714-824-8960. This number is for a baud rate of 9600. Set the modem for 7 data bits, 1 stop bit, and even parity. At the "csi-ts1" prompt, type "MLVL." A request for terminal type follows, and after that, instructions for using the system.

University of Colorado, Boulder: (CARL) 303-758-1551. The system is fully automated, and one is connected with no additional information. Many libraries in the western states support access to CARL, the Colorado Alliance of Research Libraries.

University of Michigan: (MIRLYN) 313-577-0335. Set software for 7-1-E. After connecting, press "enter" and at "%Terminal=" prompt, press enter until the prompt "Which Host?" appears. Type "MIRLYN" and then a variety of terminal types will be offered from which a selection can be made.

University of Minnesota: (LUMINA) 612-625-6009. After connecting and pressing "return," a prompt for terminal type appears. Enter PA (which indicates public access) and a menu will appear with LUMINA as the first option.

University of Oregon: (JANUS) 503-346-3565 (2400 baud); 503-346-4391 (1200 baud). At the "UOnet" prompt, type "c janus," and press "enter." At the "login:" prompt, type "janus" again, and at the password type "janus."

Vanderbilt University: (ACORN) 615-322-3551. At the "user I.D." prompt, the user may type in any name. At the "Local" prompt, type "C CTRVAX" and at the request for "User name" type "ACORN."

Alternatively, many researchers and students will have access to the Internet and the library online server, "Telnet," which can access the "Internet Libraries." Telnet is a server program that links online libraries worldwide into a massive bibliographical network and that can be accessed on screen, usually through an institutional modem. If Telnet is available, the code of a cooperating library can be entered at the Telnet prompt. Successful connection is usually indicated by a screen identifying the library and offering initial search options. As above, most libraries will ask for "terminal emulation type" and will offer basic directions for use and for logging off. Some institutions will also offer the "Gopher list of Internet-accessible libraries" program now based regionally at Yale University and the University of Texas at Dallas: "Gopher" offers an international listing of online libraries with their electronic addresses and with basic information for entering and using their databases and for logging off. Some of the libraries listed in Gopher can, moreover, be accessed through Gopher itself, which will connect to Telnet with the proper command.

Results will vary: researchers will find that many libraries have a large capacity for searches, welcome outside use, and are very user-friendly, that others are frequently so busy that outside users will not be able to gain access during peak use periods, and that still other libraries will simply deny access to outside use through Telnet, unless a further entry code is used. Some of these codes are available through "Gopher."

When using the Telnet server for any library, the program can create a "capture file" on the user's hard drive with the command "Alt-C." Once created, the capture file can be retained as a repository for downloaded information: any screen can be "dumped" into the capture file with the command "Alt-D." The result is a copy, in ASCII, of the original screen separated from preceding entries by a hard page. The "dump" command automatically places new information at the end of the extant capture file. Thus, the user in Michigan can do bibliographical searches in California or New Jersey and dump the results into the capture file on his own hard drive, yielding a file that includes all relevant author, title, and publication information plus data on the location and call number of the book in the library searched.

A sampling of libraries and electronic addresses:

Harvard University: HOLLIS.HARVARD.EDU
University of California: MELVYL.UCOP.EDU
University of California at Berkeley: GOPAC.BERKELEY.EDU
University of Michigan, Ann Arbor: HERMES.MERIT.EDU [at Host prompt, enter MIRLYN]
University of Chicago: OLORIN.UCHICAGO.EDU
Yale University: ORBIS.YALE.EDU
Leiden University: RULUB3.LEIDENUNIV.NL
Utrecht University: RUUT.CC.RUU.NL
University of Heidelberg: VM.URZ.UNI.HEIDELBERG.DE

III. Scholarly Projects, Services, and Databases on CD-ROM

Bibliographical Information Base in Patristics. Director, René-Michel Roberge, Faculté de Théologie, Université Laval, Cité Universitaire, Québec, Canada G1K 7P4. This database organizes and stores information on books and articles on Patristics; to date the contents of articles from some 300 periodicals have been electronically stored, and these materials may be searched through a thesaurus.

Center for Bibliographical Studies and Research. The North American project of the Eighteenth-Century Short Title Catalog is located at the Center for Bibliographical Studies and Research, Rivera Library-016, University of California, Riverside, Riverside, CA 92521-0154. The newsletter of the ESTC, *Factotum*, is edited by J. L. Wood at the British Library and distributed through the Riverside office. The Center is currently working on the machine-readable versions of Pollard and Redgrave, and Wing.

Center for British Studies. C.B. 184, University of Colorado, Boulder, CO 80309-0184. Thanks to the revolution worked by the reproduction of materials in microform, the holdings of this Center constitute one of the strongest collections of British primary sources in the United States.

Starting with a good reference library, the directors have assiduously collected many of the major microfiche/microfilm collections mentioned in this Appendix, as well as many others that do not bear on topics related to church history. One of the noteworthy strengths of the center is the vast collection of historical materials on sacred music.

Chadwyck-Healey, Inc. 1101 King St., Alexandria, VA 22314. Chadwyck-Healey has produced Migne's *Patrologia Latina* on CD-ROM.

Eighteenth-Century Short Title Catalog. The University of California, Riverside and the British Library, Great Russell Street, London WC1B 3DG. The CD-ROM version of ESTC was produced by the British Library. See the Center for Bibliographical Studies and Research.

Institute for Scientific Information. 3501 Market Street, Philadelphia, PA 19104. 800-336-4474; 215-386-0100. ISI European Branch, 132 High Street, Uxbridge UB8 1DP, UK 44-895-270016. ISI publishes *Current Contents/Arts & Humanities* biweekly, which reproduces the table of contents of journals (for example, the table of contents of *Revue D'Histoire Ecclésiastique* will be found in English), and their citation index covers the most important journals in the humanities; these services are available online through major research libraries and can be searched through BRS and DIALOG.

Medieval and Early Modern Data Bank. Department of History, CN 5059, Rutgers, The State University of New Jersey, New Brunswick, NJ 08903. 201-932-8316; 201-932-8335. This effort, sponsored jointly by Rutgers University and by the Research Libraries Group, Inc., concentrates on quantifiable data such as parish records, currency exchange rates, tax and probate records, and business data. It will also support inquiries on Latin and vernacular place names, and it may be searched through RLIN.

Past Masters. Intelex Corporation, Route 2, Box 383, Pittsboro, NC 27312. 919-542-4411. This series provides full critical texts of the main works of such leading figures as John Locke, George Berkeley, René Descartes, Gottfried Wilhelm von Leibniz, and Søren Kierkegaard, to name a few. The texts are supplied on standard diskettes (the collected works of Kierkegaard, for example, require ten megabytes of disk space), but they are supplied with VIEWS, a powerful search and retrieve software program produced by Folio Corporation. Recently Intelex has produced an electronic copy of Aquinas's *Summa Theologica* in English and Latin.

Philosophy Documentation Center. Bowling Green State University, Bowling Green, OH 43403-0189. 800-444-2419; 419-372-2419. Publishes journals and bibliographies on all topics in philosophy and provides guides for searching The Philosopher's Index.

Thesaurus Linguae Graecae Project. University of California, Irvine, Irvine CA, 92717. 714-824-7031. Many research libraries possess the CD-ROM version of the TLG, but custom searches are available for a modest fee; the database can be supplied on tape, and limited online access through networks may also be arranged on an individual basis. The project publishes the *Thesaurus Linguae Graecae Newsletter* twice yearly.

IV. Materials in Microform

A. Major Microfilm, Microfiche Collections

The following directory of companies and organizations is not intended to provide an exhaustive survey of all the relevant publishers of research materials in microform. It does, however, offer the student some sense of the variety of documents now available. Similarly, the descriptions of collections will not include every group of documents that are important to the study of church history and theology, though the annotations are designed generally to reflect the company's strengths in these fields.

> American Theological Library Association
> Preservation Programs
> 820 Church Street, Suite 300
> Evanston, IL 60201-3707
> 708-869-7788

The ATLA "PREFIR" program (Preservation Filming in Religion) was developed to preserve primarily nineteenth-century theological and biblical monographs and earlier serials on microfiche and microfilm. ATLA currently possess about 14,000 monographs in these media, and they are adding several thousand titles a year, with Phase Four (1989-90) concentrating specifically on church history. Descriptive brochures are available, and individual items may be ordered directly from ATLA.

> Center for Reformation Research
> 6477 San Bonita Ave., St. Louis, MO 63105
> 314-727-6655

The Center has about 10,000 items in microform, including both manuscript and printed sources, pertaining to the late medieval period and the Reformation, and these are available through interlibrary loan. Besides the magisterial reformers, the collections include the works of some Catholic theologians and leaders of the Radical Reformation. The finding guide that describes these materials is found in the Sixteenth Century Bibliography series (vols. 12-19) published by the Center. The Center serves the academic community not only through the library with a 2,500-volume reference collection, but as the administrative headquarters for The American Society for Reformation Research, The Sixteenth

Century Studies Conference, and The North American Committee for the Documentation of Free Church Origins.

Chadwyck-Healey Ltd.   Chadwyck-Healey Inc.
The Quorum Barnwell Road   1101 King St.
Cambridge CB5 8SW   Alexandria, VA 22314
England   800-752-0515
(0223) 311479   703-683-4890

The company has published on microfiche the *Répertoire Bio-bibliographique des Auteurs Latins, Patristiques et Médiévaux,* the *Répertoire des Fins de Textes Latins Classiques et Médiévaux,* and the *Répertoire d'Incipit de Sermons Latins Antiquité Tardive et Moyen Age;* these three catalogs of *L'Institut de Recherche et d'Histoire des Textes* are critically important for the study of classical and medieval Latin texts and their authors. The company has also specialized in the microfiche publication of English County Record Societies, and many of the published documents of the record societies are available as individual volumes. Guides to collections have also received serious attention; for example, catalogs of the books of the John Rylands University Library of Manchester and of the Lambeth Palace Library, as well as numerous indices of manuscript collections in both North America and the UK, are available. Chadwyck-Healey is the microform publisher of large numbers of the English-language books and pamphlets in *The Nineteenth-Century Short Title Catalog;* in this long-term endeavor they are publishing major works within clearly defined subject areas, such as "Beliefs and Religion" on microfiche.

The Genealogical Society of Utah
Genealogical Department
50 East North Temple Street
Salt Lake City, Utah 84150

The Genealogical Society possesses one of the largest collections of filmed manuscripts in the world, and the collection is truly international in scope. The holdings are especially valuable for local history, since the Society is oriented around vital records organized primarily with the needs of the genealogist in mind. Many denominations beyond the Church of Jesus Christ of Latter Day Saints are represented, including the Society of Friends, Presbyterian, Congregational, Lutheran, Reformed, and Roman Catholic. Some states, for example, New York, are particularly well represented in their local church history collections. Virtually all of the English nonparochial birth and baptismal registers of the Nonconformists, and many Anglican vital records as well, are available on film, and all filmed materials may be obtained through local stake libraries on loan. The acquisition policy is aggressive, with ongoing projects of filming records in such places as Union Theological Seminary in Virginia and the Presbyterian Historical Society in Philadelphia.

General Microfilm Company
70 Coolidge Hill Road
Watertown, MA 02172
617-926-5557

This company has a very large collection of books dated before 1701 that is international in scope. For example, they have 524 rolls of microfilmed materials from the Low Countries and some 622 rolls of German books before 1601. Collections of books similar in extent from France, Spain, Italy, Russia, and Scandinavian countries are also available. The company has a comparatively small microfilm and microfiche collection on topics that are specifically related to the history of the church: the "History of Ideas in Europe," with a focus on Catholic responses to the Protestant Reformation (189 titles on 2,282 microfiche mostly from Union Seminary, New York), the Shakers in America, the Jesuits in New France, sixteenth- and seventeenth-century French works on Canon Law, and a collection of written directories from the Catholic Church (1857-72). Individual items may be purchased and legible paper copies of most titles on microform may also be ordered.

Harvester Press
Microfilm Publications
Ship Street
Brighton
Sussex BN1 1BD
UK

Harvester has filmed many modern British political documents, but the company also has a substantial medieval collection, including literary and historical manuscripts in the Cotton Collection in the British Library. The church court records of Ely and Chichester (1400-1660) are on film, and they have the most important items from the Tanner Collection in the Bodleian Library on Church and State from 1550 to 1700. Harvester has a series entitled "Church Authority and Power in Medieval and Early Modern England" that provides access to English Episcopal registers from 1215 to 1650.

The Historical Commission, SBC
901 Commerce Street
Suite 400
Nashville, TN 37203-3620
615-244-0344

The Historical Commission of the Southern Baptist Convention has taken a very aggressive approach to preserving Baptist materials on an international scale. Many dissertations as well as primary sources are available, and individual items are priced separately and very reasonably. The collections range widely in the type of document, from church minutes, to archival items, to associational and convention annuals, to rare books and pamphlets. The collections are not narrowly limited to the Southern Baptist Convention; rare books by and about Baptists of all branches have been copied from major depositories in both the U.K. and the U.S., and these collections range chronologically from the sixteenth-century Anabaptists to the modern period, including, most recently, the addition of materials from Soviet and other Eastern European countries. A vast array of Baptist periodicals, including Black Baptist and non-English periodicals, are available on film. The Commission actually invites requests for the filming of specific documents that have not been filmed before.

Inter Documentation Company
P.O. Box 11205
2301 EE Leiden
The Netherlands
31-71-142700

IDC is one of the world's leading publishers of rare documents in microfiche, with major collections on the Protestant Reformation, including early sixteenth-century pamphlets in German and Latin, the Radical Reformation, Mennonite sources, Dutch pamphlets (through 1684), the history of religion in Latin America (1830-1970), and massive numbers of missionary society publications. IDC has reproduced the 266-volume Simler manuscript collection of sources for church history and the Reformation. In addition, the company has major collections on the Catholic Reformation and French Reformed Protestantism. Eastern church history, particularly Russian materials, has recently been added to the company's collections, and IDC is presently working on a vast project on Methodism. These microfiche are extremely well produced, but expensive. The American distributor for IDC is Norman Ross Publishing Inc., 330 West 58th Street, New York, NY 10019 (tel. 1-800-648-8850).

Library of Congress
Central Services Division
Washington, DC 26540

The Library of Congress will supply information on almost any conceivable topic, including their microfilm resources.

Lost Cause Press
4002 Glenview Ave.
Glenview, KY 40025-9999

Lost Cause Press is less well-known than other publishers of microform materials, in part because each series is sold as a unit at prices that are prohibitive for individual scholars. The company, however, has a massive microfiche collection, including nineteenth-century American literature and history, antislavery materials from the Oberlin College Library, and theology and church history collections for Britain and the United States, and Canada. The theology and church history collections are designed to be "representative," but they are dominated by items from the nineteenth century, though one will find some seventeenth- and eighteenth-century materials interspersed. The company has some 7,200 volumes on Afro-American materials, and 2,600 more on slavery. Finally, Lost Cause Press has copied the works of The Parker Society on early Anglican theologians.

Microform Academic Publishers
Main Street East Ardsley
Wakefield
West Yorkshire WF3 2AT
England
(0924) 825700

Microform Academic Publishers has a strong collection of missionary society records and Anglican parish registers, particularly for London and the southeast, and for Yorkshire. The company has both printed and manuscript materials on British and American history, including, for example, the Holkham illuminated manuscripts of the fourteenth and fifteenth centuries, many English newspapers, Joseph Priestley's letters to Theophilus Lindsay, West Indies Mission Records of the Church Missionary Society, the records of the Society for the Propagation of the Gospel, and numerous British M.A. theses and Ph.D. dissertations. The company possesses a wide variety of miscellaneous documents that bear upon the history of the church, such as diaries of clergy, sermons, registers, monumental inscriptions, catalogs, and a few more well-known medieval manuscripts. Recently a new series that runs to over one hundred rolls of film was completed on "Religion, Radicalism and Freethought in Victorian and Edwardian Britain."

Readex
58 Pine Street
New Canaan, CT 06840

Readex is responsible for the Early American Imprint Series. It is also the major supplier of *Early American Newspapers* (1704-1820) on microfilm.

Primary Source Media
12 Lunar Drive
Woodbridge, CT 06525
800-444-0799
203-397-2600

In addition to its substantial collection of microfilmed medieval manuscripts, Primary Source Media, formerly Research Publications, is particularly strong in its modern history program. In the *Eighteenth Century* project, the company is publishing every important text of the *Eighteenth Century Short Title Catalog*. When completed, this project will offer the scholar ready access to more than 200,000 titles, or almost every important work published in English between 1700 and 1800. Primary Source Media has a major collection entitled "British Culture: Series Two, British Theology" that runs to 12,826 fiche. This company has also filmed Charles Burney's and John Nichols's large collections of English newspapers, 1662-1820 in their *Early English Newspapers* series. Many major research libraries subscribe to these collections, and reels may be obtained on interlibrary loan. Searching guides for both *The Eighteenth Century* and *Early English Newspapers* are available from Research Publications, and the reel numbers for the former are listed in each entry in the online and CD-ROM versions of ESTC. The company is copying Joseph Sabin's *Bibliotheca Americana* on microfiche; and the records of the Moravian Mission among the Indians of North America, a collection on Social Problems and the American Churches, and a collection on Utah and the Mormons, are available. Primary Source Media has microfilmed many volumes of the papers of the American Board of Commissioners for Foreign Missions, and guides are available that describe the nature of the materials. Their History of Women collection includes a massive array of pamphlets, periodicals, books, and manuscripts.

K. G. Saur, Inc.
175 Fifth Ave.
New York, New York 10010
212-982-1302

Saur is publishing a microfiche edition of major biographical dictionaries. Included in this compilation are American, Australasian, British,
French, German, Italian, Scandinavian, Spanish, Portuguese, and Latin
American biographies. Saur's "British Biographical Archive," for example,
draws upon 324 sources and includes a quarter of a million biographies
on 1,400 fiche. The company's "American Biographical Archive" cumu-
lates some 350 original biographical reference works and gives particular
attention to less well-known persons, including women, African Americans, and native Americans. The tremendous value of these works lies
in the fact that they are arranged alphabetically and reproduce all of the
articles for a person in sequence on the same fiche.

Scholarly Resources Inc.
104 Greenhill Avenue
Wilmington, DE 19805-1897

Scholarly resources has a large microfilm collection of materials for
women's studies in relation to peace and prohibition; it also has a major
African American studies collection. Scholarly Resources has more than
130 rolls of microfilm on early American newspapers. The only specific
acquisitions in church history on film are the Billy Sunday Papers and
the Washington Gladden Collection.

University Microfilms International
300 N. Zeeb Road
Ann Arbor, MI 48106

UMI has now reproduced on 35mm microfilm most of the pamphlets
and books listed in the *Short Title Catalogs* of Pollard and Redgrave, and
Wing. (See the Bibliography under Modern British Sources for their *Early
English Books*, series I and II.) This project involves the copying of virtually every substantial title in the English language from the beginning
of printing in England in 1475 until 1700 (in the case of Pollard and
Redgrave, over 26,000 of 36,000 total, and with Wing, about 50,000 of a
total of 100,000 titles). The project for the earlier period is now complete
(1,999 rolls), and for the late seventeenth century it is ongoing (2,143
rolls to date). In the guides that are available for each collection, the
catalog numbers in Pollard and Redgrave, and Wing are cross referenced
to the microfilm reel numbers. These items are available on an individual

basis, and if they have not filmed the book you require, your request will be added to a list of prioritized documents yet to be filmed. UMI's very large *American Culture Series, 1493-1875* runs to over 600 rolls of microfilm and includes some titles in church history and theology, but this collection is dwarfed by the *American Periodicals Series, 1741-1900* which contains many relevant journals and runs to nearly 3,000 rolls.

World Microfilms
Microworld House
2-6 Foscote Mews
London W9 2HH
England
071-266 2202

This company is probably the largest publisher of medieval manuscripts in the world. Their considerable collections include the manuscripts of Trinity College, Cambridge (413 rolls), Queens' College, Cambridge, Lincoln Cathedral Library (one of the most important manuscript collections in western Europe), and Lambeth Palace Library, including many biblical, patristic, and theological studies. Medieval and Renaissance manuscript collections at six Oxford colleges (the theology collection from Balliol alone runs to 55 rolls) and at Trinity College, Dublin, and the early manuscript collection of the Westminster Abbey Library have been filmed. The illuminated manuscripts in the Victoria and Albert Museum are currently being prepared for publication. These projects are ongoing, so that new titles are added at regular intervals. The Archives of the Huguenot Community in London are available, as are the Society of Friends' "Digest of Registers of Births, Marriages and Burials" and "The Great Book of Sufferings" from the Friends House Library in London. In the Quaker collection one will find diaries of Quaker women. In addition, a number of nineteenth- and twentieth-century Baptist, Quaker, and Methodist periodicals are available. But World Microfilms has not limited its reach to nonconformist and dissenting denominations; it has filmed many Anglican records as well. Many seventeenth-nineteenth–century Anglican materials are available — for example, bishop's visitation returns and the archives of the Society for Promoting Christian Knowledge. The company has also filmed the Fulham Papers of the Lambeth Palace Library and the Tractarian pamphlets at Pusey House.

B. Microform Guides and Sources

"Basic Baptist Historical Materials on Film." *Baptist History and Heritage* 4 (1969): 1-139.

Bibliographic Guide to Microform Publications. Boston: G. K. Hall, 1987- . This annual publication replaces the *National Register of Microform Masters,* 1965-75, 6 vols., Washington, DC: Library of Congress, 1976-83, which was discontinued in 1983. The new guide lists all the microform materials cataloged by the Library of Congress and the New York Public Library (which, for practical purposes, can be considered an exhaustive list).

Black Studies: Select Catalog of National Archives and Records Service Microfilm Publications. Washington, DC: National Archives, 1973. Covers black churches, sects, and religious movements on film.

The Center for Reformation Research Microform Holdings from All Periods: A General Finding List. 8 vols. Sixteenth-Century Bibliography, 12-19. St. Louis, MO: Center for Reformation Research, 1977-79. This Guide lists the Center's nearly 10,000 documents on microform. The Center for Reformation Records also has finding aids for their own holdings for "Sixteenth-century Roman Catholic theologians," "Evangelical theologians of Württemberg," and "Gnesio-Lutherans, Phillipists and Formulators."

Eakle, Arlene H., Arvilla Outsen, and Richard S. Tomson, comps. *Descriptive Inventory of the English Collection.* Finding Aids to the Microfilmed Manuscript Collection of the Genealogical Society of Utah, 3. University of Utah Press, 1979.

Early American Newspapers. New Canaan, CT: Readex, 1962- . This collection includes most newspapers published before 1821 and is available on microcard at many research libraries.

Early English Books, 1475-1640, Selected from Pollard and Redgrave's Short Title Catalog: A Guide. Ann Arbor: University Microfilms International. Guides may be obtained from University Microfilms International.

Early English Books, 1641-1700. Selected from Donald Wing's Short Title Catalogue. Continues the project noted above in *Early English Books, 1475-1640.*

Early English Newspapers. Woodbridge, CT: Research Publications. Most of the massive holdings of the Charles Burney and John Nichols collections are now available on microfilm. Since 1985, Research Publications is also working on a wide array of provincial papers under the title *Eighteenth Century English Provincial Newspapers.*

Guide to Microforms in Print. Author, Title, and *Guide to Microforms in Print. Subject.* Westport, CT: Meckler, 1978- . Three separate volumes beginning in 1961, and with international coverage in 1974, now appear annually in two volumes. This is a cumulative listing of microform titles, including books, journals, newspapers, government publications, archival material, and collections which are currently available from micropublishing organizations throughout the world.

Hale, Richard W., Jr. *Guide to Photocopied Historical Material in the United States and Canada.* Ithaca: Published for the American Historical Association by Cornell University Press, 1961. Includes a section on church records, and though dated, still serves as a good point of entry for those searching microfilm collections.

Microform Review. Westport, CT: Meckler, 1972- . This quarterly publication is the best source for gathering information on new collections. Two cumulative indices are available.

Newspapers in Microform: Foreign Countries, 1948-1983. Washington, DC: Library of Congress, 1984.

Newspapers in Microform: United States, 1948-1983. 2 vols. Washington, DC: Library of Congress, 1984.

Register of Microfilms and Other Photocopies in the Department of Manuscripts, British Library. List and Index Society, Special Series, 9. London: The Department of Manuscripts, British Library, 1976.

The Thomason Tracts, 1640-1661: An Index to The Microfilm Edition of the Thomason Collection of the British Library. 2 parts. Ann Arbor: University Microfilms International, 1981. A compilation of books, pamphlets, newspapers, and manuscripts collected by George Thomason, including more than 23,000 separate items concentrated in the mid-seventeenth century. The index is keyed to Wing's Short Title Catalogue.

United States Newspaper Program: National Union List. 4th ed. Dublin, OH: Online Computer Library Center, 1993. This union catalog is available in microfiche and online through OCLC. *Newspapers in Microform* must still be consulted.

V. Specialized Research Techniques

Bits & Bytes Review. John J. Hughes, ed. Whitefish, Montana: Bits & Bytes Computer Resources, 1986- . This newsletter on computer products and resources in the humanities appears nine times a year.

Floud, Roderick. *An Introduction to Quantitative Methods for Historians.* London: Methuen & Co., 1973. Though dated, Floud still provides the most accessible introduction to the basic concepts of quantitative research.

Guide to the OCLC Database and the Special Collections Therein (Dublin, OH: OCLC, 1984).

Havlice, Patricia Pate. *Oral History: A Reference Guide and Annotated Bibliography.* Jefferson, NC: McFarland, 1985.

Hockey, Susan. *A Guide to Computer Applications in the Humanities.* Baltimore: The Johns Hopkins University Press, 1980. Especially valuable for guidance in the analysis of text.

The Humanities Computing Yearbook. New York: Oxford University Press, 1988- .

Hurd, Julie M. *Online Searching in Religion Indexes.* Evanston, IL: American Theological Library Association, 1989. This book is designed as a guide to ATLA's online databases, and it provides helpful directions for the use of Ovid Online and DIALOG.

Kraft, Robert. "Offline." *Religious Studies News.* Atlanta: Scholars Press, 1985- . Kraft's column is an excellent source of new information on the use of computers in biblical and religious studies.

Reiff, Janice L. *Structuring the Past: The Use of Computers in History.* Washington: The American Historical Association, 1991. The best single volume on the topic.

Shillingsburg, Peter L. *Scholarly Editing in the Computer Age.* Athens, GA: University of Georgia Press, 1986.

VI. Software Products and Companies

Bibliostax. Pro/Tem Software, Inc., 3790 El Camino Real, Suite 389, Palo Alto, CA 94306. 415-323-4083. For the Macintosh.

Instant Recall, 2.0. Chronologic Corporation, 5151 North Oracle, #210, Tucson, AZ 85704. For the Personal Computer.

Microsoft Word. Microsoft Corp., 16011 N.E. 36th Way, P.O. Box 97017, Redmond, WA 98073. For the PC and Mac.

Nota Bene. Nota Bene, New York. 285 West Broadway, Suite 460, NY, NY 10013-2204. 800-462-6733. For the PC.

NoteBook II. Pro/Tem Software, Inc. Also available with discount for American Historical Association members through Oberon Resources, 147 East Oakland Ave., Columbus, OH 43201. For the PC.

Pro-Cite. Personal Bibliographic Software, Inc., P.O. Box 4250, Ann Arbor, MI 48106. For the PC and Mac.

Sonar Professional. Virginia Systems, 5509 West Bay Court, Midlothian, VA 23112. 804-739-3200. For the PC.

Statistical Package for the Social Sciences. SPSS Inc., 444 North Michigan Ave., Chicago, IL 60611. 800-543-5833. PC and Mac.

WordPerfect. WordPerfect Corp., 1555 N. Technology Way, Orem, UT 84057. For the Mac and PC.

VII. Guides to Word Processing

An Author's Primer to Word Processing. New York: Association of American Publishers, 1983.

Chicago Guide to Preparing Electronic Manuscripts for Authors and Publishers. Chicago: University of Chicago Press, 1987. N.B. that many publishers prefer electronic manuscripts to word-processed camera-ready copy. Some require ASCII text. The *Chicago Guide* offers instructions and, among other things, lists acceptable codes for electronic manuscripts.

Cunningham, Michael, ed. *Using WordPerfect 6.1 for Windows.* Indianapolis: Que, 1994.

Cunningham, Michael, ed. *Using WordPerfect 5.1 & 5.1+ for DOS*. Indianapolis: Que, 1995.

Cunningham, Sheila, ed. *Using WordPerfect Version 6 for DOS*. Indianapolis: Que, 1992.

Mansfield, Ron. *Mastering Word 6 for Windows*, 2nd ed. Alameda, CA: Sybex, 1995.

Person, Ron, and Karen Rose. *Using Word Version 6 for Windows*. Indianapolis: Que, 1993.

Simpson, Alan. *Mastering Word Perfect 6.1 for Windows*. 2nd ed. Alameda, CA: Sybex, 1995.

Zinsser, William. *Writing With a Word Processor*. New York: Harper & Row, 1983.

Index of Names